Black Magic Killers

Black Magic Killers

Nigel Cawthorne

Magpie Books, London

Constable & Robinson Ltd
3 The Lanchesters
162 Fulham Palace Road
London W6 9ER
www.constablerobinson.com

Most of the material in this book was first published in the UK in 1995 as
Satanic Murder by True Crime, an imprint of Virgin Publishing Ltd.

This edition, with additional material, is published by Magpie Books,
an imprint of Constable & Robinson Ltd, 2008.

A copy of the British Library Cataloguing in
Publication Data is available from the British Library

ISBN 978-1-84529-790-9

Printed and bound in the EU

1 3 5 7 9 10 8 6 4 2
B paperback

Contents

Introduction

There are many reasons for murder – poverty, jealousy, the unbearable pressures of marriage and family, and the ever-popular crime of passion. These motives are all too human and understandable. They speak of human frailty. Others kill for political or religious reasons. They cloak themselves in idealism and claim they want to change the world for the better. But those who kill for Satan have a far more absolute motivation. They believe that if they can abandon the last remaining moral scruple they will gain ultimate power. So it is hardly surprising that Hitler and other high-ranking members of the Nazi party toyed with the occult.

Satanic ideas have been around since the beginning of Christianity. They have some of their roots in paganism and pre-Christian religions. But it was only when Christianity teased out a God of love that the empire of evil was left open for another master.

However, modern Satanism has little to do with ancient gods and age-old traditions. Most satanic rites are the inventions of modern men and are designed to ritualise their perverted desires. They put pure motiveless, senseless murder in a theatrical setting.

This may be all very well for those who practise it. They get their kicks. But the innocent victims have done nothing to deserve or invite their fate. Often they find themselves victims of multiple rape, horribly tortured, mutilated and even abused after death. Worse, the victims are often children.

Such atrocities are not confined to a bygone age. Nor do

they take place in exotic places. Devil worship is as much alive in rural Sussex as in the voodoo island of Haiti. And its tentacles spread right through society.

In 1992, Nebraska state senator John W. DeCamp – a Republican – published a book making the most startling allegations about satanic influence in the Republican administration. Two years earlier, DeCamp had been chairman of a senate committee investigating the collapse of a savings and loan company – the American equivalent of a building society – called the Franklin Credit Union. The Franklin Credit Union was run by Larry King, the rising black star of the Republican party who sang the national anthem at the Republican convention in 1984 and 1988. DeCamp's investigation alleged that the Franklin Credit Union was not a savings and loan company at all, but a front for a drugs and paedophile ring. Young boys were being recruited from Boys' Town, the children's home made famous by the 1932 Spencer Tracy film of that name, and girls were being taken from the Omaha Girls' Club.

The children were drugged and forced to pose for nude photographs. Some were transported around the country – and even abroad – for sexual purposes. DeCamp alleges that powerful newspaper barons, police chiefs and politicians in Nebraska are all implicated.

The children were kept in order and terrified into silence by the satanic rituals of their captors. They gave evidence to DeCamp's enquiry that other children had been ritually mutilated and murdered during devil-worship ceremonies. Some said they had been forced to eat the flesh of other murdered children. Two of the children said that they had been to paedophile parties where senior members of the Republican party were present. Children were forced to perform obscene sexual acts, including oral and anal sex, with each other and with adults. One of these parties had taken place at Southfork – home of TV's *Dallas* – when the Republican convention had been held in Texas.

According to DeCamp's book, one girl had been taken to two of these parties in Washington and Chicago where

2

George Bush – then Vice President – had been present. De-Camp does not suggest that Mr Bush took part in any of these acts with children, or even that he was aware of what was going on. But it is deeply disturbing that a senior politician can trace the satanic influence so deeply into a major political party.

The Republican Party is also, of course, the party of the 'moral majority', America's Christian fundamentalists. But it must be remembered that Christian fundamentalists believe in Satan too. They believe that Satan exists; they do not follow him. What's more, they are all too ready to kill for that belief.

The year 2000 marks the end of the millennium. There are those on both sides of the fence who believe that the apocalypse is upon us, that the last great battle between God and Satan is beginning. In the years to come, we can only expect the body count to climb.

1

The Rapes of Sussex

In Saxon times, Sussex was divided into a series of administrative districts known as rapes. One of them, the Rape of Bramber, was the backdrop to a number of mysterious deaths in the 1970s and 1980s.

The Rape of Bramber is in West Sussex. It runs from Worthing to Shoreham on the coast, and north to Horsham, between the Adur and Arun rivers. The Bramber Rape cuts across the South Downs at the so-called 'Devil's Triangle'. Local legend says that when the Devil heard that inhabitants of Sussex had become Christians, he tried to drown them by digging the Devil's Dyke, a huge trench that runs down to the sea. The earth from the excavation was piled up into three downland hills – Rackham, Chanctonbury and Cissbury. The hills of Chanctonbury and Cissbury are topped by ancient circles, which seem to be the site of modern-day pagan or satanic rituals. They are also the favoured sites of UFO-spotters.

Those who believe in such things say that the ley lines that run through Chanctonbury and Cissbury Rings meet at Clapham Wood on the A27, just outside the villages of Clapham and Patching. Normally, there would be no reason to think that there is anything special about this wood. But David Bennett, the churchwarden of Clapham church, used to record nightingales singing there. Then in the early 1970s he found that the night birds were no longer to be heard. The woods had fallen strangely silent. Other woodsmen noticed that the teeming wildlife – the foxes, badgers, rabbits and squirrels that used to inhabit the woods – had also disappeared. The woods had become a dank place, smelling of sulphur, stagnation and death.

People walking in the woods also reported strange feelings – headaches, dizziness, stomach cramps, a sudden weakness of the limbs. Some drivers on the A27, which borders the woods, said that they felt a strange force on the steering wheel, tugging it out of their hands, as if a magnet were pulling them towards the woods. And two hikers ran from the woods one evening when a patch of mist suddenly transformed itself into the shape of a bear.

During the late 1970s and early 1980s there was a series of strange fires in the area – nine during the autumn of 1978 alone. They may have been the work of an arsonist, but one occurred in the engine of a car which caught fire on a section of the road called Long Furlong where drivers regularly reported their engines going faulty.

Local UFO-spotters reported increased activity in the area of the woods. Strange lights were seen and crop circles appeared in the wheat fields of Patching. And a mandrake plant, long established in Clapham Wood, was mysteriously uprooted in 1978. Mandrake, with its hallucinogenic properties, has long been associated with the occult, particularly with the followers of the Greek demon Hecate.

Local dogs started disappearing. In April 1975, a three-year-old chow, owned by Peter Love of Patching, was being taken for a walk by his son in an area of the wood known as The Chestnuts. The dog ran in among the trees and did not return when called. Despite a thorough search of the area, no trace of the dog was ever found. The following week a two-year-old collie, owned by Clapham farmer John Cornford, disappeared at the same spot. Again a thorough search was instigated, but no trace was ever found. A golden retriever owned by a Mr E. F. Rawlins from Worthing was found partially paralysed after running into the woods. It had to be put down. A collie belonging to Mrs E. T. Wells of Durrington became frantic if taken near the woods and a pug suffered what amounted to an epileptic fit there – though, later, a vet could find no cause

5

for the dog's symptoms. A horse also went missing in the wood. The rider dismounted to relieve himself, leaving the animal tied to a tree. When he returned, it had gone. It has not been seen since.

Charles Walker, a researcher into the paranormal, began investigating the bizarre goings-on in the woods in 1978. One evening in the autumn, he received a phone call from a well-spoken gentleman who said that he had background knowledge on some of the strange events that had been reported in the local press. Walker was not surprised by the phone call. He had made strenuous efforts to find out whether the woods were being used by an occult group, and, as part of his investigation, he had had a number of letters published in local newspapers soliciting information.

The caller asked Walker to meet him in Clapham Wood, at the crossroads in The Chestnuts, in half an hour. Intrigued, Walker drove down the A27 to Clapham. He parked in the small lay-by off the dual carriageway which was otherwise empty that night. He got out of the car and he pushed open the wooden kissing gate into the wood itself. It was pitch black that night and Walker had trouble negotiating the brambles as he trudged up the pathway. Soon he left the flash of headlights and the sound of the traffic far behind him.

At the top of the hill, there was a signpost which marked a crossroads where two bridle paths intersected. This was the rendezvous. There was no one there, so Walker walked on a little, then he walked back past the signpost again. He walked back and forth several times. There was still no one there, but he began to sense that he was not alone.

Then, from among some bushes, Walker heard a voice: 'Don't attempt to look for me! For your safety and mine, it is imperative you do not see who I am.'

Walker froze. The voice was the one he had heard on the telephone. In the darkness, the concealed informant explained that he was an initiate in a satanic sect called the Friends of Hecate which had been formed there in Sussex.

The woods were used by the sect for their meetings, once a month. And the disappearing animals were used as sacrifices which had to be made at each meeting.

They were now standing near the place where the sacrifices were made, though when the weather was bad 'other arrangements were made', the hidden informant said. The group had been using the woods for around ten years. They intended to use them for another ten years when they would 'select other areas in which to spread the word'. The informant said that all he was saying could be confirmed by another initiate who was hidden in the undergrowth with him.

Walker was scared. How many other members of the sect might there be hidden in the darkness? But he took some comfort in the thought that his enquiries might have been misinterpreted and the group might think that he was a potential convert interested in joining.

Then came the terrible warning: 'There are people in high places involved, holding positions of power and authority, who will tolerate no interference,' said the disembodied voice. 'We will stop at nothing to ensure the safety of our cult.'

This final threat terrified Walker. Barely a week before, on Hallowe'en, the retired vicar of Clapham, the Reverend Harry Neil Snelling, had gone missing.

Reverend Snelling had been rector of Clapham and Patching from 1960 to 1974 and, in retirement, lived in nearby Steyning. During his time there, he had set up the local branch of the Samaritans. Walker knew that Hecate was goddess of suicides and untimely deaths. The Reverend Snelling had been in good spirits on the day he disappeared. He had been to the dentist in Goring. On the way, he had chatted to other passengers on the bus. On the way home, he called his wife from a phone box in Findon. When she told him that the car was out of action and that she would not be able to come and pick him up, he said that he would walk home over the Downs.

When the Reverend did not turn up, Mrs Snelling called

the police. Twenty-five officers were called in to search the area. Tracker dogs and a light aircraft also assisted. They found no trace.

The locals were particularly concerned about the safety of Father Snelling. There had been several unexplained deaths in the area. The body of a young woman was found on the Downs in April 1972. Police Constable Peter Goldsmith had been working as the coroner's officer at the time. He was forty-six, six feet six inches tall and a former Royal Marine Commando. His wife was a state registered nurse. They had two daughters and the family fitted in well in the village of Steyning where they had moved two years earlier. After the woman's body was found, PC John Grigson, a friend of Goldsmith, said that Goldsmith was quiet and nervous, and seemed to be worried about something. One day, Goldsmith and Grigson were burning old paperwork concerning former inquests when Goldsmith remarked: 'All those suicides and sudden deaths come back to me and make me feel sick. I will never do this again.'

On 2 June 1972, PC Goldsmith called in at the police station. He was last seen at around 3.30 p.m., carrying a brown canvas holdall and walking in the direction of the Downs where the young woman's body had been found. When he did not return home that evening, his wife reported him missing. And when he did not report for duty the following morning, a massive man hunt was organised. Ninety-five policemen, some of them mounted, twenty-six dog handlers, a diving team, and a helicopter were used to comb every inch of the surrounding area. The hunt continued throughout June, July and August. A number of leads were followed up, but none were fruitful. The police, family and friends were baffled.

Then on 13 December 1972 – six months after PC Goldsmith had disappeared – a farmer from Fulking, Edward Llewellyn Harris, was out beating for a shooting party at Pepperscombe. At around 3 p.m., he stumbled across a badly decomposed body in a thicket of brambles. It was less than half a mile from the spot where the body of the unidentified young woman had been found. The body was identified as that of PC Goldsmith, but no cause of death could be established. There were no obvious injuries and no sign of a struggle. Goldsmith's body was not lying as if he had suddenly collapsed with a heart attack. He was lying on his side, as if he had crawled into the thicket and gone to sleep before he died.

More puzzling was that it was mid-summer when he disappeared. At that time of the year, the thicket would have been impenetrable. The bramble thorns would have ripped his clothes and flesh to shreds. What's more, the thicket was in an area that had been thoroughly searched.

Another body was found in Clapham Wood on 4 August 1975. It was discovered by Hugo Healy and his wife who were out searching for a missing horse. The body belonged to Leon Foster. It had lain there for three weeks. Again, it was badly decayed and no cause of death could be established. Like Goldsmith, Foster had lain down as if to go to sleep. There was a makeshift bed of straw near the corpse.

Although Foster was sixty-six, he was in good health. He walked the Downs regularly. His sister-in-law, Mrs Edna Foster, is adamant that he would not have taken his own life. The autopsy showed that he had not eaten or drunk anything for several days before he died.

Walker nearly died himself. A few weeks after the mysterious meeting with the Friends of Hecate, he was hit by a car while cycling home. The car sped off without stopping, leaving him with head and back injuries and a partial paralysis which lasted for weeks.

The following spring, Walker returned to Clapham. After a visit to the church, he spotted a medieval barn, in the grounds of the manor, which is said to be the oldest building in the village. Walker remembered that his mysterious contact had said that in bad weather the cult 'made other arrangements'. So he climbed over the wall of the manor ground and walked over to the barn. The door was open so he went in. Inside, the barn was decorated like some sort of satanic chapel. On the west wall there was a huge mural depicting the Devil surrounded by flames. Christian churches have the altar to the east, the direction of the rising sun. Devil worshippers pray to the west. After taking a photograph, Walker left the barn, to be confronted by a man with a shotgun. He shouted angrily and chased Walker, who managed to escape. Around that time, a number of casual visitors to the woods found their way barred by men with shotguns.

Another researcher into the paranormal, Toyne Newton, turned up in the area with a photographer. Newton says that the locals were suspicious to the point of open hostility, while his photographer was cross-questioned by the police.

It was not until three years after Reverend Snelling had gone missing that there was any clue to his fate. In August 1981, the Worthing police received a letter from a young Canadian tourist named Michael Raine. It enclosed the Reverend Snelling's credit card and a rough sketch showing the woods and marking the spot where Raine said the skeleton could be found. In his letter, Raine explained that he had been walking in the woods when he had happened upon human remains. The next day, Raine said, he was due to travel to Africa, so decided to make his report by post rather than in person.

With the aid of Raine's map, the police found the Reverend Snelling's body. It was in an area that had been thoroughly searched before. It was not on his route home from Findon to Steyning. In fact, it was on a restricted area owned by the Ministry of Defence – a fact that, as a local man, would have been well known to the Reverend Snelling. The body was identified from the wallet, a signet ring, and dental and medical records. There were no broken bones and no obvious cause of death. The coroner recorded an open verdict.

A month later, Mrs Jillian Matthews went missing from her home in Worthing. She said she was going to the shops and would be about an hour. Again, a search proved fruitless. One of Mrs Matthews' friends visited Steyning where the missing woman's ex-husband lived but that too drew a blank. Her body was found six weeks later in the same general area as the other corpses. Andrew Martin and Alan Budd from Clapham came across it when beating for a pheasant shoot. A local gamekeeper claims to have been on the exact same spot two weeks before and seen nothing.

Again, the body was badly decomposed, but it was possible to ascertain that she had been raped and strangled. Her underclothes were missing and were never found. There was no reason for her to have gone to the woods, some miles from her home, and no particular reason why she should have been dumped there. The police issued a statement in November 1981 saying that the investigation was in difficulties due to the fact that a number of people in the Steyning area were 'reluctant to talk directly to the police'. A confidential line was set up and forty officers conducted house-to-house enquiries. As in the cases of PC Goldsmith and the Reverend Snelling, the investigation led no further.

Toyne Newton wrote a series of articles about the goings-on in Clapham Wood. When the last of them appeared, he received a disturbing letter. It confirmed the existence of a group calling itself the Friends of Hecate – although that name had been deliberately omitted from the articles. And it said that the group was much more than a black coven. The letter said that the group met in Clapham Wood and in a barn by the church. Most of the group were local people from Clapham and Patching, but the leaders – a man of about forty-five, a woman of sixty and another woman of about thirty – came from London. When they turned up, the letter said, 'there is a human sacrifice'.

2

From Early Satanism to
Jack the Ripper

The notion of human sacrifice is common in religion. As many as 20,000 people a year were killed in Aztec and Nahua ceremonies in pre-Columbian Mexico. Ancient Celts sacrificed young women by drowning. The Mayans drowned maidens in sacred wells, while in Peru young women were strangled. The British stamped out human sacrifice in India, while the spread of Buddhism stopped it in Tibet.

Christianity itself is based on the concept of human sacrifice. The son of God was killed to atone for the sins of the world. That sacrifice is even commemorated by the eating of his flesh and the drinking of his blood in the form of bread and wine. However, the essential element of Christianity is that these acts of sacrifice and cannibalism are symbolic. For some, though, that is not enough. They take what they euphemistically call the 'left-hand path' – that is, the occult or satanic path.

Paganism or witchcraft have their roots in pre-Christian religions. But Satanism is an inversion of Christianity and grew up beside it. Many religions have similar demonic figures. The Mexican god of hell, Mictlantecauli, is almost exactly like our image of Satan, a goat-like figure with horns and a tail. The ancient Egyptians and Babylonians had Apepi and Tiawath who were similar. In Teutonic myth, there is Loki, the god of fire, who is the personification of evil.

The Christian idea of the Devil begins in Jewish tradi-

12

tion. The word 'satan' comes from Hebrew. It means an opponent or enemy, so there are numerous 'satans'. These appear frequently in the Old Testament. Only in the Book of Job is Satan a single character. He appears with the sons of God standing before the throne of Jehovah and, although he is God's opponent, in the cruel test Job is subjected to, he is in no sense the personification of evil.

Things changed when the Jews lived in exile among the Babylonians, who had a pantheon of evil spirits. The Children of Israel also seem to have picked up on the Greeks' child-god Astaroth and the Persian Asmodeus, the lieutenant of the Prince of Evil, Ahriman. By the time the New Testament was written, Satan had become established as a figure in his own right. The Gospel of St Matthew refers to him as the 'Prince of Demons'. In his letter to the Ephesians, St Paul writes of Satan ruling over the evil beings in the lower heavens and tempting the good into wickedness. However, Satan's development did not stop there.

Witchcraft – which derives its name from 'wicca', the Saxon word for 'sorcerer' or 'prophet' – was a powerful influence. Widespread across pre-Christian Europe, it was based on the worship of the irresistible forces of nature. As women were the most obvious conduit of nature, people worshipped the Moon Goddess and priestesses held sway.

However, men had a rival tradition based on their role as hunter and herder and developed the idea of the Horned God. For example, the Greek god of unreason, alcohol and fertility, Dionysis, was a Horned God. He was half man, half goat. The followers of the Horned God celebrate him, not on equinoxes and solstices which had significance for those who planted and harvested, but on 2 February, 31 March and 31 October – Hallowe'en – which correspond to the times animals come in season. When Christianity began to spread across Europe, it condemned rival religions as the work of its own Satan. So the image of this Horned God was co-opted and became the popular picture of the Christian Devil.

A goat figure was also introduced by the Knights Templar, an ascetic order established by two French knights in 1119 to protect pilgrims on the dangerous journey to the Holy Land. They worshipped a pagan idol called Baphomet. This was a goat endowed with a woman's breast and an erect human penis. Usually, it wears a five-pointed star or pentagram around its neck. The sect was suppressed in the thirteenth century and the Templars' rites are now seen as satanic.

The idea of devil worship was carried on by the monks of central Europe, known as the Cathars and, later, the Bogomils. These monks believed in both God and the Devil who struggled to rule the world. They mortified the flesh, practised savage flagellation and were vegetarians – on the grounds that animals were produced by sexual intercourse and were, therefore, sinful. They did eat fish though, in the mistaken belief that fish did not copulate. The Cathars discouraged marriage on the same grounds. But they did practise sodomy. Apparently, it was permitted as it did not risk the sin of procreation. The Cathars believed that they were the elect of God, while those who opposed them were pawns of the Devil – just like many of the wilder cults of the twentieth century. They knew they could not take on the power of the Catholic church and win so, rather than opposing the church directly, they sought to undermine it by infiltrating its ranks. And in subverting it, they developed what later became the Black Mass.

In 1208, Pope Innocent III denounced the Cathars as satanist and began a purge. This drove the Cathars further underground. So, like the Inquisition that followed it, the anti-Cathar Crusade used torture and summary execution to achieve its ends. Nevertheless, the evidence it deduced shows a remarkable consistency.

In 1275, the inquisitor Hugues de Baniols heard the confession of a sixty-year-old woman, Angéle de la Barthe, in Toulouse. She was accused of having sexual intercourse with the Devil. The resulting child, she said, was a demon who ate only the flesh of dead babies and she murdered children and dug up fresh corpses to feed it.

In 1335, In Toulouse, sixty-three men and women were tried for witchcraft and sorcery. One of the defendants, Catherine Delort, admitted to killing two of her aunts and said that, at the group's Sabbats, children were killed and eaten. Another of the accused defended these actions by saying that although God was King of the Heavens, Satan was Master of the World. The Sabbats, or ceremonies, took place on a large piece of flat, high ground with a wood or grove at one end. An altar was built out of stones. On it stood an image of Satan – a goat-like creature, but with a human body, horns and an erect penis. The worshippers carried torches, lit from a flame burning between the horns of the idol. The priestess was usually a young girl. She prayed to the Lord Satan to save her from the treacherous and violent, then planted a kiss on the idol. In some accounts, she kissed the rump; in others, the erect phallus.

Hallucinogenic herbs mixed with alcohol were then taken and the priestess would lie naked across the altar. A male worshipper would take over, playing the part of the Devil. A version of the Christian creed, substituting the word Satan for Christ, was recited. Then the body of the priestess was mutilated and burned. An orgy followed, often involving children and generally employing sodomy rather than vaginal intercourse.

Some of these ceremonies were presided over by rogue priests, in the Cathar tradition. Black turnip was substituted for bread in the communions and water replaced wine, while urine was sprinkled over the congregation instead of holy water. Sometimes children were sacrificed.

The legendary French knight Gilles de Rais followed in this tradition. Born in 1404, he was a bodyguard and confidant of Joan of Arc. When she was burnt to death – a ritual in which de Rais took great pleasure, some say – he retired to his estates in Brittany. There, he squandered his fortune on art and lavish court life. When his family obtained a decree from the king to prevent him from selling off or mortgaging any more of his inheritance, he turned to alchemy and the occult. He gathered around him a group of satanists and started practising ritual magic in the cellars of his château at Tiffauges.

His servant, Poitou, was sent out to procure children – usually boys between six and twelve. The children were tortured and sexually abused. Then they were killed, often at the point of orgasm. Once they were dead, their mutilated bodies would be sexually assaulted again, then ritually burnt. Under threat of torture, de Rais confessed that he and his followers murdered over eight hundred children in the name of Satan.

Even by the seventeenth century the Cathar tradition had not died out completely. In 1633, French priest Urbain Grandier, well known as a womaniser and a deflowerer of virgins, was accused of seducing nuns into devil-worship. With the nuns from his local convent, he had organised orgies in his own church in the name of the Persian god Asmodeus. His home was searched and a pact with the Devil was found. It was written backwards in Latin and signed in Grandier's own blood.

Around the same time, there was an outbreak of Satanism at the Monastère de Saint-Louis de Louvier in Paris. Father David, the confessor there, encouraged the nuns to go about their devotions in the nude. They took communion stripped to the waist and practised lesbianism in the chapel. When Father David died, his place was taken by Father Mathurin Picard. He introduced the Black Mass, where the nuns had sexual intercourse with a devil figure – priests dressed as animals, reading from 'a book of blasphemies'. Communion wafers would be stuck to the penises of the priests as they entered the nuns. A new-born baby was crucified and two men who had come along to watch were murdered when they tried to leave. And when the nuns gave birth, the babies were killed, cooked and eaten.

In 1673, two priests told Paris Police Commissioner

Nicholas de la Reynie that they had heard a string of disturbing confessions from wealthy men and women. A number of them had told the priests that they had murdered their wives and husbands. The priests would not breach the sanctity of the confessional and refused to give their names. However, a meticulous detective, de la Reynie decided to investigate the matter.

The middle of the seventeenth century is known in France as the Age of Arsenic. Arsenic was used in the facial cosmetics that were the rage then. Murder by poison was also fashionable, especially among the upper classes. At first, de la Reynie thought he was after a gang of crooks who were selling so-called 'succession powders' to aristocrats. 'Succession powders' were poisons that would dispose of an unwanted spouse while allowing the poisoner to succeed to their property and titles.

Suspicion fell on a fortune-teller named Marie Bosse. De la Reynie sent an undercover policewoman to consult Bosse on the best way of getting rid of her troublesome husband. Bosse sold her some poison and was arrested. Bosse's husband, two sons and another fortune-teller called La Vigourex, who had slept with all the members of the Bosse family, were also arrested. And when the Bosses' home was searched, a huge cache of poisons was found. Facing torture, La Vigourex and the Bosse family eagerly provided the police with a list of their clients. Many of them turned out to be members of the court of Louis XIV, and rich and powerful people.

It took some nimble political footwork, but in 1679 de la Reynie persuaded Louis XIV to set up a committee of enquiry, known as the *Commission de L'Arsenal*, to investigate the matter. De la Reynie conceded that the investigation might well prove embarrassing for members of Louis' court, but he argued that if something were not done the next victim might be Louis himself. The investigation was conducted in a room draped in black, lit solely by candle-light, and consequently became known as *'L'Affaire de la Chambre Ardente'*.

In *La Chambre Ardente*, Marie Bosse and La Vigourex claimed that they were part of a devil-worshipping ring led by *La Voisin*. Her real name was Catherine Deshayes. She was the wife of a failed haberdasher who set up in business making skin-cleansing treatments using arsenic compounds. Her experiments led her to learn a good deal about chemistry and she subsequently developed a number of potions which promoted what she claimed was inner cleanliness. As a sideline, Madame Deshayes took up astrology. Her clients were the rich and fashionable. To lend weight to her readings, she developed a network of informers through Parisian society. These were exclusively women and included Marie Bosse and La Vigourex. Most of them adopted pseudonyms to disguise their identities. Madame Deshayes became La Voisin.

In her astrological business, La Voisin could predict that a woman's husband was going to die mysteriously. If the woman seemed pleased at the prospect, La Voisin could help the process along a bit by selling the woman some poisons. The business proved so lucrative that Madame Deshayes could soon afford to pay 30,000 *livres* for a secluded house in a run-down area of Paris. It was protected by a high wall and hidden behind tall trees. Madame Deshayes lived there with her husband, who was now a successful jeweller, her twenty-one-year-old daughter, Marie-Marguerite Montvoisin, and a lodger, Nicholas Levasseur – an executioner by trade.

De la Reynie put the house under surveillance. An undercover police officer overheard one of Deshayes' assistants in a bar drunkenly describing acts of devil-worship. The police picked up two of the people who had attended meetings there. Under interrogation, they said that Deshayes and a sixty-six-year-old priest, L'Abbé Guibourg, regularly conducted Black Masses. During the ceremony, a naked woman would lie in front of the altar with her legs open. Guibourg, wearing an alb with black phalluses embroidered on it, would rest a chalice and wafers stolen from the local church on her stomach. Intoning words from the Catholic mass, with 'the Infernal Lord Satan' substituted for the words 'God' and 'Christ', he would press the wafer against the breasts and vulva of the woman. A child would urinate in the chalice and the contents would be sprinkled over the worshippers. Then the wafer was inserted into the woman's vagina, while Guibourg chanted: 'Lord Satan sayeth "In rioting and drunkenness I rise again. You shall fulfil the lusts of the flesh. The works of the flesh are manifest – they are drunkenness, revelling, immodesty, fornication, luxury and witchcraft. My flesh is meat indeed." '

An orgy of indiscriminate sex followed.

The police raided Deshayes' home. In a pavilion in the garden, they found a room completely draped in black with a white cross at one end. There was an altar, covered in black with black candles on it. They were made from the fat from human flesh. Under interrogation, Deshayes' daughter Marie said that animals had been sacrificed and their blood drunk. Then she admitted that there had been human sacrifices too. During one ceremony, she said, Guibourg had intoned: 'Astaroth, Asmodeus, prince of friendship, I beg you to accept the sacrifice of this child which we now offer you.'

Guibourg then held an infant up by its feet and slit its throat, so that the blood drained into the chalice on the belly of the naked woman. Guibourg then smeared the blood on his penis and on the woman's vagina and had sex with her.

The children used in these sacrifices belonged to Deshayes' inner circle and included the child of Deshayes' own goddaughter, François Filastre. Others were provided by a midwife. Occasionally living foetuses were taken from unsuspecting women by Deshayes, who had another sideline as an abortionist. Foetuses' and babies' entrails were also distilled for occult use, while the rest of the bodies were burned in a stove.

The situation was potentially explosive as the worshippers included the Marquise de Montespan, Françoise-

Arthenais de Mortmart, who had been the king's mistress for twelve years. Fearing that she was losing the king's favour she attended three 'Love Masses' where she tried to secure his affections by acting as the naked altar. Much of the evidence had to be hushed up. Nevertheless, Catherine Deshayes and L'Abbé Guibourg were arrested and confessed to murdering hundreds of children during satanic rituals during a career that spanned thirteen years. Over a hundred men and women were condemned to death, slavery in the French galleys and banishment. Madame Deshayes herself was burnt to death in 1680.

There were sporadic reports of similar practices in Britain. In 1541, the English parliament outlawed witchcraft and Satanism. In 1562, they became capital offences. And in 1563 'witchcraft, sorcery and necromancy' were also outlawed in Scotland.

The seventeenth century saw the rise of the witchfinder and over 30,000 people were put to death after being found to be witches. Confessions were usually wrung from the accused under barbaric torture. But in 1662, a young attractive red-haired woman named Isobel Gowdie freely confessed to the elders of her local kirk in Lochloy, near Auldearne in Morayshire, that she was a practising witch. Bored by marriage to a dull farmer, Gowdie said that she had attended Sabbats for fifteen years. There she had sex with the Devil. Her initiation into Satanism began one night in Auldearne church. A large black hairy figure read a liturgy from a black book from the pulpit. She was required to renounce Christ. Then the Devil sucked blood from her shoulder. A few nights later she went to a meeting where the Devil had sex with her and twelve other women worshippers. At later meetings, two children were sacrificed in the Devil's name and their bodies and blood were used in satanic rites. There were similar instances in Britain's North American colonies. In 1648, in New England, Mary Johnson admitted consorting with the Devil and murdering a child.

* * *

In the eighteenth century, Britain was scandalised by satanic goings-on among the aristocracy. They occurred at Sir Francis Dashwood's infamous Hell-Fire Club, which he began in 1721 while still in his teens. Although he remained a committed Christian throughout his life, Dashwood claimed to have used the Black Mass to evoke the Devil in the form of a black cat or a goat-like figure. Despite the condemnation of George I, Dashwood continued his activities. In 1728, Dashwood attempted to 'fornicate his way across Europe'. He visited Rome and attended the ceremonial scourging of Christ in the Sistine Chapel on Good Friday. During the ceremony, Dashwood pulled a real whip from under his coat, cried 'Il Diavolo' and viciously lashed the congregation. He was ejected from the Sistine Chapel and, later, expelled from Italy for the outrage. He returned to England where he continued his debauchery.

Dashwood's Hell-Fire Club was by no means the only satanic organisation in eighteenth-century England. Young bucks amused themselves at The Banditti, The Blasters and The Sons of Midnight. These clubs emulated the French obsession with debauchery and devil-worship. There were at least three Hell-Fire Clubs in London and three more in Scotland. They offered the excessive use of alcohol, drugs and free sex.

Dashwood's club was undoubtedly the most exclusive. Membership boasted Frederick, Prince of Wales, the Earl of Bute – who became Prime Minister, the Earl of Sandwich, an Oxford professor, the Archbishop of Canterbury's son, Thomas Potter, the poet Charles Churchill, member of parliament John Wilkes, novelist Lawrence Sterne and satirist George Selwyn. Dashwood himself rose to be Chancellor of the Exchequer in Bute's government. Meetings were held in The George and Vulture in George Yard, London. A naked girl spread-eagled on the bar-room table was used as an altar. A communion wafer was pushed up her vagina and the sacrificial wine was drunk from her navel and when the Black Mass was over, there was an orgy.

21

When Dashwood married in 1745, his Hell-Fire Club ceased its activities. But in 1753, it resumed again at Medmenham Abbey, near West Wycombe in Buckinghamshire. A complete satanic temple was excavated in the chalk caves there. Members were now called 'monks' and wore red habits. The caves were hung with inverted crosses and various idols. One resembled a bird with its head turned around so that its phallus-shaped beak protruded from its back. Women would ride this, ready for the mass orgies that would follow. Monks also had individual cells where they could perform private rituals. Prostitutes dressed as nuns were shipped in from London for rites and orgies. Virgins were much in demand. Counterfeiting virginity was a major occupation at the time and some of the women were mere girls.

There are some indications that the rites performed in the Hell-Fire Caves may have included sacrifices, possibly human. But all the records of the club were burnt by Paul Whitehead, the man who ran the club, shortly before he died in 1774. Dashwood turned the Buckinghamshire militia out for his funeral and his heart was placed in a mausoleum built over the caves. It was said to be as black in death as it was in life.

Satanism went underground after the death of Dashwood in 1781. But two books published in France in the 1890s by Karl Huysmans, a veteran of the French Sureté, claimed that devil worship was rife from Paris to Hong Kong.

The only place where the British met with a devil-worshipping cult out in the open was in India. The Hindu equivalent of Satan is the goddess of destruction and bloodshed called Kali. She is a fierce, terrifying aspect of Devi, the supreme goddess. While Devi's other faces are tranquil and peaceful, Kali is depicted as a hideous, black-faced hag, smeared with blood, with bared teeth and a protruding tongue. She has four hands holding a sword, a shield, the severed hand of a giant and a noose. She is naked except for a necklace of skulls and a belt of severed hands, and is often depicted dancing with the dead body of her lover Siva.

Kali is said to have developed a taste for blood when she tried to kill the demon Raktavija. The problem with attacking Raktavija was that a thousand new demons were created each time a drop of his blood fell to the earth. In order to vanquish him, Kali stabbed him with a spear and drank his blood before it could touch the ground. Although Kali may not look much like Satan in his western depiction, she demanded blood sacrifice and was associated with the goat. At her temple at Bindhachal, near Mirzapur on the Ganges, some 700 miles from Calcutta, goats were sacrificed day and night and rivers of blood cascaded down the temple steps. Suppliants from all over India would make their pilgrimage there. Within the temple walls they would flagellate themselves into ecstasy.

But Kali's terrible influence spread far outside the confines of the temple. She had adherents from the Indus to Bengal. They were the secret society of stranglers called the Thuggee, or Thugs, who terrorised the travellers of India for hundreds of years. They had their own hierarchy, rites and traditions. They strangled travellers on the road and stole their possessions. But they did not consider themselves thieves. Each murder was carried out according to a rigid ritual and the victim was considered a sacrifice to Kali herself. The Thuggee believed that when Kali had strangled another demon, Rukt Bij-dana, at the dawn of the world, two men had been formed from the sweat of her brow and they – and their sons and their sons' sons – had been sent forth into the world to strangle.

The Thuggee enjoyed the secret protection of rajas and rich men, both Muslim and Hindu. The lower castes were too terrified to complain. They could all too easily become victims. The Thuggee worked in bands and, each year at the end of the rainy season, they would make a pilgrimage to Bindhachal and hand over a share of their loot to the priests of Kali. In return, they would be told what area they were to work in the following year, what fees would be expected and what rituals they would be expected to perform. Then they would be given the protection of Kali and go about their murderous business.

They worked in absolute secrecy and strict rituals had to be observed. Firstly, they would seek out a group of travellers, preferably of their own caste. They would befriend them and join their caravan. Then, when the omens were right, they would strangle them. The Thuggee member would use a *rumal*, a yellow handkerchief with a silver rupee tied in the middle as a garotte, and shove his knee deep in the victim's back to hasten the victim's demise. The body was then cut with ritual gashes and buried or thrown down a well. Any of the victim's possessions that had no value were burnt. The rest, along with any attractive children, were taken as the Thuggee swiftly moved on, leaving no trace other than a secret sign that could only be read by other Thuggee.

The profits raised on the goods were not the motive for their killings, the Thuggee maintained. They considered themselves honourable and honest, and would never stoop to common thieving. The killing was done for Kali. Any material benefits accruing to the murder were thanks to Kali. She had been merciful enough to provide the assassin with a living while he continued the sacred slaughter.

The son of a Thuggee would follow his father into the craft. He would begin as a scout, then become a grave digger. After that he graduated to becoming assistant strangler, then a strangler himself. A boy's first murder was celebrated as a rite of passage, like puberty or circumcision. There would be elaborate ceremonials involving the sacred pick-axe or *kussee* which every gang carried. The *kussee* was thought of as a tooth from the mouth of Kali and without it no murder could be sanctified.

The Thuggee had a secret language and other rites and rituals that surrounded the murders. There were special sacred groves where their murders were carried out and they would bury their victims in a circular pit with the corpses packed tightly around a central core of earth. This prevented jackals digging up the bodies and the murders being discovered. After each murder, the Thuggee would consume a lump of consecrated yellow sugar – or *goor* – which they believed altered them. Once a man has tasted the *goor*, they said, he would be a Thuggee, no matter how rich he was.

When the British first came to India, they tolerated the Thuggee. It was a local custom and should be respected, the old timers said. The Indians themselves rarely complained about it. They were far too frightened. The Thuggee permeated all levels of society and any complaint would surely get back to them.

When Thuggee were prosecuted, they would almost always be acquitted. Local judges too were intimidated. The Thuggee could strike at any place, any time, and no one felt safe from the wrath of Kali. It was estimated that the Thuggee killed up to 40,000 people a year. At some times of the year, the chances of completing a journey safely were just one in three. In 1830, one gang murdered 108 people in just three months and individual Thuggee boasted more than a thousand victims. The gangs themselves had up to 300 members.

In 1802, the British Army celebrated the signing of the Treaty of Amiens with a parade, led by military bands, outside the temple of Kali herself. In 1827, three Thuggee turned informer and four others were charged with murder. But a British circuit judge dismissed the case and charged the informers with giving false evidence. They were sentenced to five days riding backwards on donkeys around the city of Jubbulpore, followed by five years in jail.

All that changed in 1830 when Lord William Bentinck was appointed Governor-General. With reforming zeal, he was determined to put an end to what he called 'the most dreadful and extraordinary secret society in the history of the human race'. He made Captain William Sleeman Superintendent for the Suppression of Thugs and gave him fifty mounted irregulars and forty sepoy infantrymen. He established his headquarters in Saugor. There he ran an intelligence operation to build up a complete picture of the history, rituals, customs and practice of the Thuggee. He traced their activities on a ten-foot map, the most detailed ever made of India up to that time.

Sleeman was ruthless. Convicted Thuggee were branded and tattooed with the words 'Convict Thug' on the shoulder or 'Thug' on their lower eyelids. Then they would be hanged. Those willing to give information on other Thuggee would be spared, though they would never be freed. Sleeman argued that 'like tigers, their thirst for blood would never be appeased'. This manner of proceeding was very effective. Many were prepared to speak out and it yielded more and more information. Sleeman found Thuggee everywhere. They worked as the trusted servants of Europeans and as senior officials to the Indian princes. Many served in the Indian Army and several worked for British Intelligence.

The Thuggee felt no remorse for what they had done. Killing had brought them a sense of elation rather than guilt and they were proud to have followed in the footsteps of their fathers and grandfathers. One man who had personally killed 931 victims explained to Sleeman the joy of outsmarting and befriending travellers, who were constantly on their guard against the Thuggee, then suddenly killing them. When Sleeman accused him of thieving, he said: 'Thieving? Never. If a banker's treasure were before me and entrusted to my care, though in hunger and dying I would spurn to steal. But let a banker go on a journey and I would certainly murder him.'

However, even the Thuggee realised that their goddess Kali was losing the battle with Sleeman's Christian god. They blamed themselves for this. They had always believed that their powers were supernatural and they had an occult partnership with the tiger.

'Those who escaped the tigers fell into the hands of the Thugs,' said one. 'And those who escaped the Thugs were devoured by tigers.'

But now, they said, Devi had withdrawn her protection on account of their transgression: 'We have sadly neglected her worship.'

They were also overwhelmed by the power of the British. They told Sleeman: 'Before the sound of your drums, sorcerers, witches and demons take flight. How can Thuggee stand?'

Sleeman went on to track down the patrons and bankers who backed the Thuggee – the 'capitalists of murder', he called them. Some did not require much persuading that investing in the Thuggee was not a very safe bet any more. One banker in Omrautee withdrew his funds and invested them in the East India Company which, at that time, had just secured a monopoly of the opium trade in China.

By 1841, the Thuggee had virtually been stamped out. Several thousand Thuggee had been tried and hundreds hanged. The rest were imprisoned or transported to penal settlements on the Andaman Islands. The less blood-thirsty were held in Jubbulpore and were taught weaving, carpet-making, carpentry and bricklaying. Later, a walled village was built near the jail, where their wives and families lived. Until the end of the century, foreign visitors would come and peer over the wall at what Sleeman hoped were the last members of this terrible sect.

However, in 1970, a bus driver and his father were accused of sacrificing a ten-year-old boy to Kali. Villagers claimed that they felt giddy after eating a sacred chapatti which the accused had distributed after they had worshipped the goddess.

Back home in London, in the late Victorian era, there was another killer who performed ritual murders which seem to have had some occult overtones. His name was Jack the Ripper. He killed five women for certain in a ten-week period from 31 August to 9 November 1888, though he may have been responsible for the deaths of four more. All five had their throats slashed and were disembowelled and mutilated. The killer paid special attention to the destruction of the breasts and female sexual organs. Interestingly, if you plot the five murders on a map, they mark out the points of a pentagram, the five-pointed occult star.

The murders all took place in the Whitechapel area of London's East End, which was well known for vice at the time. In 1888, there were 62 brothels and 233 boarding houses catering to prostitutes and their clients in the narrow lanes there. Pox-ridden, middle-aged, alcoholic prostitutes hung around in alleyways and doorways, offering their sexual favours standing up. Usually they would simply bend down and hoist up their skirts so their client could enter them from the rear. This made it particularly easy for Jack the Ripper to pull a knife and despatch his victim before she realised what was happening.

Forty-five-year-old Emma Elizabeth Smith was possibly the first victim of the Ripper. On the night of 3 April 1988, she solicited a well-dressed gentleman. Later that night, she collapsed in the arms of a constable, saying that she had been attacked by four men. They had cut off her ear and shoved a foreign object up her vagina. She died a few hours later.

Then on 7 August 1888, Martha Tabram was stabbed to death. There were thirty-nine frenzied wounds on her body, mainly around the breasts and sexual organs. Both Smith and Tabram, like the Ripper's later victims, had their backs turned when they were attacked.

The first of the women known for certain to have been killed by the Ripper was forty-two-year-old Polly Nichols. Her body was found in Buck's Row at 3.15 a.m. on 31 August 1888. She did not cry out. The attack took place under the window of a sleeping woman who did not wake. The body revealed that she fought for her life, but was overcome by her attacker. Her throat had been slashed twice, so deeply that she had almost been decapitated. There were deep wounds around her vagina, but no organs had been removed. Pathologists examining the corpse concluded that the killer had some medical knowledge. Polly had almost certainly turned her back on her killer for an assignation there on the street. While she was turned away from him, he pulled out a knife, put it to her throat and pushed her forward on to it as he slashed her. This explained the depth of the wound and would have meant that all the blood would have sprayed forward and not over the assailant, leaving him clean to make his escape unnoticed.

The police realised that they had a maniac on their hands. Detectives were sent out into the East End, searching for men who mistreated prostitutes. The name 'Leather Apron' came up several times in the investigation. A shoemaker called Pizer was picked up. He used a leather apron and sharp knives in his trade, but his family swore that he was at home on the three occasions women had been attacked.

On 8 September 1888, forty-seven-year-old Annie Chapman was bragging in the pubs of Whitechapel that the killer would meet his match if he ever came near her. She was wrong. Later, she was seen talking to a 'gentleman' in the street. They seemed to strike up a bargain and went off arm-in-arm. Half an hour later, she was found dead in an alley-way. Her head was only connected to her body by a strand of flesh. Her intestines were found thrown over her right shoulder, the flesh from her lower abdomen over her left. Her kidneys and ovaries had been removed. The killer had taken them with him. He had also left a piece of leather near the corpse. The police realised that this was all too convenient. The killer was obviously an avid reader of the newspapers and had read of the arrest of Pizer. He also left a blood-soaked envelope with the crest of the Sussex Regiment on it. It had been reported that Martha Tabram had been seen in the company of a soldier shortly before her death and the newspapers said that her wounds could have been caused by a bayonet or army knife.

Three weeks after the death of Annie Chapman, the Central News Agency received a letter that gloated over the murder and the false clues. It regretted that the letter was not written in the victim's blood, but it had gone 'thick like glue' and promised to send the ear of the next victim.

The letter was signed 'Jack the Ripper'. On 30 September 1888, the Central News Agency received another letter from the Ripper, apologising that he had not enclosed an ear – but promised that he was going to do a 'double'.

At 1 a.m. that night, forty-five-year-old 'Long Liz' Stride, a Swedish prostitute whose real name was Elizabeth Gustaafsdotter, was found in a pool of blood with her throat slashed. The delivery man who discovered her body heard the attacker escaping over the cobblestones. Around the same time, forty-three-year-old prostitute Catherine Eddowes was being thrown out of Bishopsgate Police Station where she had been held for creating a drunken disturbance. As she walked towards Houndsditch she met Jack the Ripper. He cut her throat, slashed her face and cut at her ear, though it was left still attached. He removed her intestines and threw them over her shoulder. The left kidney was missing altogether.

The murder of two women in one night sent London into a panic. Queen Victoria demanded action, but the police seemed powerless. East-End resident George Lusk set up the Whitechapel Vigilance Committee to patrol the streets. Two weeks later, Mr Lusk received a small package through the post. It contained half Catherine Eddowes' kidney. The other half had been fried and eaten, according to the accompanying note which was again signed 'Jack the Ripper'. Queen Victoria concluded that the Ripper must be a foreigner. No Englishman would behave in such a beastly way, she said. A cabinet meeting was called to discuss the matter. They ordered checks on all the ships tied up in the London docks. This proved to be a huge waste of police manpower.

The last victim that was certainly the Ripper's was un-like the others. She was young, just twenty-four, and attractive. Her name was Mary Kelly and she only turned to prostitution occasionally to pay the rent. She was killed indoors and she also cried out.

On the night of 9 November 1888, she was seen on the street soliciting a 'well-dressed gentleman'. Sometime between 3.30 and 4 a.m., the woman sleeping in the room above Kelly's heard Kelly scream: 'Oh, murder'. In the morning, the rent man found her mutilated corpse.

Being indoors and undisturbed, the Ripper had been able to spend more than an hour on his grisly task. Mary Kelly's clothes were found neatly folded on a chair so it is thought that she took her 'gentleman' back to her room and undressed herself ready for sex. It was then that he pulled out his knife. This time she had been facing him, saw the murder weapon and cried out. He slashed her throat, almost decapitating her, but blood splashed on his clothes, which were found burnt in the stove. Then he set about her corpse. Both breasts were cut off and placed on the table, along with her nose and flesh from her thighs and legs. Her left arm was severed and was left hanging by the flesh. Her forehead and legs had been stripped of flesh and her abdomen had been slashed open. She was three months pregnant at the time of the attack. Her intestines and liver had, once again, been removed and her hand was shoved into the gaping hole left. There was blood around the window where the Ripper was thought to have escaped, naked except for a long cloak and boots.

Other murders followed that may have been the work of the Ripper. The headless corpse of Elizabeth Jackson, a prostitute working in the Chelsea area, was found floating in the Thames in June 1889. In July that year, Alice McKenzie, a prostitute in Whitechapel, was found with her throat cut from ear to ear and her sexual organs cut out. And street-walker Frances Cole, also known as 'Carroty Nell' because of her flaming red hair, was found in Whitechapel with her throat cut and slashed around her abdomen. A policeman saw a man stooped over the body, but he ran away before the constable could get a good look at him.

The description of the Ripper that has seized the public imagination comes from a friend of Mary Kelly's who saw her with a man that night. He was five feet six inches tall, about thirty-five, well-dressed with a gold watch chain dangling from his waistcoat pocket. Kelly was seen in conversation with him.

'You will be all right for what I have told you,' he said.

'All right my dear,' she replied, taking him by the arm. 'Come along, you will be comfortable.'

A few hours later a chestnut vendor saw a man matching that description, wearing a long cloak and silk hat with a thin moustache turned up at the end and carrying a black bag.

'Have you heard there has been another murder?' he said.

'I have,' the chestnut seller replied.

'I know more of it than you do,' said the man as he walked away.

There are a huge number of theories as to the identity of the Ripper. The police had 176 suspects at the time. The most popular is the mad Russian physician Dr Alexander Pedachenko who worked under an assumed name in an east London clinic that treated several of the victims. A document naming him as the Ripper was said to have been found in the basement of Rasputin's house in St Petersburg after the mad monk's assassination in 1916. However, some have pointed out that Rasputin's house did not have a basement.

A Dr Stanley is another popular suspect. He is said to have contracted syphilis from a Whitechapel prostitute and thus took vengeance on them all. He fled to Buenos Aires where he died in 1929, after confessing all to a student.

V. Kosminski, a Polish Jew who lived in Whitechapel, threatened to slice up prostitutes. He went insane and died in an asylum. East European Jewish immigrants, who were unpopular in London at the time, were regularly blamed for the Ripper killings. It was said that the murders were ritual Jewish slaughters performed by a *shochet*, a butcher who kills animals according to Talmudic law. This theory was given some little credence by the confused message 'The juwes are not the men that will be blamed for nothing' that was scrawled on a wall in Whitechapel after the murder of Catherine Eddowes. 'Juwes', the Masonic spelling of 'Jews', also gave rise to the theory that the murders had been some Masonic rite. The police commissioner Sir Charles Warren was himself a high-ranking Mason. He had the graffiti removed to prevent inflaming anti-Jewish feelings in the area, he said. Sir Charles Warren resigned after the murder of Mary Kelly, admitting his utter failure to solve the case.

Another Polish immigrant, Severin Klosowich – alias George Chapman – was also suspected. He was a barber's surgeon in Whitechapel and kept sharp knives for bloodletting and for the removal of warts and moles. He poisoned three of his mistresses and went to the gallows in 1903.

Thomas Cutbush was arrested after the murder of Frances Cole for stabbing women in the buttocks. He died in an insane asylum.

The insomniac G. Wentworth Bell Smith who lived at 27 Sun Street, off Finsbury Square, was a suspect. He railed against prostitutes, saying, 'They should all be drowned.'

Frederick Bailey Deeming confessed to the Ripper's murders. He had killed his wife and children in England, then fled to Australia where he killed a second wife. He was about to kill a third when he was arrested. It is thought that his confession was an attempt to delay, if not evade, the gallows in Australia.

Dr Thomas Neill Cream poisoned prostitutes in London and went on to murder more in the United States. He is said to have told his hangman 'I am Jack . . .' as the trap was opened.

The police's prime suspect was Montague John Druitt, an Oxford graduate from a once-wealthy family. After failing as a barrister, Duritt became a school teacher, but he was a homosexual and was dismissed for molesting a boy. He moved to Whitechapel where he was seen wandering the streets. In December 1888, his body was fished out of the Thames. There were stones in his pockets – he had drowned himself.

Salvation Army founder William Booth's secretary was also a suspect after saying 'Carroty Nell will be the next to go' a few days before the slaying of Frances Cole. Alcoholic railway worker Thomas Salder was arrested after the murder of Alice McKenzie. He also knew Frances Cole, but was released due to lack of evidence.

Sir Arthur Conan Doyle, creator of Sherlock Holmes, believed that the Ripper was a woman. His theory was that 'Jill the Ripper' was a midwife who had gone mad after being sent to prison for performing illegal abortions.

The spiritualist William Lees staged a seance for Queen Victoria to try and discover who the Ripper was. The results frightened him so much he fled to the Continent. The Ripper, he believed, was none other than the Queen's physician Sir William Gull. Gull's papers were examined by Dr Thomas Stowell. They named Prince Eddy, the grandson of Queen Victoria who died of syphilis before he could ascend to the throne, as the Ripper, Stowell says. Another suspect is James Kenneth Stephen, a homosexual lover of Prince Eddy. The two of them were frequent visitors to a homosexual club in Whitechapel.

The painter Frank Miles, a friend of Oscar Wilde's, has also been named as the Ripper.

But most intriguing of all is newspaper reporter Roslyn D'Onston. A failed doctor and drug addict, he was said to have killed the women in order to write about the murders for his paper. It is said that his stories carried details that the police never released. He himself named a Dr Morgan Davis as the murderer. In 1890, he become involved with Mabel Collins, the editor of *Lucifer*, the magazine of the Theosophical Society. He later went into business with Baroness Vittoria Cremers, who revealed in the 1920s that she had found neckties caked with dried blood in D'Onston's room. She said he had told her that they belonged to Jack the Ripper. They eventually found their way into the possession of the satanist Aleister Crowley, who claimed that D'Onston was indeed the Ripper and that his ritual murders were done for magical purposes in an attempt to become invisible.

* * *

Crowley was the man who brought Satanism into the twentieth century. Born in 1875, his parents were Plymouth Brethren. Early on, the young Crowley rebelled against this strict and joyless sect. He took to drink and drugs, slept with his mother's maidservant and asked for the body of his still-born sister for experimentation. When he was refused, he dismembered a live cat instead.

At Trinity College, Cambridge, Crowley became interested in the occult and, in 1898, joined the Hermetic Order of the Golden Dawn which boasted Irish poet W. B. Yeats as a member. The Order based its beliefs on the *Kabbalah*, a thirteenth-century commentary on the first five books of Moses by a Spanish Rabbi. This claims that the spiritual world is divided into ten emanations of God, life on Earth being the lowest of the ten. Members of the Order also believed in magic. Although most of the Order's ceremonies involved dressing up in ludicrous costumes and worshipping bizarre Egyptian deities, some involved the ritual deflowering of young girls. In 1901, two members of the Order were jailed for rape during these rites.

Crowley also believed magic could be evoked by bizarre sexual practices but managed to escape trouble with the law, largely because he confined his activities to a remote house in Scotland. In 1904, Crowley and his wife were in Cairo where they claim to have evoked a god called Aiwas who dictated *The Book of Law*. This said that Christianity was about to be swept away and replaced by a new religious order. Its Messiah would, naturally, be Crowley. Aiwas also encouraged Crowley to take all the drugs he could lay his hands on. Crowley's message was simple. Satan was not an external force. He was found within the heart of every man and woman, and was the source of unlimited power. He could be released simply by discarding all moral scruples.

'Do what thou wilt shall be the whole of the law,' said Crowley.

Crowley was soon involved in a bitter struggle with Samuel Liddell Mathers, who ran the Hermetic Order of the

Golden Dawn. The Order itself was already in trouble because of its occult connection. Around that time a thirty-three-year-old bohemian woman in London named Norah Emily Farnario had joined. She had been interested in New Age thinking and her interest spread to the occult which she studied under Mrs Moina Mathers, Samuel Liddell Mathers' wife. Mrs Mathers initiated Norah into the Order of Alpha and Omega, an occult off-shoot of the Hermetic Order of the Golden Dawn.

In the autumn of 1929, Norah Farnario travelled to the remote island of Iona, one of the Inner Hebrides off the west coast of Scotland, which she believed to be her spiritual home. She rented a room in a croft and the islanders left the strange interloper largely to her own devices. But they became concerned when she started babbling about being in touch with the 'world beyond'. Without warning, Norah grew hysterical. She packed her bags and tried to leave the island. But it was a Sunday and the islanders, being strict Christians, did not allow the ferry to operate on the Sabbath. On Monday morning, her landlady found her bed had not been slept in and her clothes were neatly folded beside it, but there was no sign of Norah. There was no immediate cause for concern as Norah was a strange woman and often went for long walks on the moors at night. But when she did not turn up by the following afternoon, a search was begun.

The next day, her body was found. It was spreadeagled high up on the moor, naked except for her robe of the Order of Alpha and Omega and a silver chain around her neck. The soles of her feet were cut and bleeding as if she had been running away from something. Her face was contorted into an expression of sheer terror. In her hand was a long-blade knife, used in the Order's rituals. She had been cutting a cross in the turf when she died. On the death certificate, the cause of death is given simply as 'heart failure'. Occultists believed that she had been killed by some psychic means by Mrs Mathers.

Samuel Liddell Mathers decided that this was quite

enough bad publicity and censured Crowley, who quit the Order of the Golden Dawn and started his own Order of the Silver Star. He soon picked up a young disciple called Victor Neuburg who became the centre-piece of Crowley's occult ceremonies. These usually involved sodomy within a pentagram and a circle. In Paris, Crowley and Neuburg conducted a series of rituals. Worshippers danced within a pentacle painted on the floor, while Neuburg had his buttocks scourged. An inverted cross was carved on his chest, then he was ritually sodomised. Blood was drunk and faeces were eaten. A large number of snakes were released and a frog was baptised 'Jesus of Nazareth', then crucified and stabbed. Plans were made to kidnap, rape and murder a young girl, and cut her body into nine pieces which would be offered up to nine demons. It is unclear whether this was done.

Crowley then announced the death of Christianity, proclaimed the coming of Horus, the Egyptian Satan-figure and began referring to himself as 'The Great Beast' – the description of Satan used in the Book of Revelations. And he published many of the details of occult 'experiments' he had conducted with Neuberg.

In 1912, German Freemason Theodore Reuss visited Crowley in Scotland. Reuss was head of a secret magic sect, based in Germany, called Ordo Templi Orientus (OTO). He accused Crowley of revealing the sect's secret rituals. Crowley convinced Reuss that he had stumbled on the rituals by his own devices and Reuss invited him to join OTO. Within five years, Crowley had completely taken over OTO, which increasingly became a vehicle for Crowley's Satanism. 'My master is Satan; resist not Evil,' he proclaimed.

To escape the growing interest of the press and impending bankruptcy caused by his addiction to cocaine and heroin, Crowley moved to a derelict farmhouse in northern Sicily, which he converted into a satanic temple and renamed The Abbey of Thelema, where he is believed to have kept the Ripper's blood-stained neckties. The floor of the central hall had a circle and a pentagram painted on it. The walls were covered with obscene and blasphemous paintings. One depicted Baphomet, the Knights Templars' goat figure, sodomising a man. At one end of the hall was an altar which was adorned with a whip, a phallus and Crowley's *Black Book of Rituals*. Worshippers gathered there for Black Masses. Crowley would eat a communion wafer smeared with the excrement of his new lover Leah Hirsig. He would disembowel a live cat, collect its blood and drink it. In one ceremony Leah Hirsig had sex with a goat which had its throat cut at the climax of the ritual. Again the blood was collected and consumed.

However, in 1923, when a child went missing from a nearby village, Crowley was accused of kidnapping and killing it. No charges were brought, but within a week Mussolini ordered Crowley's expulsion.

When Reuss had a stroke, OTO broke up, but there were still enough people in Germany to support Crowley's activities. Crowley set about writing *Magick in Theory and Practice*, which is intended as a handbook for the beginner. In it, Crowley emphasises the importance of animal and possibly human sacrifice. He concludes: 'A male child of perfect innocence and high intelligence is the most satisfactory and suitable victim.'

In a footnote, Crowley claims to have performed such human sacrifices on average 150 times a year from 1912 to 1928 – killing over two thousand children. And he was unrepentant. In a court case in 1934, Crowley was asked: 'Do you believe as a magician in bloody sacrifice?'

He replied, 'Yes.'

'You say for nearly all purposes human sacrifice is best?'

'Yes, it is,' he said.

However, apart from his own confession, there is no evidence that he killed children and no charges were ever brought against him.

Crowley's *Magick in Theory and Practice* remains the bible of modern satanists. After its publication, Crowley subsided into poverty, brought on by his heroin and cocaine addiction. He died in 1947 in Brighton. His body was cremated in a Black Mass, much to the outrage of the good people of Sussex.

3

Wartime Witchcraft

It is well known that Adolf Hitler was obsessed with the occult. His interest began in his twenties when he met a young man called Adolf Lanz, a failed Cistercian monk, who changed his name to Dr Jorg Lanz von Liebenfels. Lanz became a disciple of German mystic Guido von List who worshipped the pagan god of war, Woden. During the 1870s, von List had a huge following in Germany and one of the symbols he used in his ceremonies was a hooked cross, the ancient symbol of good fortune known as the swastika. Von List's group evolved into the Thule Society, a pagan group that restricted its membership to high-ranking German Army officers and the professional classes. Meanwhile Lanz began a new Order of New Templars at the ramshackle Werfenstein Castle on the banks of the Danube. From the flagpole of the castle, he flew a flag with the swastika on it.

Lanz had a number of wealthy and intellectual followers, but none was more fanatical than Hitler. He avidly read Lanz's outpouring in the cult's magazine which was devoted to the occult and racial mysticism.

When the Nazi Party was in its infancy, Hitler decided that it should have a symbol to rival the Communist Party's hammer and sickle. Another occultist, Friedrich Kohn, came up with a suggestion. Kohn belonged to the German order which believed that there was a world-wide Jewish conspiracy, underpinned by occult practices, and the only way to fight it was for Nordic Freemasonry to respond in kind. He suggested a black swastika, symbolising the triumph of Aryan will, on a white disc, symbolising racial purity, with a red background, symbolising blood. Hitler agreed, only he turned the swastika back to front in what has been interpreted as a black magic gesture. It is that reversed swastika that became the emblem of the Nazi Party.

Another believer in the occult who was influential in the Third Reich was Karl Haushofer. Born in 1869 in Bavaria, Haushofer came from a military family and after graduating from Munich University he joined the German army. In the early years of the twentieth century, he became interested in mysticism and travelled to India and the Far East. He became convinced that the Indo-Germanic people had originated in Central Asia and that it was they who gave nobility and greatness to the world. In Japan, he also joined a secret Buddhist society. During World War I, it is said that his ability to predict where shells would fall was uncanny. He was promoted to the rank of General.

After the war, he returned to Munich University where he began teaching his own theory of the 'Science of Geo-Politics'. This was thinly disguised nationalist propaganda. He promoted the idea that it was the destiny of the German people to rule Europe and Asia. The heartland of Central Asia was, of course, the Indo-Germanic people's homeland and must be recovered. It would be the centre of unassailable world power. He ran a journal called the *Geo-Political Review*, in which he expounded his views of Aryan superiority. He also said that on his travels he had discovered a race of supermen who lived in a vast cavern beneath the Himalayas in a place called Agharti. Similar ideas had been put forward by the Rosicrucians who had themselves influenced the Order of the Golden Dawn.

One of Haushofer's students was Rudolf Hess and Hess became his assistant. When Hess and Hitler were jailed for their failed putsch against the Bavarian government, Haushofer visited Hess in prison and met Hitler. He began visiting Hitler daily and many of Haushofer's ideas were incorporated in *Mein Kampf*. Hess later said that

41

Haushofer was the secret Master Magician behind the Reich. His ideas of 'cones of power' were incorporated in the staging of the Nuremberg rallies and he brought lamas from Tibet and members of the Green Dragon Society from Japan to Germany to lend the war effort mystical backing.

Heinrich Himmler, head of the SS, was another believer in the occult. The SS used occult practices and worshipped the Nordic god Woden in ceremonies in the castle at Wewelsburg in north-west Germany where Himmler had built a temple known as the Hall of the Dead.

However, during World War II, such harmless practices as astrology and palmistry were banned in all German occupied countries. Even occult organisations such as the Thule Society and the German Order, who had backed Hitler from the outset, were outlawed. Occult practice was to be confined to those at the top of the Nazi Party.

Whatever help the occult may have lent Hitler, his experiment in pure evil failed. But even in defeat, Hitler did not give up his belief. He delayed his own suicide until the pagan festival of Walpurgisnacht, 30 April 1945.

During World War II, there were some strange goings-on in Britain too. On the afternoon of 18 April 1943, three boys were birds' nesting in Hagley Wood in Worcestershire. The woods were part of the estate of Hagley Hall, the ancestral home of Lord Cobham. It was late in the afternoon and the light was already failing when they decided to have a look in an old wych elm. One of them clambered up it. Hidden under the spindly branches, he discovered a large hole in the trunk – just the place a bird might nest. Peering down into the cavity, he saw what looked like a grimacing face. He took a stick and prodded at it. Slowly it dawned on the boy that what he was prodding was a skull. Shaken by the experience, the boy and his two companions ran off home and told their parents. They informed the police. By then it was dark and it was too late to examine the tree that night. So the local bobby, Sergeant

Skerratt, placed a guard on the tree overnight. In the morning, detectives from the Worcestershire CID turned up. They set about examining the hollow in the tree. First they managed to retrieve the skull. Then they found a spine, a shoulder blade and some human ribs, still with pieces of rotten clothing clinging to them. And at the bottom of the hole, they found a single crêpe-soled shoe.

The tree and the surrounding area were photographed and Sergeant Skerratt took detailed measurements of the hollow. It was about three-and-a-half feet off the ground and it was just two feet across at its widest. The trunk itself had been cut off at about five-and-a-half feet and the resulting tangle of branches would have made it very difficult to shove a body into the hollow. The surrounding area was cordoned off and a thorough search was made. A shin bone was found knotted in the roots of a sapling nearby. A little further away detectives found one of the hands buried. Most of the skeleton was eventually found and remnants of the victim's clothing were strewn through the undergrowth. The job of reconstructing the body fell to West Midlands pathologist Professor J. M. Webster. The local newspaper, the Wolverhampton *Express and Star*, billed him as 'as famous as any figure who ever helped solve a crime excepting, perhaps, Sherlock Holmes'.

Webster had set up Britain's first forensic science laboratory in Sheffield in 1929 and he had established the West Midlands forensic laboratory before the war. Meticulously, he pieced the body back together and built up a remarkable picture of the victim. She was a brown-haired woman, around five feet tall and about thirty-five years old when she died. She had a cheap ring on her wedding finger. The words 'Rolled Gold' were stamped on it. It was worth about 2/6, or 12½p. She was wearing blue crêpe-soled shoes, a cloth skirt with a zip and a peach-coloured taffeta underskirt, and a dark blue knitted woollen cardigan, fastened with a light blue belt. Professor Webster drew up a detailed artist's impression of the victim and a dummy was prepared to give the police a more accurate idea of the missing woman. The front teeth in the victim's lower jaw were noticeably irregular. This should have made her readily identifiable. However, no dentist came forward who had treated her. Detailed notices in all the dental journals elicited not a single response.

Professor Webster estimated that the victim had been dead for around eighteen months. Part of her clothing had been stuffed deep into the cavity of the jaw. This had happened before she had died and Professor Webster believed that the woman had probably asphyxiated. But he could not be sure. Her body had been jammed into the hollow in the tree, feet first, shortly after she had died – certainly before rigor mortis had set in. She could not have squeezed in there when she was alive.

The inquest opened on 28 April 1943 at North Worcestershire Coroner's Court in Stourbridge. The verdict was 'murder by person or persons unknown'. This did not help the police with their enquiries. They were still no closer to finding out who the dead woman was, let alone the identity of those who had killed her. They tried checking through their missing persons' files. But the bombings and wartime disruption made this a monumental and ultimately fruitless task. At the same time, they checked with clothing manufacturers in the hope that they could trace the woman through the distribution chain.

Her unusual blue crêpe-soled shoes seemed to offer some prospect of this. The police found the manufacturer and tracked down all but four pairs of that type of shoe sold. But none of the purchasers gave a clue to the identity of the unknown victim.

Searching back in their records, the police discovered that two men – a teacher and a businessman – had reported hearing screams emanating from Hagley Wood in July 1941. A constable had assisted the two men in searching the woods, but nothing suspicious had been found. The date of this report would be consistent with Professor Webster's estimated time of death. On the other hand, there was not a shred of other evidence to tie the two events together. Another report showed that gypsies had been camping in the woods at that time. The police had stepped in following a minor domestic dispute. The hypothesis that the victim was a gypsy was appealing. It would explain the difficulty in tracing her. But enquiries among the Romany community drew a blank.

The police had only one thing to go on. Although the victim was clearly an outsider, the perpetrator must have had good local knowledge. The wych elm was less than half a mile from the main road from Kidderminster to Birmingham in an area popular with picnickers, hikers and courting couples. But the hollow was so well hidden, it seems inconceivable that anyone who had not spent a great deal of time in Hagley Wood would have happened upon it by chance. But why would anyone choose such an inconvenient and inefficient way of concealing a corpse? The victim would have had to be dismembered directly after the murder, the bulk of the body jammed into an awkward confined space and the rest of the corpse and clothing disposed of piecemeal. Why not simply bury the body in one piece?

Letters to the local papers suggested that the woman's murder was part of a black magic ritual. Mysterious messages were also chalked on the walls of empty buildings in Wolverhampton, Old Hill and Halesowen. They said: 'Who put Bella down the wych elm, Hagley Wood?' Sometimes the graffiti artist used the name 'Luebella'. Both names are diminutives of 'Elizabeth' and are commonly associated with witchcraft.

Hagley Wood had a reputation as a witches' haunt. But the police found no current indications of occult activity. However, there are plenty of superstitions surrounding corpses and trees. According to folklore, the spirit of a witch could be confined in a hollow tree. In ancient times, blood sacrifices were offered to damaged trees and the wych elm in Hagley Wood was actually only a living stump, the main trunk being severed. Another indication that this had been an occult killing was that one hand had been cut off and buried some distance from the corpse. There is no rational reason why it was removed. Despite the tight squeeze, it could have been fitted into the hollow. However, in occult practices, the severed hand of a corpse – especially one taken from a hanged man on the gallows – has magical powers. It can be used to find treasure, paralyse enemies, charm open locks and perform supernatural robberies. If a lighted candle is put in the hand, or one of the fingers is set alight, light from the flame is supposed to put all those who see it into a death-like sleep. To have these mystical properties, the 'hand of glory' has to be dried and pickled in a special way. The name comes from the French *main de gloire* and is related to the mandragora plant which has narcotic properties.

Interesting though all that may be, it did not get the police any closer to finding the identity of the victim or the killer. Their only hope was to find the author of the messages chalked up on the walls. These had been carefully printed in capital letters about three inches high and must have taken some time to complete. But the perpetrator was never seen and no one acting suspiciously was ever reported in the vicinity. The investigation of the corpse in Hagley Wood had ground to a halt.

Interest in the corpse in Hagley Wood was rekindled nearly two years later with the mysterious death of a seventy-four-year-old farm labourer called Charles Walton. He lived not too far away in the quaint village of Lower Quinton in Warwickshire. Partially crippled by rheumatism, Walton could not walk without the aid of a stick, but on the morning of 14 February 1945 he set off to do some hedge-laying for local farmers. At 9 a.m. he left the picturesque thatched cottage he shared with his niece, Edith, and trudged off on the mile or so to the fields below Meon Hill, a lonely spot. He carried with him a pitchfork and a hedge-trimmer's slash-hook.

Walton was a man of regular habits. He would return home each day at 4 p.m. for his tea. So when he had not appeared by 6 p.m., Edith became concerned that he had

had an accident. With neighbour Harry Beasley, she went looking for the old man. But they could not find him. As it grew dark, they became more and more worried. Edith got in touch with her uncle's employer Alfred Potter. By torchlight, they went to search Meon Hill. Late that night, they found the old man's body stretched out under a willow tree. Potter went over to examine it and he shouted over to Edith: 'Don't come any nearer! You mustn't look at this!'

Potter stayed by the body, while Beasley escorted Edith back to her cottage and called the police. When they turned up, they were horrified by what they found. Walton was pinned to the ground by the neck. He had been run through by his own pitchfork. The prongs protruded a full six inches into the ground. It took two policemen to pull it out. The sign of the cross had been cut into Walton's chest with the slash-hook. The hook itself was embedded in a huge gash in the victim's throat. And there were gashes along the outsides of his arms, as if he had tried to defend himself. The old man's walking stick was found nearby. It was bloodstained and had also been used as a weapon by the attacker.

Professor J. M. Webster, the pathologist who had reconstructed the body found in Hagley Wood, was called in to make an initial examination at the scene of the crime. Then Walton's body was carried back to the village on a five-barred gate.

Superintendent Simmons from Stratford-upon-Avon, just eight miles to the north, was initially put in charge of the investigation. He imagined that his task would be relatively simple. There were only five hundred people in Lower Quinton – there could be few secrets in such a small community and it would be difficult for the killer to hide. However, there were few clues at the scene of the crime, no obvious motive and the villagers were deeply suspicious of outsiders. Interviews revealed only that Charles Walton was a reclusive man. He had few friends and there was no reason to suspect he had any enemies. The report in the local newspaper, the *Stratford-upon-Avon Herald*, claimed that it was a random murder committed by 'a lunatic or someone maddened by drink'. The case was so baffling that, within two days of the murder, Detective Superintendent Alec Spooner of the Warwickshire CID called in the legendary Fabian of the Yard.

Superintendent Robert Fabian was Britain's most famous policeman. His career at Scotland Yard spanned twenty-nine years and included spells as head of the Flying Squad and the Vice Squad. After the war, Fabian appeared frequently on television. Feature films were made of his most famous cases and he made lecture tours of South Africa and The United States, where he was given the freedom of New Orleans. In 1960, he was decorated with the Police Medal for Gallantry, after defusing a bomb in London.

Fabian hurried to Lower Quinton, arriving at dawn on 16 February. But he found that local policemen had already combed the murder site, trampling any clues and making it impossible to reconstruct what had happened. And the clumsy removal of the pitchfork and the slash hook had obliterated any fingerprints that may have been on them. But this was wartime and Fabian had special techniques available to him that would not have been feasible before. He called the Royal Air Force base at Leamington. They sent out an Avro Anson reconnaissance plane to take aerial photographs of the area. These were detailed enough to pick out footprints and bloodstains, but Fabian had a more prosaic use for these reconnaissance pictures. He used them to construct a large-scale map so that he could trace the movements of everyone from the village on the day of the murder.

So far the local residents had not been very forthcoming. Only Alfred Potter admitted to seeing Charles Walton at work that day, though Meon Hill was open country and anyone working out there would have been clearly visible. With the map and details of everyone's movements, Fabian might be able to jog a few memories in the village. As well as being deeply suspicious of the police, the villagers had their own theory of who the killer might be. They claimed that there was something deeply un-English about the way Walton had been killed. Plainly foreigners were to blame. Luckily, there were plenty to hand.

By 1945, there were over 40,000 prisoners of war being held in Britain – with hundreds of thousands of others being held in camps in the United States, Canada, North Africa and on mainland Europe. As the war dragged on to its conclusion, security got pretty lax. Few if any prisoners wanted to return to the war and no POW held in Britain ever got back to Germany. In fact, the only recorded case of a German making a 'home run' was from Canada, when the United States was still neutral. However, trouble in prisoner-of-war camps was not uncommon. A week before the murder, there was a break-out in northwest England. Seven Germans got away. They were quickly recaptured. In the process, one was killed and four were injured. And there was a break-out in Atherstone in Warwickshire a month later.

There was a prisoner-of-war camp at Long Marston, just two miles from Lower Quinton. It would have been easy enough for a POW to slip out of the camp, commit the murder and slip back in again without being spotted. Local police had been to the camp the night after the murder. But there were 1,043 prisoners of war there – Germans, Italians, Ukrainians and Slavs. The prospect of interviewing them all was daunting. With nothing else to go on, Fabian called in Special Branch language expert Detective Sergeant David Saunders and began a long round of interviews. Eventually, they came up with a suspect. Several of the prisoners had seen an Italian serviceman desperately trying to scrub bloodstains out of his coat. When questioned, the Italian stubbornly refused to talk. Plainly he had something to hide. His coat was sent away for forensic examination. A tin watch was missing from Watton's body and Fabian had called in a mine-detecting team from the Royal Engineers. So far they had drawn a blank, so Fabian

49

put them to work in the area where the Italian had been seen acting suspiciously. What they unearthed were some home-made animal snares. The blood on his coat proved to be that of a rabbit. The Italian had been supplementing his meagre POW rations with a bit of poaching. That's why he had kept quiet.

Fabian was quickly running out of any reasonable line of enquiry. However, a fellow officer mentioned that there was a bizarre precedent for the killing. In 1875, an old woman called Ann Turner had been killed by one John Haywood. According to the report at the time, he had stabbed her with a pitchfork before 'slashing her throat with a billhook in the form of a cross'. Surely this could not be a coincidence. Then one evening, Fabian was walking up near the crime site on Meon Hill. A huge black dog came bounding past him and disappeared down the hill. A few minutes later, Fabian happened on a farm lad and asked him if he had lost a big black dog. The boy blanched and he ran away from the detective in panic. That night, Fabian mentioned this intriguing incident in the local pub, the College Arms. Villagers told him that there was a local legend surrounding a ghostly black dog. Its appearance, they said, was supposed to be a harbinger of death. Many years before, a fourteen-year-old ploughboy had seen the dog nine times. The last time he saw it, it suddenly turned into a headless woman as it rushed past him, emitting an eerie rustling sound. The following day, the boy's sister died. Superstitious twaddle, surely. But with nothing else to go on, Fabian had the story checked out. He discovered that such an incident had indeed been reported in 1885. And the ploughboy who had seen the dog was none other than Charles Walton – who had now, sixty years later, been murdered on Meon Hill.

Up to this point, the locals had been wary. Now they clammed up completely. Before when Fabian walked into the College Arms, the locals might have given him the time of day. Now the place fell silent and, when Fabian walked in, everyone else walked out. The enquiry hit a brick wall.

The mere mention of Charles Walton's name would prompt talk of a dead heifer, failed crops and veiled mentions of the evil eye. There was also talk of the Rollright Stones.

A few miles from the village of Lower Quinton are seventy or so standing stones arranged in a circle that has exactly the same diameter as the inner circle of Stonehenge. The local legend is that they were formed when a witch confronted an invading army. She transformed the leader into the 'King Stone' – which is the largest of the group – and the king's followers became the ring of stones known as 'Whispering Knights'. It is said that the stones periodically come to life and drink the nearby stream, that their exact number can never be counted and that they can induce fertility in a barren woman. It was whispered that Charles Walton had seen witches dancing up there when he was a boy. Indeed, the Rollright Stones have undoubtedly been a focus for occult activity. In the 1970s, the police found the charred remains of a puppy there after one midnight ceremony.

Disquieting things began happening around the village. A calf died mysteriously at a local farm. A police car ran over a hound in one of the narrow lanes near the village. A black dog was found hanged by its collar from a bush near where Walton had been murdered. Meanwhile the police enquiries were getting nowhere. Every one of the villagers was interviewed. In addition to the questioning of the prisoners of war, efforts had been made to track down gypsies and tinkers who might have been in the area at the time. They were detained as far away as Somerset and Salisbury. But no one could shed any light on the murder.

On 20 February, the inquest into Walton's death was opened, but, after a brief hearing, it was adjourned for a month. However, it was revealed that his clothing had been tampered with. Many of the villagers, it seemed, believed that Walton had a money belt. Fabian believed that money was the motive for the crime. Edith Walton said that her uncle had lent Alfred Potter substantial sums of money.

The war had hurt Potter's business and his farm was in dire financial straits. Potter was supposedly a pillar of the community. He was a member of the British Legion and sidesman at the local church. He was a cricket fan and a race-goer. He was also known to be a violent man when drunk. Walton was on his land when he was killed and he had a compelling motive: the repayment of Walton's loans were long overdue. The problem was that there was no documentary evidence that the loans had ever been made. So the evidence against Potter was not strong enough for charges to be laid against him.

At the second inquest hearing, Potter was cross-questioned by the coroner. Not only was Potter the only person to have seen Walton at work on the day of his death, there were huge inconsistencies in his story. At first, he said he had seen Walton at about 12.30 p.m. from a distance of about 500 yards in his shirtsleeves. But Walton had been wearing a short-sleeved shirt that day. Potter admitted drinking in the College Arms on the day of the murder and later said that he had been helping another farmer rescue a heifer that had fallen in a ditch at the time he had said he had seen Walton. But the coroner excused these contradictions because of the shock Potter had suffered in discovering the body. As the police had no concrete evidence to offer, the coroner found that Charles Walton had been 'murdered by person or persons unknown'.

Fabian remained convinced that Potter was the culprit and that he manufactured the evidence of occult activity to disguise the financial motives for the murder. They also ensured the silence of other superstitious villagers. To that extent Fabian and Spooner believed that the occult was involved in the murder. However, other occult experts believed that there was more to it than that. The murder had occurred on 14 February which, that year, was not only St Valentine's Day but Ash Wednesday too. It was also the Druidic festival of Imbolc and Candlemas, one of the four main witches' Sabbats. With the dark talk of failed crops and heifers dying mysteriously, the idea was floated that Walton had been slaughtered as part of a fertility ritual. Others speculated that Walton himself was part of an occult group and had been killed because of it.

Distinguished Egyptologist and expert on the occult Dr Margaret Murray – the author of *The Witch Cult in Western Europe* and *The God of the Witches* – visited Lower Quinton in 1950. Belief in the occult was very deep, she concluded. Walton, she believed, had been a blood sacrifice and his killer was a countryman following country ways. But Dr Murray agreed with Fabian in one respect. Both were certain that the people of Lower Quinton knew who had killed Charles Walton. They were just not saying. Margaret Murray also made a study of the case of the body in Hagley Wood and became convinced that the murdered woman was 'another victim of the devil-worshippers'. Others ridiculed the idea of occult involvement. The local church warden said: 'I think she was a gypsy and that she was tried and condemned by her tribe of Romanies.'

Following Dr Murray's investigations, the Wolverhampton *Express and Star* took up the case again and a journalist calling himself 'Quaestor' – the seeker – wrote a series of articles linking the body in Hagley Wood with the murder of Charles Walton. He traced two of the boys who had been birds'-nesting the day the corpse was found. Both were afraid of returning to the wych elm. The third boy had apparently died of shock after their ghastly find. Following the publication of Quaestor's articles, the *Express and Star* received a stream of letters, one which came from a woman calling herself 'Anna'. She said that the victim had been a Dutch woman and that the 'person responsible for the crime died insane in 1942'. This was an attractive theory as it would explain why the police could not trace her clothing or dental records. The police interviewed 'Anna' and were clearly impressed by her story. They made further enquiries in Holland. But no arrest was ever made and the victim's identity was never revealed.

4

The Church of Satan

During World War II, Aleister Crowley established new OTO lodges in Britain and authorised two American Army officers to set up branches in California. German OTO member Karl Germer, after initially being interned by the Nazis, was deported to the US in 1941 and also established new lodges there.

One of these was the Church of Thelema in Pasadena. It was run by Jack Parsons who was a rocket scientist and had developed jet-assisted take-off during World War II. Earlier he had been a disciple of Wilfred Smith, whose devil-worshipping parties at Agape Lodge during the 1930s had attracted the Hollywood crowd. In 1946, Parsons attempted to bring the 'Whore of Babylon' down from the Astral Plane and incarnate it in the womb of a woman. The experiment took place over the first three days of March. While chanting various incantations, Parsons had sex repeatedly with a willing devotee while another OTO member, science fiction writer L. Ron Hubbard, made notes. When Crowley heard about this bizarre experiment, he wrote it off as 'idiotic'. Indeed, the woman did not even get pregnant. The experiment left Parsons exhausted. And Hubbard ran off with Parsons' girlfriend and $10,000 of his money and started the Church of Scientology.

Parsons changed his name to Belarian Armiluss Al Dajjaj Antichrist and blew himself up in a chemical explosion in the basement laboratory of his home. Hubbard later claimed to have studied extensively and in person with Crowley.

When the 1960s came along, with its explosion of drugs and hedonism, Satanism was ready to win new converts. Throughout the British Isles, there were reports of graves being disturbed and magical symbols being painted on the walls of churches. In Ayrshire, Scotland, in 1964, a minister reported finding in a disused seventeenth-century church a partially burnt bible, an inverted cross and a smashed chalice. And, in the small town of Helikon in Switzerland, a group calling themselves the Seekers of Mercy were broken up by the police after a young girl in their care had died in mysterious circumstances. An investigation revealed that the group's 'church' had black candles and a fully equipped torture chamber. She had been sexually assaulted and brutally whipped while tied to an inverted cross.

Then on 30 April 1966 – Walpurgisnacht – the First Church of Satan was established in San Francisco. Its founder was former circus artist and animal trainer Anton Szandor LaVey. In the early 1960s, he quit the circus to work as a conjurer and hypnotist. Slowly his interest in magic grew and he set up a circle of students studying the black arts. His satanic beliefs were very much in the Crowley mould.

'There is a demon inside man and it must be exercised not exorcised – channelled into ritual hatred,' he said.

LaVey claimed that satanic ages last 1,458 years. The last one, where God was on top and Satan was cast down, started in AD 508. Consequently, the new satanic age began in 1966 and this time Satan was on top. 1966, LaVey proclaimed, was 'Year one, Anno Satanas'.

LaVey caught the mood of the time. He claimed that Christianity had brought restraint, mortification, self-denial, discipline and conformity. Instead, satanism offered indulgence, vitality and gratification. Sins, he argued, were really virtues as they brought physical and emotional pleasure. Within five years, he claimed 10,000 disciples world-wide. His church was recognised as a legitimate religion with resulting tax-free status in the US. He also produced two books, *The Satan Bible* and *The Satanic Rituals*. These works have been cited repeatedly in murder trials.

The First Church of Satan attracted a lot of devotees in California because of LaVey's unashamed showmanship. He called himself the Black Pope, dressed all in black, shaved his head and grew a goatee beard. His home in San Francisco was in the middle of a block with empty lots each side. The only things that grew in the barren garden were weeds. There was a mangy lion in the back yard. The house itself was totally black. Even the curtains were black. A human skeleton hung at the end of the hallway. The living room was full of stuffed animals, including a fully grown wolf and raven. His wife claimed to be a fully fledged witch and her hair hung a full three feet below her shoulders.

LaVey would use a pantomime devil-suit for his ceremonies and be greeted by the cry: 'Hail Satan.' His congregation would also be masked and robed in theatrical style. There was the obligatory nudity. A naked woman lying across the altar was, of course, *de rigueur*.

LaVey also took Satanism to the people. He choreographed ceremonies using topless dancers from seedy San Francisco bars. One of them was Susan Atkins who played a blood-sucking vampire in LaVey's 'Witches' Sabbath' at Gigi's nightclub in North Beach. She went on to become a leading member of Charles Manson's 'Family'.

The Black Pope revelled in his celebrity and boasted Sammy Davis Junior and veteran actor Keenan Wynn among his followers. Another member was Jayne Mansfield. But her lawyer, Sam Brody, was very much against her involvement, fearing that it would hurt her public image. On 29 July 1970, Mansfield and Brody were driving in San Francisco when a truck crashed into them, decapitating Mansfield. LaVey claimed prior knowledge. He said that he had put a curse on Brody and warned Mansfield to stay out of cars with him. This was dismissed as nauseating opportunism, but it helped put LaVey and his First Church of Satan in the public eye.

LaVey was employed as an adviser on the film *Rosemary's Baby* and had a walk-on part as the Devil himself. He was also technical director of the movie *The Devil's Rain*, starring John Travolta. This show-biz sell-out alienated some of his more committed followers. And when he started selling posts in the higher echelons of the church to his Hollywood friends, his followers split.

US Army Officer Michael Aquino led one break-away group and founded the rival Temple of Set which was also recognised as a legitimate church by the Federal authorities. The Temple of Set claims that it aims to teach 'responsible and ethical knowledge of the Black Arts' and to become 'the pre-eminent repository of the wisdom of the "left-hand path" '.

Aquino claimed to be worshipping not Satan, but the ancient Egyptian god Set. He too rushed into print with *The Book of the Coming Forth by Night*, which again expounded the Crowleyan view that Satan was inside man and must be released. Despite the more secretive and intellectual approach of his satanic church, Aquino also courted the theatrical. He modelled himself on Damien Thorn from the *Omen* series of films. While it is easy to dismiss him as a harmless crank, Aquino had top security clearance given to him by the US Army. He served on the World Affairs Council and at NATO and it was feared that at least twelve other members of the Temple of Set were in Army Intelligence. A police report noted that Aquino had worked in the Army's psychological warfare department and when the Army tried to dismiss him because of his involvement with Satanism, he sued for discrimination and won, arguing that his right to freedom of religion was guaranteed by the First Amendment to the Constitution. He was later promoted to lieutenant colonel, even though his increasingly fascist leanings were disturbing members of his own satanic organisation. Aquino's satanic theories kept harping back to Heinrich Himmler and his Hall of the Dead ceremonies.

The collapse of the First Church of Satan generated a

number of other spin-off cults. One, the Temple of Baal, claims in its advertising to be a 'spiritual organisation dedicated to dominance, conquest, murder and slavery'. Another, the Warlords of Satan, are said to crave 'nothing less than to turn human beings into prey'.

In May 1970, eighteen-year-old Patricia Hall – also known as Inca Angelique – was arrested with three male drifters for the rape and cat-o'-nine-tails flogging of a teenage girl in a wax museum's hall of mirrors on Bourbon Street in New Orleans. She threatened to turn the arresting officers into frogs and claimed to have been baptised by the Black Pope in San Francisco, though LaVey denied all knowledge of her. She was later extradited to Florida, where she was convicted of the stabbing of a sixty-six-year-old man.

Around the same time there were two strange murders in Morgantown, West Virginia, with occult overtones. But the evidence is itself bizarre.

On 18 January, Mared Malarik and Karen Ferrell, two nineteen-year-old students, went missing from the campus of Morgantown University. The police could not find a single clue as to their whereabouts. Then, on 6 April, the Morgantown police received an anonymous letter telling them that the bodies of the two women could be found in a wooded area some twenty-five miles outside of town. It gave the exact location of the bodies. The author signed himself with the Greek letter delta and said he would reveal himself when the bodies were located. At first the police dismissed the letter as the work of a crank. But a second letter came on 12 April, giving a map of the area showing where the bodies could be found and adding that they were lightly covered with leaves and had been partly eaten by wild animals. This time the police went out to the site. They found the two headless corpses of the women exactly as the letter-writer had described. A third letter from the mysterious 'delta' was received on 21 April 1970. It told the police where they could find the women's heads. But after an extensive search of the area, they could not be found.

However, the author of the letters then came forward. His name was Fred Scanning and he lived in La Vale, Maryland, some eighty miles from Morgantown. He had a friend named the Reverend R. Warren Hoover, who was a psychic. Hoover had a spiritual guide called Dr Spencer, who had been a practitioner in London in the 1800s. Hoover would go into a trance and speak in the voice of Dr Spencer, while Scanning recorded what he said. The tapes said that the two women had been murdered as part of the initiation rites of a satanic sect and identified the murderers as a white man with blue eyes and blond hair and a black man from West Virginia who was five feet seven inches tall. The police promptly arrested Scanning and Hoover for the murders, only to release them without charging them.

Five-and-a-half years later a prison inmate with a history of making false confessions wrote to the police saying that he had killed Mared Malarik and Karen Ferrell. His story directly contradicted the forensic evidence and he retracted his statement before the case came to court. Nevertheless, he was found guilty and sentenced to life, and another murder file was closed.

The collapse of the Church of Satan also gave rise to a huge increase in the reports of human sacrifice during satanic rituals all across the USA. And the ideas propounded by LaVey in his books continued to influence thousands of people.

In June 1971, in Vineland, New Jersey, a teenager called Mike Newell was found drowned in a sandy wash, his hands and feet bound together with adhesive tape. Newell was the leader of a thirty-strong group of devil worshippers at school. Their practices included putting a hamster in a box with walls studded with nails and shaking it. Newell believed that if he died violently, Satan would put him in command of 'forty leagues of demons'. He told two members of his group that if they did not help him commit suicide to keep his 'satanic appointment' he would kill someone else. So the two teenagers accompanied him to the wash, bound his hands and feet and pushed him in.

LaVey's *Satanic Bible* and *Satanic Rituals* were cited by the assistant attorney-general in a murder trial in Sandford, Maine, where teenage devil-worshipper Scott Waterhouse was accused of killing twelve-year-old Jezelle Cote. Jezelle had been reported missing on the evening of 29 April 1984. That afternoon she had gone to meet friends in a wood on Pike's Hill. But she did not turn up. And when she did not return to her home in Jackson Street for dinner, the police were called. The next day her body was found floating in the Mousam River which ran through the town.

For some time, there had been rumours of a teenage satanic sect in the town. The previous Hallowe'en, a number of teenage girls had received death threats signed 'the Cult'. Several youths were prosecuted, but the police failed to prove that there was really a cult operating in Sandford. The culprits' behaviour was written off as juvenile pranks.

But the murder of Jezelle Cote was no prank. A youth answering eighteen-year-old high-school student Scott Waterhouse's description was seen with Jezelle walking near the river. Waterhouse already had a record for theft and the police discovered that he, too, had been making death threats to young women. In his locker at school, they found satanic notebooks. He listed rules for satanic conduct, questions and answers about Satan and essays contrasting Christian and satanic beliefs. Most bizarre of all there was a letter to Waterhouse purporting to have come from Jesus Christ. Waterhouse had also drawn satanic graffiti on the walls of his home. He copied satanic logos from Ozzy Osbourne and Black Sabbath, wrote the ubiquitous '666' and drew sheep being killed in some form of ritual.

Waterhouse's defence contended that he had been seduced into Satanism by reading LaVey's works and that his consumption of marijuana and LSD had pushed him over the edge. But the jury would entertain no talk of diminished responsibility and convicted him for first degree murder. Judge William Broderick also dismissed Waterhouse's obsession

61

with Satanism as mumbo-jumbo. After all, LaVey's books do not explicitly advocate murder or child sacrifice. They simply promote hedonism and the pursuit of untrammelled power. Waterhouse killed because he enjoyed it, the judge said, and sentenced the eighteen-year-old to life imprisonment without the possibility of parole.

Later that year, there was a double satanic murder in Nevada. On 5 November 1984, fifty-eight-year-old Carl Gordon and his wife Colleen were getting ready for bed at their home in Washburn Road on the outskirts of Las Vegas when an intruder came crashing through the window. Colleen was dragged into the bedroom and shot twice in the head. Carl was shot seven times. Their nineteen-year-old grandson Dale Flanagan who lived in a caravan at the back of their property was charged with the murder. It turned out that he was a member of a teenage satanic sect. The murder had been planned at a coven meeting a few weeks before. In exchange for a suspended sentence for voluntary manslaughter, one of the members, Thomas Akers, turned state's evidence. Another member, Michael Walsh, pleaded guilty and was sentenced to four life terms. Another four members, including Dale Flanagan, pleaded not guilty. They were convicted anyway. Flanagan and Randy More, who had loosed the lethal bullets, were sentenced to death. Roy McDowell got life and Johnny Lucket got life without possibility of parole.

In 1983, a teenager in Oklahoma City fell under LaVey's spell. When seventeen-year-old Sean Sellers broke up with his girlfriend, he turned to LaVey's satanic teachings for comfort. He had been interested in the occult since he was twelve when he had started playing Dungeons and Dragons. Sellers grew the nail of the little finger on his left hand long and painted it black. He carried vials of his own blood around with him and made a show of drinking them in his high-school cafeteria. He formed a 'coven' with his only friend Richard Howard and held ceremonies in a derelict farmhouse where they took drugs. On 7 September 1985, Sellers borrowed a .357 Magnum pistol from

Richard's grandfather and the two boys went to the Circle K supermarket. The night clerk there, Robert Bower, had once refused to sell Sellers a six-pack of beer. Sellers and Howard chatted to Bower for a while over the counter. Then, without warning, while Bower sipped a coffee, Sellers pulled out the gun and shot him in the head. Afterwards he boasted around school that he knew how it felt to kill.

Some six months later, on Wednesday 4 March 1986, Sellers handed in an essay that frightened his teachers. It began with a quotation from LaVey's *The Satanic Bible*: 'Behold the crucifix, what does it symbolise? Pallid incompetence hanging from a tree!'

Sellers went on to describe his conversion to Satanism: 'Satanism taught me to be a better person for myself rather than for the benefit of others ... Why should I not have sex or worship other gods? I treat others not as I would have them treat me, but as they treat me.'

The essay concluded disturbingly: 'I am free. I can kill without remorse. I have seen and experienced horrors and joys indescribable on paper.'

The school contacted Sellers' mother about the essay. She was shocked, but she knew she had not been the most attentive of mothers. Vonda Sellers Bellofatto had become a mother at sixteen and was soon deserted by her husband, Sean's father. When she remarried she promised her son that they would have a settled home life. Her new husband was Paul Leon 'Lee' Bellofatto, a Vietnam veteran and former Green Beret, eleven years her senior. He tried to be a good father to his stepson and wanted to adopt him. But he was a long-distance truck driver and Sean's mother would go off on long-haul jobs with him, leaving Sean to his own devices from the age of fourteen. While she was away, Sellers was free to indulge his growing obsession with Satanism. He started collecting ritual paraphernalia and keeping bottles of blood in the fridge.

Vonda largely left her husband to discipline Sean, and Lee Bellofatto did talk to his stepson about his belief in

Satanism. But when Vonda heard about the essay from the school she was overcome with guilt for neglecting him. She sat down and wrote her son a long and supportive letter. She left the letter in his room and went to bed.

Vonda and Lee Bellofatto were already asleep when Sellers came home that night, and he never read the letter. Instead, he lit two candles – one white one, one black one – and prayed to his god Satan. Then he snuffed out the candles. Barefoot and stripped to his undershorts, he crept along the landing of the family duplex in the quiet suburb of Summit Place. In his hand was his stepfather's .44 Smith and Wesson pistol. He opened the door of the bedroom where his stepfather and mother were sleeping and crept in. He paused beside their waterbed to make sure they were sound asleep. Then he raised the gun to his stepfather's head and pulled the trigger. His mother woke and clutched at her husband's dead body only to have her son turn the gun on her. The first bullet passed through the side of her mouth. She did not die immediately. Flailing around in a groggy panic, she tried to identify the killer in the darkness. No one will ever know whether she realised that it was her own son. A second shot hit her in the side of the head. Blood spurted from the gaping wound and she slumped motionless on the pillow.

Sellers showered and dressed, then returned to his mother's bedroom and ransacked it. He removed the security bar from the patio door and forced it to make it look as if there had been a break-in. Then he drove over to Richard Howard's house, where he hid the gun. He spent the rest of the night bragging about what he had done – killing your own mother, after all, is pretty high up in the pantheon of evil.

Next morning though, Sellers tried to establish an alibi. At 8.30 a.m., he went to the pizza restaurant where his mother worked and asked to see her. He said he had stayed overnight with a friend, he was going to be late for school and he needed her to write a note for him. The restaurant owners said that his mother was not due until 9 o'clock, so

Sellers said he would go home and catch her there. Half an hour later, neighbours saw Sellers running up and down the street, shouting. It took several minutes before anyone could calm him down enough to find out what had happened. When they did, he asked them to call an ambulance.

Detective Ron Mitchell of Oklahoma City Police Department interviewed Sellers later that morning. He seemed to answer all of Mitchell's questions candidly. His clear blue eyes gave the impression of innocence. He could account for his movements, consented to be fingerprinted and gave permission for the house to be searched. But Mitchell had a hunch there was more to Sellers than met the eye.

Although the duplex showed signs of a bungled burglary, Mitchell felt that it was unlikely that Sellers' mother and stepfather would have slept through it. And on closer inspection, it was plain that the patio door had been forced from the inside.

When Mitchell contacted the school, he heard about Sellers' satanic essay. A visit to the school revealed that Sellers had bragged about a killing, which Mitchell immediately tied to the random slaying of Robert Bower. Then, when he interviewed Richard Howard, he got the clinching proof. Howard told Mitchell what had happened and led him to the gun Sellers had used to kill his mother and stepfather. And on Thursday 6 March 1986, Sellers was charged with three counts of first degree murder.

In a pre-trial motion, Sellers' lawyer, assistant public defender Bob Ravitz entered an insanity plea. But schoolmates testified that, when Sellers was asked what he would do if he was caught for the murder of Robert Bower, he said that he would plead insanity. And a psychologist diagnosed him not as insane, but as a sociopath, meaning that he was simply incapable of feelings of remorse. This meant he was the most dangerous type of criminal. The insanity plea was thrown out.

Next Ravitz argued that, although Sellers was seventeen and technically an adult, he should be tried as a minor. The

65

assistant district attorney Wendell Smith countered with a psychologist's report saying that a sociopath like Sellers was unlikely to respond to treatment. Treatment centres often release offenders after as little as two years. This was far too short a time to keep a dangerous criminal like Sellers out of society. Judge Manville T. Burford agreed and Sellers was tried as an adult.

The trial began on 24 September 1986 in front of Judge Charles Owens at Oklahoma City County Courthouse. Sellers pleaded not guilty. But throughout the rest of the trial he remained completely silent. The material evidence against Sellers was overwhelming. All that remained for the prosecution, led by district attorney Robert Macy, was to demonstrate a rational motive for the killings. His schoolmates were called. They testified that Sellers resented his mother because she disapproved of his girlfriends – dismissing one or more as 'white trash'. They also testified that he had complained that his mother was 'pushing him around' and said that it would be better if she was out of the way.

'I've killed people for less than that,' he told one girl.

In defence, Ravitz claimed that his client was the victim of satanic possession. He called in expert witnesses from a group called BADD – Bothered About Dungeons and Dragons – which claimed that the game was the way most children learned about the occult. Some of these were parents who had lost children under mysterious circumstances and their emotive testimony was very effective. To show that Sellers and his mother were not at odds, Ravitz read out the letter his mother had written to her son the day before she died: 'I'll always love you,' she wrote. 'If you let me in, I'll help you. I'll always be here when you need me, no matter what, until the day I die.'

This was the first time Sellers had heard what his mother had said in her letter and he broke down.

Ravitz also showed that although Californian detective Curtis Jackson, an expert on satanic murder, was on hand, the local police had paid him scant attention. Jackson's theory was that Sellers had killed his stepfather and mother as part of a ritual blood sacrifice. Their murders, and that of Robert Bower, had taken place on or near festivals associated with blood sacrifices in the satanic calendar. Sellers, he maintained, had slipped helplessly into a demonic state of mind. He was 'possessed'.

The jury retired for over twenty-four hours before finally dismissing this idea. They found Sellers guilty on all three counts of first degree murder. Macy asked for the death penalty.

Public opinion was running heavily against Sellers. The media made his 'possession' defence look like the work of a cynical manipulator. On 14 October 1986, Sellers was sentenced to death by lethal injection and became the youngest inmate on Oklahoma's death row.

This brought him national celebrity. *People* magazine ran a feature on the boy who murdered for the Devil in their December 1986 issue. He appeared on *The Oprah Winfrey Show* and on *Geraldo*, the network show of investigative journalist Geraldo Rivera. Sellers used the media exposure to get over his side of the story. He said he loved his mother and stepfather and that he had been driven by a demon to kill. He had now renounced Satan and had become a born-again Christian. The sentence, he claimed, was cruel and unjust.

In fact, the death sentence on Sellers was never carried out. Oklahoma had had a moratorium on death sentences since 1976. In 1987, Sellers took part in a nationwide study of juvenile murderers. New psychological tests diagnosed him as schizophrenic and he was declared insane.

In 1982, twenty-six-year-old Julian Dominguez stabbed his fifty-two-year-old father to death in San Antonio, Texas, because he thought that his father was the Devil. He stabbed him thirty-four times with a ten-inch blade.

'I thought I had just killed Satan,' he told the judge.

Drenched with blood, he fled the building. He confessed all to his cousin the next day. He was convicted of murder.

In June 1985, several informants in Toledo, Ohio, reported

attending Hallowe'en festivals in woods nearby where human sacrifices were offered to the Devil. The police went to work with spades and dug up the area. They found a nine-foot wooden cross with ligatures attached, a headless doll with nails driven through its feet and a pentagram attached to its arm, a number of axes and knives, a book on anatomical dissection, sacks of neatly folded children's clothes and sixty boy's left shoes. And in 1986, there was another spate of reports of satanic activity in El Paso, Texas.

On 2 February 1986, Lloyd Gamble killed his seventeen-year-old younger brother with a shotgun. He was a self-confessed satanist and fan of the Australian heavy metal band AC/DC, who occasionally include satanic imagery in the lyrics of their songs. Gamble claimed that he had murdered his brother to 'release him to a higher plane of consciousness'. He had picked 2 February for the killing, because it was Candlemas.

In 1987, a pair of severed female legs were found behind a church in Brookville, Indiana. They were identified as those of Monica Lemen, a twenty-one-year-old waitress from Cincinnati. A few days later, John Fryman was arrested for the murder. A search of his mobile home revealed satanic literature, black candles, a gravestone altar and other paraphernalia.

Throughout the 1980s, cemeteries from Vancouver, British Columbia to Sarasota, Florida, reported a steep climb in the numbers of graves that had been opened and bodies stolen, apparently for use in satanic rituals. And according to police records, vandalism, arson, burglaries and animal mutilations have been committed from Maine to California by satanic gangs of heavy-metal rockers called 'stoners'.

In 1988, two members of the rock band Rigor Mortis, Joseph Beeson and petty criminal Edward 'Eddie the Rotting Corpse' Bennett, were found guilty of a satanic slaying. This can hardly have come as a surprise to their fans as the band's most memorable lyrics went:

'Blood is dripping from the walls,
Someone's going to die.
You hear screams of pain and agony
As children are nailed on crosses.
Kill 'em, let's kill 'em dead.'

Pure poetry.

The truth is far more banal. Beeson and Bennett were arrested after ritually sacrificing small animals and holding drugs, booze and heavy metal parties in a derelict building. Out on bail, they fled. In Las Vegas, they held up a corner store, shot the twenty-one-year-old girl behind the till dead and wounded a customer. In Utah, they took refuge with another band of satanists. Naturally, they boasted about the murder. However, some of the other cult members did not think that the random shooting of a young girl really counted as a satanic sacrifice and told the police. Joseph Beeson pleaded guilty to murder and attempted murder and was given two life sentences. This proved to be a death sentence. In 1990 he was stabbed to death by the inmates of Utah State Prison at Ely. Meanwhile, Edward Bennett awaits a judicial death sentence on Death Row.

Terry Belcher, Robert McIntyre and Malisa Earnest used prayers from LaVey's *Satanic Bible* when they strangled seventeen-year-old Theresa Simmons on 22 January 1988.

Belcher and McIntyre were just sixteen and Earnest seventeen when the highway patrol stopped them driving a van with Georgia license plates just outside Gonzales, Louisiana. The occupants claimed that they were from Douglasville, Georgia, and were heading for New Orleans for a holiday. But a computer check found that the van had been reported stolen by Robert McIntyre's parents. The three teenagers were put in the cells while the police tried to contact their parents. After a while, Malisa's cellmate asked to speak to an officer. She told him that Malisa had been rambling on about satanism and said that she had taken part in a human sacrifice in Douglasville. Under interrogation, Malisa confirmed the story. She said that she and a Theresa Simmons had hitched a lift and been picked up by the two boys, McIntyre and Belcher. They had smoked marijuana and drunk a little together. Then the two boys started raving on about Satan and devil-worship. They decided to offer up Theresa as a sacrifice to the Devil and she was buried in the woods somewhere in Douglasville.

The police did not take the story too seriously, but decided to check it out anyway. They soon discovered that Malisa Earnest and Theresa Simmons had recently run away from a home for disturbed children and that a week before Malisa was picked up, Theresa had called a friend to say that they had been picked up by two weird boys. That was the last anyone had heard from her.

The three were taken to Atlanta where McIntyre refused to talk. But Belcher told the police everything. He praised the Devil and freely admitted to being a satanist. He had begun the year before, sacrificing small animals and drinking their blood. He had recruited McIntyre to his coven, then Malisa. She had been persuaded to bring Theresa along. The three of them took it in turns to strangle her with a leather thong, then they buried her in some scrubland near the house. Belcher was unrepentant and lectured the court on Satanism. He also turned chief prosecution witness against McIntyre. Both were sentenced to life. Malisa Earnest was sentenced to three years as an accessory.

But LaVey's works are not the only inspiration to murder. In 1990, David Biro, an avid student of Crowley's *Magick in Theory and Practice* and *Necronomicon*, shot dead two neighbours, one of whom was pregnant. In his room, a note was found saying, 'I am Cain. I kill people.' Later he bragged about the murders.

That same year, twenty-three-year-old Joe Bergamini shouted: 'Don't worry, I won't die, Satan', as he stabbed his mother to death with a knife and badly wounded his father. Neighbours in the Ozone Park area of Queens, New

York, heard screams. Moments later Bergamini's twenty-five-year-old sister started pummelling on the door, shrieking that her parents had been killed. The police arrested Joe Bergamini near the scene of the crime but he failed to respond when charged.

It would be nice to think that such things were confined to America. Sadly they are not. Take the case of Andrew Newell. He was brought up in a conventional Christian home on the outskirts of Telford, near Birmingham. He was baptised as a Christian in 1986, but Christianity failed to give him the answers he was looking for. Soon after, he left home and moved into a flat in Telford's Brookside council estate which he shared with a friend, Philip Booth. They were both fans of pseudo-satanic rock group Iron Maiden and went to their gigs. They also began dabbling in various occult religions, including Satanism.

On Saturday 8 November 1986, they went to a party and got extremely drunk, returning home in the small hours of Sunday morning. At 6.55 a.m., Philip Booth died after being stabbed in the heart.

When Detective Chief Superintendent David Cole arrived at the scene, he found Booth in the living room, naked. There were huge amounts of blood. Four wounds in the chest were grouped closely together. One had pierced the heart. The odd thing was that there was only one defensive wound, on one of his wrists. Clearly he had not been trying to fend off the attack.

In a case in the bedroom – which Newell specifically asked the police not to open – Cole found candles, a knife, a ceremonial cloth, books on the occult and some papers with two verses of an Iron Maiden song transcribed on them. The words described a satanic sacrifice, and under the last line, Newell had written the words 'Satan', 'Lucifer', 'Baphomet' and 'Belial'. And he had painted an inverted cross in human blood. One of the books described how to make an altar and the case and the things in it were drenched in Booth's blood. It was clear that they had been used to make an altar on which Booth had been sacrificed.

71

On 9 December 1987, Newell was found guilty of murder at Shrewsbury Crown Court – the first successful prosecution for satanic murder in England. However, the conviction was reduced to manslaughter by the Court of Appeal on the grounds that the trial judge had not given sufficient weight to Newell's claim that he had killed Booth in self-defence.

That same year, eighteen-year-old devil-worshipper Paul Bostock was arrested near Leicester for stabbing a young nurse over thirty times during a savage sex attack. During questioning, he also admitted to killing another woman two years earlier when he was just sixteen. He had tied her up, gagged her and then stabbed her repeatedly. She was buried just outside Leicester, where he lived, with a piece of paper covered in satanic symbols. He made regular trips to her grave. On one of these trips, he had met the nurse and killed her too. When his home was searched, other evidence of his involvement with the occult was found.

Then in August 1987, nine-year-old Christel Devilet disappeared while on holiday in the seaside town of Coxyde in Belgium. Her parents and her two older brothers searched the town and discovered that she had been seen at the entrance to the Luna Amusement Park with a fat woman. The police were called in, but could find no further clue to the whereabouts of the missing girl. Six days later, her body was found in a canal across the border in Dunkirk, France. She had been raped and murdered and her body was terribly mutilated. The autopsy revealed that the cuts and burns on her body had been inflicted in some sort of ritual. A small fire had been lit on her abdomen as if her body had been used as an altar. The pathologist could also give a good estimate of the length of time the body had been in the water. From knowledge of the current, the French police could work out where the body had been put into the canal.

They found a man who had been walking his dog on the tow path there at about the right time. He had seen a white Peugeot with Belgian number plates parked there. Back in

72

Coxyde, the Belgian police traced the owners of the twenty-nine white Peugeots in the area. One of them belonged to Claude Bouck, a man in his thirties. His wife, the police noted, was rather fat. In the cellar under the Boucks' house, the police found a satanic temple and a torture chamber with all the devilish devices needed to torture and kill Christel Devilet. They also found traces of blood on the floor of Christel's blood group. Confronted with the evidence, they confessed, without regret, that they had offered the nine-year-old girl up as a human sacrifice. They were sentenced to life imprisonment.

And in 1989, in Swansea, twenty-five-year-old Ian Harris, a long-time dabbler in the occult, was reading the tarot with his girlfriend, twenty-one-year-old Mandy Jackson. He dealt her the two cards for The Devil and Death. Taking this as a sign, he dowsed her in petrol and set her on fire. As she tried desperately to put herself out, he left. She died horribly. He too was sentenced to life imprisonment.

The murders of Christel Devilet and Mandy Jackson were brutal and horrifying. But recently, in Nottingham, there was a satanic murder that might almost be said to have an amusing side to it. In 1993, Christopher Rogers, the forty-year-old deputy head of Manchester City Council's education committee, went to dinner with thirty-seven-year-old carpenter Colin Henry, who lived with his homosexual lover in Catton, Nottingham. The three of them enjoyed wearing women's underwear and shared a taste for sado-masochistic pornographic videos.

Councillor Rogers was a practising satanist, while Henry was a devotee of witchcraft – indeed, he was a high priest in a local coven. Late that night when they were really drunk an argument broke out. Henry claims that Rogers was trying to convert him to Satanism and called his belief in witchcraft 'stupid'. He pulled a knife and stabbed its six-inch blade into the councillor's chest.

Henry pleaded not guilty to murder, claiming that Rogers had boasted of abducting and torturing to death five young men. The jury were unimpressed. Henry was

73

convicted and sentenced to life imprisonment at Nottingham Crown Court in February 1994. What the Sunday papers enjoyed most about the case was the fact that Councillor Rogers had been wearing a black PVC basque when he died. He also had flower shapes scratched around his nipples, arms and buttocks.

Not quite so entertaining is the case of thirty-four-year-old Karl Teufel who turned up at a fancy dress ball in Retz, Austria in 1973, dressed as the Devil. He was new to the district, but had found work as a mechanic in a garage owned by Anton Schelzer. He met and married thirty-two-year-old Gertrude Felsenbock and moved into a house she had bought on the edge of the forest. Two weeks after they married, they went to a fancy dress ball in Retz. This marked the end of the region's carnival and the beginning of Lent. Teufel carried the traditional toasting fork and wore a horned mask and red costume with cloven boots and a tail. He thought this was very appropriate because Teufel means 'Devil' in German. His tail particularly drew attention. The girls pulled it and made jokes about it. Their favourite was a pun – in German the word for tail is 'schleppe', while the word for 'limp' is 'schlapp'. Gertrude made the mistake of laughing at this *double entendre*. Teufel did not find it very funny.

For two days after the ball, Teufel did not turn up to work. His boss, Herr Schelzer, went round to his house to find out what the matter was. When there was no reply, he tried the door. It was unlocked, so he ventured in. In the bedroom, he found Gertrude's naked body. She was dead. The autopsy report estimated that she had died approximately two hours after the end of the ball. After a session of frantic sex, she had been strangled.

Karl Teufel had disappeared. The following day a search party was sent out into the forest. They found him, still in his Devil costume, cavorting about in the trees. He shouted at the police. 'I am the Devil. My home is hell.'

He gave himself up without a struggle. Unfit to plead, he was sent to a hospital for the criminally insane.

5

The Process Church

The Process Church of the Final Judgement was the brain-child of Robert Sylvester DeGrimston Moore, who was born in Shanghai on 10 August 1935. He was educated at Winchester and studied architecture at Regent Street Poly-technic in London. While a student, he became involved in the Church of Scientology, founded by former OTO member L. Ron Hubbard. By 1962, DeGrimston had become a senior member and ranking officer of the Church. And just as Hubbard claimed to have studied in person under Crow-ley, so DeGrimston claimed to have studied in person under Hubbard.

At the Church's London headquarters in Fitzroy Street, DeGrimston met Mary Anne MacLean. She was born in Glasgow in 1931. She had spent time in reform school and had briefly been engaged to the boxer Sugar Ray Robin-son. But when she met DeGrimston she was earning a living as a nightclub hostess on the fringes of the social circle that included Christine Keeler and Mandy Rice Davis. One of her boyfriends was the osteopath Dr Stephen Ward, the only man to stand trial in the Profumo scandal. He had a deep and long-standing interest in the occult.

DeGrimston and MacLean set up an informal group who practised what they called compulsion therapy. This attempted to rid participants of all manner of compulsive behaviour by examining the complex motivations behind it. By 1963, the group's ideas began to deviate from those of Scientology, so DeGrimston, MacLean and their followers left the Church and set up on their own. They established the Process Church of Final Judgement which believed, like the Cathars, in both God and Lucifer. The Church preached a particularly broad interpretation of the concept of free will. The Jews, they argued, had chosen to be exterminated in the Nazi gas chambers during the Holocaust. People with birth defects had chosen them in a past life. Crazy as it may seem, this idea of total freedom struck a chord in the London of the 1960s. Beatniks and bikers flocked to the new religion, but Process made its biggest effort to recruit the beautiful people – the wealthy and well-connected who would supply the Church with funds and introduce its philosophy to the highest levels of society.

By March 1966, Process had enough money to lease a huge mansion in Balfour Place, Mayfair. DeGrimston, MacLean and twenty-five other cult members moved in. Each bought an Alsatian dog. In June, eighteen members of Process went on a six-week holiday in the Bahamas. Then they moved on to Mexico. DeGrimston leased a large piece of land at Xtul, a beach area on the Yucatan peninsula. There, Process members began practising traditional satanic rituals – the sex-and-magic rites offered up to Satan by Crowley and his followers.

Back in London, DeGrimston decided that he must try and reach a wider audience with his new theology. He opened Balfour Place to the public and began producing a magazine propounding the group's philosophy. He opened a book shop and tried to recruit the pop glitterati – the Beatles, the Rolling Stones – with some success. Marianne Faithfull posed nude, clutching a rose and apparently dead for the front cover of one issue of the Process magazine. DeGrimston also began to turn out books, explaining Process's creed in more detail. The first, *As It Is*, was published in 1967. In it, DeGrimston spelt out a clear philosophical line. Christ had said, 'Love thine enemy'. Christ's enemy was Satan. So Christ should love Satan and anyone who followed Christ should also love Satan. That love would eventually break down the enmity between Christ and

Satan. On the Day of Judgement, he said, Christ and Satan would be reconciled – Christ would do the judging and Satan would execute Christ's judgements. Of course, anyone who understood this simple truth had a duty to help bring about the Day of Judgement. DeGrimston claimed he knew how to do that. In his second book, *Jehovah on War*, he wrote simply: 'Thou shalt kill.'

DeGrimston believed that a spree of motiveless killing would hasten the Final Judgement. After all Armageddon, the terrible war preceding the Day of Judgement in the Book of Revelations, was gratuitously violent. And DeGrimston was not just talking about making human sacrifices during satanic rites. He believed that the whole of life should be one long murderous ritual.

In the summer of 1967, the cult moved to San Francisco and set up in the centre of the counter-culture, the Haight-Ashbury district. Their headquarters was at 407 Cole Street. Just two blocks down the street at number 636, lived ex-convict and drifter Charles Manson.

Later, the US branch of the Process Church moved to South Cochrane Street in Los Angeles, where Hell's Angels and drug addicts from Sunset Strip as well as minor pop and movie figures made willing converts. DeGrimston tried to form a union with the First Church of Satan, but Anton LaVey dismissed he and his followers as 'kooks'.

During the paisley period of the late 1960s, Process members were distinctive in their black suits, jumpers, robes and capes. The satanic Goat of Mendes was picked out in red stitching on the back of their capes. They wore silver crucifixes around their necks. Some members wore them inverted in the satanic manner. And the symbol of the Process Church was four 'P's joined at the foot and radiating from a central point like the arms of a swastika.

The Church was divided into three fractions which, DeGrimston said, would be reunited on the Day of Judgement. New members were free to choose which road they followed. One group followed Jehovah. They were straight-laced and puritanical. The second followed

Lucifer. They immersed themselves in the pleasures of the flesh – sex, drugs and rock 'n' roll. The third faction followed Satan. Like the followers of Christ, they were puritans – but they believed in violence, sacrifice and blood.

The Process magazine gave editorial space to spokesmen from all three factions. In issue four, the so-called Sex issue, for example, Jehovah's advocate argued that sex was defilement; it was degrading and humiliating to both the participants and to couple with another human being was to exclude God. Lucifer's advocate talked of Lucifer washing away 'all pointless guilt, all worthless fear, all futile shame . . . all embarrassment and the crippling bonds of self-restraint'. Satan's advocate talked of naked women on mortuary slabs: 'you feel the atmosphere of death as you stroke the woman and then lie upon her.' And murder is never very far away: '. . . priests in midnight garb, the congregation, men and women unclothed except for blood-red masks upon their faces, stand silent waiting for the presence of their Lord and Master Satan. A naked girl, fairhaired and in the very prime of youth, lies like a human sacrifice upon the altar . . .'

The satanist urges followers to 'sink down in the decadence of excessive self-indulgence. Let no so-called sin, perversion or depravity escape your searching senses; partake of all of them to overflowing . . . There is nothing else now, with the end of man so near. There is no dialectic but death.'

Despite the seeming evenhandedness, the whole leaning of Process was towards the satanic. On the cover of the Sex issue, there was a naked girl. She was spread-eagled across an altar, beneath an inverted cross and surrounded by hooded worshippers.

The next issue was the Fear issue. In it, DeGrimston urged his followers 'by seeking out fear in living experience, we become fear itself'. One who took that teaching on board was Charles Manson who, by this time, had joined Process.

Whichever faction Process members joined, they were expected to spend some time in satanic worship. After all, sex, blood rituals and sacrifices were a good way to maintain a hold over members. The Process Church was highly structured. It had six levels – acolyte, initiate, messenger, prophet, priest and master. DeGrimston referred to it as 'The Family' and members were assigned temple names. There were brothers, sisters and fathers – but no mothers.

Following the Fear issue of the Process magazine came the Death issue. Manson, who was about to form his own 'Family', contributed an article. It was a rambling incoherent piece, but it revealed Manson's growing obsession with death. He was following where DeGrimston led. During his time in California, DeGrimston published his third book of theology. It was called *Satan on War*. In it, he wrote: 'Release the fiend that lies dormant within you, for he is strong and ruthless and his power is far beyond the bounds of human frailty.'

These words could have been written for Manson.

Soon after, the Process Church broke up, largely because many of the original members from London had come to the US on ninety-day tourist visas which they had long outstayed. Some went back to England. Others went underground. New branches of the Process Church were set up in Chicago, Dallas, New Orleans, Toronto and Cambridge, Massachusetts. DeGrimston and MacLean headed for New York and established a branch on Cornelia Street in fashionable Greenwich Village. But the Boston branch of the Process Church was by far the most successful. It recruited through a soup kitchen it ran. Several members of rock bands joined and the Church had its own rock show on local radio.

Although the Process Church had quit California, its adherents had not. A large number of dead dogs were found in the area around Santa Cruz, just south of San Francisco. Most were Alsatians and they had been beheaded, mutilated, skinned and, often, drained of their blood. The Santa Cruz police force were unable to explain this until

Stanley Dean Baker, a twenty-two-year-old lumberjack from Wyoming, was stopped by the California Highway Patrol near Big Sur on suspicion of being a hit-and-run driver. When the registration of the vehicle failed to check out, the police searched Baker and his companion Harry A. Stroop. In Baker's pocket, they found a well-thumbed copy of Anton LaVey's *Satanic Bible* and a finger. When the officer asked him what it was, Baker replied with masterly understatement: 'I have a problem. I am a cannibal.'

The car, it turned out, belonged to James Schlosser. He was a social worker from Montana who had picked Baker up as a hitchhiker in Livingston, Montana. That night they camped on Yellow River at the foot of a hill called, appropriately enough, Devil's Slide. That night there was a thunder storm. Awoken by the lightning, Baker said that he was overwhelmed by a cannibalistic compulsion which had gripped him since he had received severe electrical burns in a car accident when he was a teenager. He killed the sleeping Schlosser, cut his heart out and ate it in ritual fashion. Then he stole his car and took a finger along with him to snack on.

A body search revealed that he was covered in occult tattoos. Baker claimed to be a practising satanist and a member of a blood-drinking cult in Wyoming, who were an off-shoot of the Process Church. They sacrificed dogs during their ceremonies and drank their blood. The group, he said, had a movable carved wooden altar, a special sacrificial knife with six blades and a portable crematorium to dispose of victim's mortal remains. This was confirmed by another member of the cult. The cult called itself the Four P Movement – or Four Pi, for short – which had obvious connections with the Process symbol. Its leader, Baker said, was a wealthy doctor or business executive living in Los Angeles known as the Grand Chingon. Neither De-Grimston nor Manson fitted that description and both had left LA by that time.

During his trial, Baker was linked to the murder of a forty-year-old Robert Salem, an internationally renowned lamp designer in San Francisco. The victim's throat had been slashed and his ears cut off, and the killers had written 'Satan Saves' on the wall. Next to it was a crude drawing of a crucified man and the word 'Zodiac'. The victim's left ear had been hacked off and was missing. And on the victim's stomach was carved the circle and cross-wire symbol of the Zodiac killer. Although Baker was never charged with the murder, the case was considered closed when he was convicted in Montana. It had also been attributed to the Zodiac killer.

Both Baker and Stroop said that Baker was alone when the crime was committed, but they were both found guilty of murder and sentenced to life. In Deer Lodge Prison, Baker would crouch in his cell and growl like an animal. After several of these werewolf incidents, he was transferred to a maximum security prison in Illinois. There he became a model prisoner, counselling other inmates with drug problems. In 1976, he applied to join the First Church of Satan, but was refused admission. After serving fifteen years of his sentence, Baker was paroled. He is now trying to cope with his cannibalistic urges in the community.

Around the same time as Baker was arrested, other weird things were happening in the Santa Cruz area. In fact, in the early 1970s, District Attorney Peter Chang described Santa Cruz as 'the murder capital of the world'. And the murders were often committed by crazed cult members with apocalyptic visions.

On 19 October 1970, prominent eye surgeon Dr Victor Ohta was found dead in the swimming pool of his palatial home overlooking Santa Cruz. With him were his wife, their two sons and his secretary. They had been tied up and shot. The house had been set on fire. When the fire truck arrived, it found its way blocked by Dr Ohta's Rolls-Royce. Under its windscreen wipers was a note. It said that Ohta and his family had been killed to save the world from materialism and pollution. This was to be the first of a series of such sacrifices and it was signed, Process-style, by the 'Knight of Wands, the Knight of Cups'. The note signed off: 'Halloween 1970. Today World War III will begin as brought to you by the people of the free universe.'

Four days later, John Linley Frazier, an unemployed mechanic who lived in a cowshed down the hill from Ohta's mansion, was arrested for the murder. He said that the Book of Revelations had told him to do it.

Two years later, Herbert Mullin sacrificed the lives of thirteen people. He called the murders 'small disasters'. His idea was that these sacrifices would avert a 'big disaster'. Under the influence of the occult, he believed that the killings would save California from a major earthquake and the cataclysmic tidal wave that would follow. The murders, which all took place in and around Santa Cruz, also helped end the war in Vietnam, or so Mullin thought.

Mullin was born on 18 April 1947 in Salinas, a farming community in Monterey County, south of Santa Cruz. His father was a World War II veteran, who worked in a furniture store, and Mullin had a sister who was some years older. The family moved to San Francisco but in 1967, when Mullin was 16, they moved back to Santa Cruz, this time to the respectable suburb of Felton. It was there that he joined the Boy Scouts. At scout camp he learned to shoot. He became a proficient marksman and, later, joined the National Rifle Association. At high school, he was a good student. He graduated forty-third in a class of 132 in June 1965. Healthy and well-adjusted, he made friends easily and was not unattractive to girls. By the time he left high school, he was going steady with Loretta Richards. But that summer, his best friend, Dean Richardson, was killed in a car crash. This was a turning point. Mullin cried for a week. He became withdrawn and depressed.

By the beginning of the autumn term, he had picked himself up enough to enrol at Cabrillo college. But early the next year he began experimenting with LSD with high school friend Jim Gianera. The following year, he graduated from junior college, got a job with the public works department and, after a six-month separation, became engaged to Loretta. That fall, he registered at San Jose State

College and slowly he began to change. He lost the Christian faith he had been brought up with and he abandoned his ambition to follow in his father's footsteps and join the Army. Instead, he applied to have his draft status changed to 'conscientious objector'.

After a drugs party, he had a homosexual encounter. Although he seems to have enjoyed it, it also filled him with feelings of self-loathing. The engagement with Loretta was broken off. He changed his major from engineering to philosophy but, six weeks later, he dropped out. Then on 21 April 1968, he was arrested for the possession of marijuana. His father paid the $625 bail and he was put on probation for a year.

In October 1968, Mullin was granted his change of status by the draft board. As alternative service, he went to work for a charity, Goodwill Industries. But that did not last. After a brief period as a trainee, he was sent to manage the Goodwill thrift shop a hundred miles down the coast at San Luis Obispo but then, suddenly, he quit. In February 1969, he went to live with his older sister Patricia and her husband Albert Bocca.

By the end of March, Mullin had changed completely. He would slip into trances and imitate Bocca's actions exactly. He talked of 'secret voices' and 'cosmic emanations'. His parents took him to a mental hospital, but he discharged himself. He got a job as a dishwasher in Mendocino. Then, in September 1969, he returned to Santa Cruz where he checked into a drug rehabilitation centre. A few days later, a forest ranger saw him meditating, seemingly in a trance, in Cowell State Park. When disturbed, Mullin attacked the man with a hunting knife.

Mullin moved in with a friend from college and got a job in a gas station. But when he made unwanted homosexual advances to the nephew of a doctor, the doctor had him committed to a mental hospital. Mullin's parents got him released and took him home, giving doctors the assurance that he would attend the Santa Cruz Mental Health Clinic as an outpatient. But his behaviour did not improve. He shaved his head and changed to a macrobiotic diet, then he dressed up as bandit and affected a Mexican accent.

He got a job as a busboy in a restaurant down at the beach, but soon quit. He left home again and ended therapy after attacking another patient with an axe. Then he flew to Hawaii with a forty-year-old woman, who was a registered drug addict. When she dropped him, he committed himself to a mental hospital on Maui. After a month, he called his parents and cadged the fare home. When they met him at the airport, they were shocked. He was talking gibberish and started ranting. They called the police and tried to have him arrested. But, as the police pointed out, he had not done anything. In an attempt to stabilise his condition, Mullin was prescribed powerful anti-psychotic drugs and was arrested again. Despite the mix up, Mullin demanded the legalisation of marijuana and LSD in court and was put in psychiatric care. But he could not be bothered to turn up for appointments.

He moved to San Francisco, where he took a $15-a-week room at the Donnelly Hotel in the city's squalid Tenderloin district. He took up boxing. A local gym thought he showed promise. But he lost his first fight on points and gave up. At that time, he knew Jean Carlisle, a professional photographer who let Mullin baby-sit her four-year-old child. Mullin told her that he was a quarter Swiss, like Einstein. This became something of an obsession for him. Then he discovered that Einstein had died on 18 April 1955. He himself was born on 18 April 1947. But, more significantly, the earthquake that had destroyed San Francisco had occurred on 18 April 1906.

Soon everything became clear – to Mullin at least. Veteran earthquake forecaster Reuben Greenspan predicted that San Francisco would be hit by another devastating earthquake. Calculating the tidal forces on the San Andreas fault by the Sun and Moon, he worked out this would happen on 4 January 1973. Greenspan had accurately predicted earthquakes this way before. Mullin believed that the way to stop this huge natural disaster was to offer up human sacrifices. He was perfectly prepared to be one himself. After a murderous spree, Mullin realised that he would be caught and sentenced to die in the electric chair – a scapegoat for a generation, he told himself. But it would be worth it if he could prevent California falling into the sea and stop the Vietnam war.

On the morning of 13 October 1972, Herbert Mullin was driving down Highway 9 when he spotted his first sacrificial victim – an old hobo called Lawrence 'Whitey' White. He was shuffling along the side of the road. Mullin drove by and parked a little way ahead. He had a baseball bat in the back of his station-wagon. He grabbed it and got out. Then he opened the hood and looked in at the engine, shaking his head as if something was wrong. When Whitey reached the car, he kindly offered his help. Then, as he leaned over the engine to take a look, Mullin clubbed him over the head with the baseball bat. The tramp crumpled, but Mullin went on hitting him over and over again, even after he was dead. Eventually, Mullin rolled his body down a shallow bank at the side of the road and hid it in some dense undergrowth. Then he drove home to his parents' house in time for lunch.

The body was found that afternoon by John Chilton who had stopped his car to take a walk. However, though Whitey was known by other hobos in the area, the police could find out nothing more about him and the investigation soon faltered. He was given a funeral at the state's expense.

Four days later, Mary Margaret Guilfoyle, a twenty-four-year-old student at Cabrillo College, had missed her bus. She knew that she should not hitchhike. There had been a series of murders of young college girls in the area at the time. But she had a job interview at 3.30 p.m. in the California Department of Human Resources employment office in downtown Santa Cruz six miles away. She had to run to catch up with the blue and white station-wagon that had stopped just up the road. She hesitated for a moment before she got in. But the driver was a guy about her age and he was slight. She could probably handle it if he tried anything. He said he was going right by the employment office, so she got in. Everything seemed fine for the first five minutes. Then he pulled off the highway. But before she could ask why, she was dead, stabbed in the chest with a hunting knife. He took her body to a deserted spot on Empire Grade, where he dumped her in a clearing. Then he ritually dissected her.

A week later, Mullin was parked outside St Mary's Church in Los Gatos, the next town to Santa Cruz in Santa Clara County. It seemed like an appropriate place to find another human sacrifice. No one had gone in or out of the church for some time. When he went in, Mullin saw a light on over one of the confessionals. It was a sign, he thought. There was a priest inside, waiting to hear confession. Mullin knew the priest must die.

Inside the confessional, Father Henri Tomei, a hero of the French Resistance who had been in America since 1961, was at prayer. He heard a rattling at the confessional door and slipped the bolt. The door flew open and Mullin stabbed the defenceless priest repeatedly until he was dead. Mullin heard a scream behind him. He quickly sheathed his knife and walked slowly out of the side exit. Then he drove home.

The pastor of St Mary's, Father Richard Nowley, heard a pounding on his rectory door. It was Mrs Margaret Reed, one of his parishioners. She had seen Mullin murder Father Tomei in the church. She gave a description. The killer was white, medium height, medium build. It could have fitted any one of a hundred thousand men in California alone. Los Gatos' Sheriff's office was at a loss. They could not find a motive for the attack. And the only clue they had was one fingerprint on the door of the confessional. In Santa Cruz, though, the police were not even looking for the killer of Mary Guilfoyle. Her boyfriend had reported her missing, but the police said the missing girl had probably run off with another man. He eventually called her parents in upstate New York. They had not heard from her and they were worried. They put an advertisement in the *Santa Cruz Sentinel* showing a picture of Mary. It was headlined: 'Urgent, have you seen this girl?' The ad gave the telephone numbers of the supervisor of Cabrillo College and Mary's boyfriend. No one called.

Three months had passed since the last murder and Mullin knew he was safe. No one had even come close to arresting him. Then on 25 January 1973, Mullin woke knowing that he had to kill his old school friend Jim Gianera. At 9 a.m. he drove up to the log cabin where he used to buy drugs from Gianera. The door was answered by Kathy Francis. Her husband was Gianera's business partner and she recognised Mullin as an old friend of Gianera's. Joe and his wife had moved, she explained, and she gave Mullin their new address. Mullin went there and Gianera answered the door. As he turned to lead Mullin into the living room, Mullin pulled a small revolver from his belt and began firing. Somehow Gianera managed to stumble upstairs. His wife emerged from the bathroom to see her husband bleeding heavily. He tried to warn her, but it was too late. Mullin killed her too. Then he drove back to Kathy Francis's cabin, shot her and her two sons, then stabbed them for good measure. The next day, Kathy's husband Bob Francis, who had been away making a drugs deal, found himself in custody, the prime suspect in all five killings.

Two days later came the news that Mullin's perverted sacrifices seemed to be working. The Paris Peace Accords, ending America's involvement in the Vietnam war, were signed.

On 7 February 1973, Mullin returned to Cowell State Park where he came across a shack that had been constructed by four teenage boys – Mark Johnson, fifteen, David Oliker and Rob Spector, both eighteen, and Scott Card, nineteen. Mullin scolded them for building such a shelter on government property. The boys were not frightened of him because they had a .22-calibre rifle with them for protection. It did not help. Mullin came back a little while later with his small black revolver and killed them all.

87

Two days later, veteran earthquake-predicter Reuben Greenspan held a press conference and said quite simply: 'I goofed.' His calculations had been wrong. There was not going to be an earthquake as he had predicted. But Mullin knew that he had not goofed at all. It was his bloody sacrifice of twelve innocent lives that had saved California.

But the killing still did not stop. On 13 February 1973, seventy-two-year-old Fred Perez went out early to fix the driveway of his rented bungalow. He was a well-known figure around Santa Cruz. After serving in the Marines during World War II, he had been a middleweight boxer under the name Freddie Bell. After a long career in the ring, he had retired to join the family fish business that had been established in Santa Cruz for one hundred and ten years. The Perez family had once owned most of the ocean front in the town, but had sold it off over the years to developers. Fred Perez and his wife now lived in retirement in a quiet residential area of Santa Cruz.

At around 8 a.m., Fred was pushing his wheelbarrow up the driveway when a station-wagon drove by. It stopped a little way up the road. A young man got out with a .22 rifle. Fred Perez was too intent on heaving the wheelbarrow up the slight incline to take any notice. The young man aimed carefully – and pulled the trigger. The old man knew nothing until the bullet hit him in the chest. It ripped through his right lung, his aorta and his heart. Perez gasped for air and crumpled. He was unconscious before he hit the ground.

Immediately across the street from the Perezes' bungalow, Joan Stagnaro was opening the lounge curtains. She heard a gunshot and looked out. A blue and white station-wagon was just pulling away. She watched as it turned right at the first intersection and saw that it had a distinctive red STP sticker on the passenger door. It was only then that she noticed Fred Perez lying bleeding in his driveway. She screamed, rousing her sons. But by the time they had run across the street, the old man was already dead. Composing herself, Mrs Stagnaro called the police. In two minutes, her description of the killer's car was out on an all-points bulletin. Patrolman Sean Upton heard the bulletin as he was driving down Highway 1. Immediately in front of him was a blue and white station-wagon with a red STP sticker on the passenger door.

'I've got him,' he radioed in. 'Send me cover.'

The Santa Cruz Police Department put out the call. Cars were already on their way when Patrolman Upton turned on his siren, pulled the station-wagon over and stopped a little way in front of it. He did not risk approaching the car alone. Instead, he switched on his roof-mounted megaphone.

'This is a felony arrest,' he said. 'We have you covered. Put your hands on the windshield and don't move.'

The driver did as he was told. When two more patrol cars arrived, officers pulled their guns. Gingerly, they approached the station-wagon. A .22-calibre rifle was propped against the front seat. But the driver came quietly.

At the police station, he was fingerprinted. He was identified as twenty-five-year-old Herbert William Mullin, five foot seven inches tall, weighing 135 pounds. He had brown hair and brown eyes. He was formally charged with the murder of Fred Perez. When cautioned, he said simply: 'I don't have to answer any questions. I choose to remain silent.'

This left the police with a puzzle. There was no obvious connection between the victim and the killer. The murder seemed motiveless. The only thing Mullin said to explain his action was: 'Satan gets into people and makes them do things they don't want to do.' The police took him to the county hospital for a medical examination. No immediate signs of illness or drug addiction were found. But there were burn marks on his penis and a bizarre collection of mystical tattoos on his arms and ankles. They read 'Kriya Yoga', 'Mahashamadi' and 'Birth'. Others on his abdomen said 'Legalise Acid' and 'Eagle Eyes Marijuana'.

Then things began to come together. In Mullin's pocket, there was a receipt for a .22 pistol bought from the Western

Auto store in Santa Cruz on 16 December 1972 for just $25. The Santa Cruz Police Department checked their unsolved murder files and discovered that the Francis family and Jim Gianera and his wife had all been shot with a .22 pistol. Armed with a search warrant, the police found the revolver in Mullin's station-wagon. Ballistics tests showed that it had been used to kill the Gianeras and the Francises. Mullin's address book had Gianera's name in it. A leather pouch four-year-old Daemon Francis had kept his marbles in was found in Mullin's apartment. And Bob Francis confirmed that Mullin had been a customer of theirs.

Mullin's parents told the police that Mullin had brought them a station-wagon full of fire wood, cut up on Empire Grade. A search there revealed Mary Guilfoyle's mutilated body hidden in the undergrowth.

When Mullin's fingerprints were checked against state records, they matched the single print lifted from the confessional at St Mary's Church in Los Gatos. Mullin was charged with seven counts of first-degree murder and bail was set at $300,000.

Two days later, on 17 February 1973, twenty-one-year-old Jeff Card came into Santa Cruz police station. He had just found the bodies of his younger brother Scott and his three friends at their camp in Cowell State Park. They had been shot with Mullin's .22 pistol and the .22-calibre rifle that was used to shoot Perez was missing from their shack. This brought the charge sheet to eleven.

Mullin refused to answer police questions and remained silent in court. A plea of *nolo contendre* was entered. This is a 'no contest' plea allowed in American courts which is a way of pleading guilty without technically admitting guilt. His court-appointed public defender Jim Jackson said: 'He's as nutty as a tree full of fish.' Only later, with psychiatrist Donald Lunde, did Mullin admit the killings.

'It was to avoid the great earthquake that was coming earlier in the year,' he said. 'And it was prevented.'

6

The Family

Charles Manson had connections to the Process Church and his chief lieutenant and hitwoman Susan Atkins was a satanist with connections to Anton LaVey.

Manson was born 'No Name Maddox' in Cincinnati, Ohio, on 11 or 12 November 1934. His mother, Kathleen Maddox could not remember which. So she plumped for the eleventh. She was just sixteen when she gave birth and had run away from home in Ashland, Kentucky, to escape her Bible-thumping mother. She supported herself by prostitution. Manson's father was a drugstore cowboy who called himself Colonel Scott. He left long before the birth. But William Manson married Kathleen briefly at that time and gave the young boy his surname.

Kathleen Maddox found motherhood difficult and regularly abandoned her son. By the time he was six, she found she was unable to support herself and her son even by prostitution, so she left him with her mother, while she and her brother, Luther, robbed a gas station. They were caught and jailed for five years.

Manson stayed with his strict grandparents for a few weeks, then was farmed out to his mother's sister, Joanne, in McMechen, West Virginia. When Kathleen was paroled, she came back for the boy. Manson was ecstatic. They began a shiftless existence together, roaming the Midwest. It was not the most stable of existences. Kathleen was always on the murky fringes of crime and Manson could never be sure whether they would stay together or he would be farmed out to someone else. Eventually Kathleen met a man who wanted her. But he did not want her young son. So Kathleen had Manson made a ward of court and he was sent to the Gibault Home for Boys in Terre Haute, Indiana. His mother visited him there and promised he would be back with her 'pretty soon'. But gradually they lost contact. Later, he was sent to the famous orphans' home, Boys' Town in Nebraska. He was kicked out for his surly manner and constant thieving.

Still in his early teens, Manson became a drifter and was soon arrested for stealing food. He was sent to Indiana Boys' School, where he escaped eighteen times. In 1951, he was arrested again for theft in Beaver City, Utah, and served four years in a federal reformatory. Reformatories, Manson found, were a great improvement on children's homes. While the harsh, often sadistic, regimes in orphanages had taught him to survive, reformatories were the universities of petty crime.

In November 1954, he was released into the custody of his aunt in McMechen, where he met miner's daughter Rosalie Jean Willis. They married in January 1955. But soon he was arrested for transporting stolen cars across the state line into California and sentenced to three years in Terminal Island Federal Prison in San Pedro near Los Angeles. Soon after, his wife bore him a son. She then divorced Manson and went out of his life, taking Charlie Junior with her.

In jail, Manson took an intensive course on how to be a pimp. Paroled in 1958, Manson set about his new career in Hollywood. His first attempt failed miserably. He fell in love with his main woman, who then dumped him. He was nothing if not tenacious and was arrested repeatedly under the Mann Act for transporting women across state lines for immoral purposes.

Manson started forging cheques. When he was caught passing a stolen cheque for $38, he absconded to Mexico. But the police still caught up with him and he was sentenced to ten years in the federal penitentiary on McNeil Island in Washington State.

Being small, just five foot two inches, Manson had a hard time in prison. He was raped repeatedly by other prisoners, many of whom were black. This left him with a lifelong racial chip on his shoulder. Manson was also introduced to the philosophy of Scientology in jail. Established by former OTO member Lafayette Ron Hubbard, Scientology is often dismissed as a cynical money-making idea. However 'the modern science of mental health', as Scientology is subtitled, has a skilfully constructed theory. This is expressed in bewildering jargon and has no scientific data, statistics or methodology to back it, but it does have a certain plausibility.

Hubbard's idea is that most mental health problems are caused by emotionally or physically painful experiences undergone when the person is in the womb, unconscious or ill. These are recorded in the body's cells as 'engrams'. When these are accidentally restimulated by events in the outside world, they cause the victim to behave seemingly irrationally. Naturally, Scientology can rid the sufferer of these engrams by reliving them when in a light hypnotic trance known as a reverie. Those who study scientology seriously, it is said, can empty their 'engram bank'. This makes them, in scientological jargon, a 'clear'.

Manson claimed to be a clear, but there is little evidence that he really took Scientology very seriously. What attracted him was the control such ideas gave him over other people. To survive in prison, Manson had already become shifty, cunning and manipulative. To this, he added the techniques of Scientology. These set him in good stead when he was released on 21 March 1967.

When he went to jail, it had been the 1950s. The world was conservative, restrained. By the time he came out, everything had changed. A new generation was turning on, tuning in and dropping out. He was thirty-two years old and he headed for the centre of it all, San Francisco. He had heard what was going on from new inmates coming into the jail, but he had scarcely believed it. Now he was in the outside world, he saw it was all true.

'Pretty little girls were running around everyplace with no panties or bras and asking for love,' Manson said. 'Grass and hallucinatory drugs were being handed to you on the streets. It was a different world than I had ever been in and one that I believed was too good to be true. It was a convict's dream and after being locked up for seven solid years, I didn't run from it. I joined it and the generation that lived in it.'

One of his first experiences on the outside was attending a Grateful Dead concert and dropping a tab of acid. People remember him dancing like a man possessed, then suddenly falling into a trance and curling up in the foetal position. He had just $30. He bought a guitar and started to busk. Suddenly, he became something of a star in the hippy Haight-Ashbury district. People also flocked to him on the campus of the University of California at Berkeley. The world was turning against the establishment and 'straight' society. Suddenly, the institutionalised reject Manson was all the rage. He soon discovered that he could use the manipulative powers he had learned in jail on the long-haired flower children that inhabited southern California. With his hypnotic stare, his unconventional lifestyle and the strange meaningless phrases he babbled, he was the perfect hippy guru. The rhetoric of Scientology was soon supplemented by what he learned from the Process Church. His contempt for authority and convention made him a hero of the counter-culture and he soon developed a penchant for the fashionable middle-class girls who had chicly dropped out of mainstream society. The first was Mary Bruner, a librarian. She was a slim, flat-chested red-head and not very pretty. But she was naive and impressionable, very much Manson's type. So he stopped sleeping in the park and moved in with her. Soon he picked up another girl called Darlene and discovered something new. By sleeping with Mary and Darlene on a strict rota basis, he found he could control both of them. He had discovered the power of sex.

The Process Church moved down to Los Angeles, so

Mary bought a VW bus and Manson got his parole officer's approval to travel down the coast. On the way, Manson and Bruner sampled communal living – and loving – in the communes that were being established throughout California. Eventually, they reached Los Angeles, where Manson intended to establish himself as a rock superstar.

On Venice Beach, he met another slim redhead, Lynette 'Squeaky' Fromme. She had just had a row with her father and was emotionally vulnerable. Manson brought her back to Mary and had sex with her. The three of them formed the nucleus of 'The Family'. This was Manson's entourage of hangers-on. They comprised a harem of young girls – who were all about ten years younger than him – and a number of docile males who would do anything he told them to. They numbered as many as thirty to thirty-five at one time. Manson controlled them through acid – LSD – and sex. Every woman who came to the Family was initiated by Manson. She would be given a tab of acid, then have a few hours of sex with him. Soon she would be joining in the skilfully choreographed orgies, where Manson would control who did what and with whom.

An early recruit was Patricia Krenwinkel. She was a former girl scout from a normal middle-class family. Her expensive education earned her a good job as a legal clerk at a big insurance company in Los Angeles. She met Manson on Manhattan Beach when she was twenty-one and abandoned everything to be with him. She ditched her car and walked out of her job without even bothering to pick up her last paycheck. Leslie Van Houten was just nineteen when she dropped out of school. She lived on the streets on a perpetual acid trip until she met Manson. Twenty-year-old Linda Kasabian left her husband and two children and stole $5,000 from a friend to join the Family. She too began to see her seamy life through a constant haze of LSD. Another redhead, Diane Lake, joined after her parents had dropped out to join the Hog Farm commune. And Ruth Ann Moorehouse, a preacher's daughter,

95

married a hapless bus driver so she could leave home and join the Family.

The woman who brought Satanism to the Family was Susan Atkins. Her real name was Sadie Mae Gutz. At twenty-one, she was a topless dancer and bar-room hustler. It was in that role that she became involved with Anton LaVey's First Church of Satan. Later, she became Manson's closest aide. But, like the others, she had to share his sexual favours. He promised each girl a baby in return for their devotion, while Susan used the situation to plant her naive satanist ideas into their receptive minds.

One of the few men in the commune was twenty-three-year-old former high school football star from Farmersville, Texas, Charles 'Tex' Watson. He had once been an honours student, but in Manson's hands he had become a mindless automaton. Another college drop-out, Bruce Davis, joined them. So did Bobby Beausoleil, former guitarist with the Digger band Orkustra and protégé of underground film-maker Kenneth Anger. Anger was a follower of Crowley and one of LaVey's magic circle. Beausoleil had played Lucifer in Anger's movie *Invocation of My Demon Brother* and taken part in a Black Mass Anger performed on stage at the premier. But Beausoleil spoiled the occasion by ripping off some of Anger's camera equipment. Anger had a locket made with a picture of Beausoleil on one side and a picture of a toad on the other. The inscription read: 'Bobby Beausoleil – who was turned into a toad by Kenneth Anger.' Two years later Beausoleil was arrested for the Manson murders, while Anger went on to write the bestselling exposé *Hollywood Babylon*.

The Family hung around on the fringes of the movie community. With three girls to every man, they were welcome at any party. Often they would sit in a circle and take acid, taking a group trip. Family member Paul Wilkins remembered that Manson was always the one who handed out the tabs. He always took less than everybody else. He was always in control.

Dennis Wilson of the 1960s Californian band, the Beach

Boys, was particularly fascinated by Manson and his life-style. The Family free-loaded on him unmercifully. He put them up, fed them and clothed them from his own wardrobe.

The Family quickly grew to the point where the bus could no longer contain them. They moved out to a huddle of shacks around Topanga Canyon. Almost every young hippy drifter on the West Coast passed in and out of the Family at that time – Joan 'Juanita' Wildebush, Sandra Good, T. J. 'the Terrible' Walleman, Juan Flynn, Cathy Gillies, Brooks Poston and Steve 'Clem' Grogan. Kitty Lutesinger, Cathy 'Gypsy' Share and Stephanie Scram became more permanent members. There were junior additions too. Susan Atkins gave birth to a son, imaginatively named Zezozoe C. Zadfrack, while Mary Brunner had a boy named Valentine Michael after Robert Heinlein's hero in the trendy cult 1960s science fiction classic *Stranger in a Strange Land.*

By and large, the girls were middle-class drop-outs. Susan Atkins was the only one with a criminal record. They brought with them money, cars, daddy's credit cards – what was needed if the Family was to survive. They formed the secret core of the Family. To join, they had to meet Manson's hypnotic gaze and perform seemingly impossible tasks. They were taught to think of themselves as an elite and the outside world as hostile, threatening and beneath contempt. And with their means of support in the outside world surrendered, Manson controlled them with threats of expulsion and, occasionally, death.

During his time in Los Angeles, Manson stayed close to the Process Church. When it courted pop stars like John Phillips of The Mamas and the Papas, so did Manson. The icons of Satanism – perhaps the satanist wing of the Process Church – began to get more important. Manson traded the VW van for a school bus, which was painted black. It was adorned with an image of the Goat of Mendes/Baphomet painted by Beausoleil. The words 'Holywood [sic] Film Production Company' were painted on the side in an attempt to avoid trouble with the police.

When Process broke up, Manson headed for the desert. Through contacts in San Diego, the Family got permission to stay out on the Spahn ranch. This was an old movie set where westerns would be shot. It was owned by eighty-year-old George Spahn. He was virtually blind. In return for being allowed to settle there, the girls cooked and cleaned for him – and, according to some, provided him with sexual favours. Lynette Fromme later told prosecuting attorney Vincent Bugliosi that she was in love with Spahn and would have married him if he had asked her to.

To enhance their counter-culture status, the Family fed themselves by collecting food thrown out by supermarkets. This was supposed to show how wicked and wasteful the 'capitalist' world was. The effect was marred somewhat by the fact that they picked up the discarded food in a Rolls-Royce. They freed themselves from the other constraints of straight society by hustling dope, 'borrowing' credit cards and 'liberating' cars and other valuables. Family member Cathy Gillies rented the Family's second home, the Baker Ranch, using Dennis Wilson's collection of gold records as a deposit.

Surrounded by compliant sycophants, the drug-addled Manson began to build huge delusions, fuelled by Susan Atkins' studies of Satanism and the teachings of the Process Church. She convinced him that his own name, Manson, was significant. Manson, or Man-son, meant Son of Man, or Christ, in her twisted logic. He was also the Devil, Susan Atkins said. Manson began to see himself as the gnostic deity Abraxas – a rooster-headed god figure with serpent's feet and in whom light and darkness, good and evil, are supposed to be both unified and transcended. He also called himself both Christ and Satan and said that after the apocalypse, the coming black-white war, he – 'the Beast of the bottomless pit' – would bring salvation.

The Beatles' *White* album, Manson believed, was full of messages directed at him and his Family. 'Sexy Sadie' was aimed at Susan Atkins, whose real name was Sadie. 'Piggies' sneered at the establishment and was a word that became very much a part of the Family's vocabulary. 'Blackbird' was a call for black people to revolt. 'Revolution 9' was aural chaos. But to Manson, 'Revolution 9' meant Revelations, chapter nine. Although he had been illiterate until his early twenties, Manson had been brought up with a thorough knowledge of the Bible. Chapter nine of the Book of Revelations talks of the coming of Appollyon, the Exterminating Angel. Manson saw himself as that too. And one verse in chapter nine reads: 'Neither repented they of their murders, not of their sorceries, nor of their fornications, nor of their theft.'

He was blissfully unaware that a helter skelter was a harmless British funfair ride and interpreted the track 'Helter Skelter' as heralding the beginning of what he saw as an inevitable race war. The blacks would rise up and wipe out the piggies – the police, authority figures, the rich and the famous, and what Manson called 'movie people' who – although they partied with him – had plainly failed to recognise his cinematic potential. Throughout this cataclysm, Manson would wait in safety in the desert. Once the blacks were in charge, being inferior, they would find themselves incapable of intelligent rule. So they would turn to him and ask him to take over as world ruler. The only problem remaining was how to provoke this Armageddon. To this end, Manson tried to recruit violent biker groups such as the Straight Satans and, later, turned to violence himself.

In the meantime, Manson believed anything the Beatles could do, he could do better. He fancied himself as something of a pop star and took one of his feeble compositions to successful West Coast musician Gary Hinman. It was then that Manson learned that Hinman had recently inherited $20,000. He sent Mary Brunner, Susan Atkins and Bob Beausoleil to Hinman's house on Old Topanga Canyon Road, to steal the money and to kill Hinman for refusing to put Manson at the top of the charts, which was where he believed his feeble effort belonged. The three Family members argued with Hinman for about two hours. Then Bobby Beausoleil lost his patience and pulled the Family's gun, a 9 mm Radom pistol. He handed it to Susan Atkins and began searching the house. With Beausoleil out of the room, Hinman tried to escape. He struggled with Susan Atkins. The gun went off. The bullet richocheted around the kitchen and embedding itself under the sink. Hearing the shot, Beausoleil ran back, grabbed the gun and beat Hinman around the head with it. Then the intruders called Manson, who drove over to Hinman's house. Manson took a sword and cut Hinman's ear. He told Beausoleil to find the money. The girls were to clean up Hinman's wounds, then they were to bring him out to the ranch. Then Manson left.

Mary Brunner stitched up Hinman's ear with dental floss, bandaged his other wounds and gave him something to drink. Then when Hinman was tied up on the hearth rug, Beausoleil and Atkins ransacked the house. But the money was not there. All they found were two pink slips – the ownership documents to two cars. Under threat of death, Hinman signed them over. At dawn the following morning, Hinman managed to reach the window and screamed for help. Beausoleil panicked and stabbed him twice in the chest and left him to bleed to death. Devil-worshipper Susan Atkins dipped her finger in Hinman's blood and wrote 'political piggie' in blood on the wall. And she drew a cat's paw, a crude version of the logo of the militant Black separatist movement, the Black Panthers. Then the three of them bundled up some blood-stained bandages and clothes. They tried to wipe their fingerprints off everything they had touched during their long stay at Hinman's house. Then they left, locking all the doors behind them. But then they began to worry that Hinman was not dead, so they climbed back into the house through a side window and smothered him for good measure. Then they hot-wired Hinman's VW van and drove to the To-panga Kitchen where they celebrated with coffee and cherry cake. Afterwards they drove back to the Spahn Ranch to tell Manson what they had done.

Hinman's body was found by friends on 31 July 1969,

four days after he was murdered. The Los Angeles Sheriff's Office – which deals with crime outside the metropolitan area – were called in. Sergeant Paul Whiteley and Deputy Charles Guenther were assigned to the case. The investigation started out easily enough. The killers had not done a very good job of cleaning up and they found Beausoleil's fingerprints in Hinman's house. On 6 August, they picked up Beausoleil. They found the knife that killed Hinman and a T-shirt drenched in Hinman's blood in Beausoleil's car. He was convicted of murder and went to jail – but without implicating Atkins or Manson.

This loyalty impressed Manson not at all and he began to plan new acts of violence. Next he tried to get his dire composition recorded by the son of Doris Day, Terry Melcher, who Dennis Wilson of the Beach Boys had introduced him to. Melcher was a big player in the music industry, but failed to see the potential in Manson's material. Manson's followers formed a death squad. They dressed in black and trained in the arts of breaking and entering in abandoned buildings. These exercises were known as 'creepy crawlies'. As part of their training, Manson told them they were to kill anyone who stood in their way.

On 8 August 1969, Manson's death squad was despatched to Melcher's remote home on Cielo Drive in Benedict Canyon in the Hollywood Hills. But Melcher had moved. This did not matter to Manson. The people he saw going in and out of the house were 'movie types'. Their slaughter would act as a warning. He sent Tex Watson, Susan Atkins, Patricia Krenwinkel and Linda Kasabian to the house armed with a .22 Bluntline Special revolver, a knife and a length of rope.

The house at the end of Cielo Drive was indeed occupied by 'movie people'. Film director Roman Polanski was away shooting a movie in London. But his wife, movie star Sharon Tate, who was eight months pregnant, was at home. Coffee heiress Abigail Folger and her boyfriend Polish writer Voytek Frykowski were visiting. So was Sharon Tate's friend, celebrity hairdresser Jay Sebring.

Manson's death squad parked their white and yellow Ford outside 10050 Cielo Drive, while Tex Watson shinned up a telegraph pole and cut the phone lines. Kasabian lost her nerve at the last minute and stayed outside. Tex Watson, Susan Atkins and Patricia Krenwinkel pushed open the wrought iron gates. At that moment a white two-seat Nash Ambassador came down the driveway. It was driven by eighteen-year-old Steven Parent. He had been visiting the caretaker. Brandishing the .22, Tex Watson leapt into the headlight beams and screamed for the driver to stop. He thrust the gun into the car window. Steven Parent begged for his life. Watson pumped four bullets into his chest.

Patricia and Susan scouted around the house, but could find no way in. So Watson started cutting his way through the screen on the window of an empty room in the front. Inside the house, Manson's disciples found Voytek Frykowski asleep on the couch. He woke to find a .22 in his face. He asked what they wanted.

'I am the Devil,' replied Watson. 'I am here to do the Devil's business. Give me your money.'

He told Susan Atkins to get some towels to tie Frykowski up. On her way back from the bathroom, she saw the others talking in a bedroom. She reported back to Watson, who told her to go and get them. Susan Atkins told Sharon Tate and her guests that the house was simply being robbed and no harm would come to them. While she was tying them up, Jay Sebring broke free and made a lunge for the gun. Watson shot him in the armpit, then stabbed him four times.

Fearing they were all going to be killed, Frykowski attacked Watson, who beat him to the ground with the pistol butt. He hit him so hard that the walnut grip of the pistol broke in two. Frykowski staggered to the door, screaming for help. Then in a frenzy, the girls stabbed Frykowski to death. There were fifty-one stab wounds on his body. Frykowski's gallant stand put some fight in the others. Abigail Folger made a break for it. But Krenwinkel caught up with her halfway across the lawn. She was knocked to the ground and Watson stabbed her to death. Sharon Tate begged for the life of her unborn child. Susan Atkins showed no mercy. While Patricia Krenwinkel held her down, she stabbed her sixteen times. Tate's mutilated body was tied to Sebring's corpse. Watson then went around kicking and stabbing the lifeless bodies. The killers spread an American flag across the couch and wrote the word 'pig' on the front door in Sharon Tate's blood. They changed their bloody clothes, collected their weapons and made their way back to the Spahn Ranch, disposing of the evidence on the way.

'I felt so elated,' said Susan Atkins. 'Tired but at peace with the world. I knew this was just the beginning of helter skelter. Now the world would listen.'

Later that night, Manson and another member of the Family returned to Cielo Drive to look for Susan Atkins' knife and clean up. They wiped Steven Parent's car clean, then cleaned off the finger prints in the house with the towel that had been used to tie up Frykowski. They left it draped over Jay Sebring's face. Manson got high on marijuana and read the reports of the murders in the newspapers as if they were reviews. To celebrate this great victory, he had an orgy with his female followers. But soon he craved more blood.

On 10 August, Watson, Kasabian, Krenwinkel and Atkins set out again. This time Manson accompanied them. Leslie Van Houten and Steven 'Clem' Grogan came along for the ride. Manson randomly selected a house in the Silver Lake area of Los Angeles. The address was 3301 Waverley Drive. He took his sword and his gun, walked up the drive to the long low house and broke in. The house belonged to forty-four-year-old grocery store-owner Leno LaBianca and his thirty-eight-year-old wife Rosemary, who ran a fashionable dress·shop. They awoke to find Manson holding a gun in their faces. He tied them up and told them they would not be harmed. He only intended to rob them. He took LaBianca's wallet and went outside to the car where the rest of his followers were waiting.

103

Manson sent Tex Watson, Leslie Van Houten and Patricia Krenwinkel back into the LaBiancas' house. He said that he was going to the house next door to murder its occupants. Instead, he drove home.

Watson did as he was told. He dragged Leno LaBianca into the living room and stabbed him four times with a kitchen knife which he left sticking out of his throat. Using his own knife, Watson then stabbed LaBianca eight times in the stomach, leaving him to bleed to death with a pillow over his face. Then Watson and Krenwinkel stabbed the helpless Mrs LaBianca forty-one times while chanting a murderous mantra. They wanted Van Houten to join in. Reluctantly, she stabbed Mrs LaBianca sixteen times in the buttocks. She was already dead. Watson carved the word 'War' on Leno LaBianca's abdomen. Krenwinkel stabbed the bodies with a carving fork, leaving it sticking out of Mr LaBianca's stomach. They tied a lamp flex around his neck and put a pillowcase over his head. They used their victims' blood to write more revolutionary slogans on the walls – 'Death to pigs' and 'Rise' in the living room and 'Healter [sic] Skelter' on the door of the refrigerator. Then the three killers took a shower together. They had something to eat and went home.

When Sergeant Whitely and Deputy Guenter – the men from the Sheriff's Office who had put Beausoleil away – read about the Tate murders, they saw similarities with the Hinman case – particularly the writing in blood on the walls. They knew Beausoleil could not have been directly involved in the Tate murders because he had been in custody at the time. But they had always suspected he was not alone and they knew that he hung out with a weird bunch of hippies at the Spahn Ranch. The people who had been with Beausoleil on the Hinman murder could be responsible for the Tate murders too, they figured. Whitely called Sergeant Jesse Buckles, who was on the team handling the Tate case at the Los Angeles Police Department, and told him of his suspicions. But Buckles dismissed the idea. He did not even report it to superior officers. After all, the LAPD already had their man.

The Tate murders had been discovered the next morning by Mrs Winifred Chapman, the housekeeper who lived out. But the young caretaker William Garretson, who lived in the guest house in the back garden, slept through the murders and claimed that he had not heard anything. He was dazed, confused and very frightened. The police leaned on him hard, but they could not break him and there was nothing beyond the circumstantial evidence that he was on the property at the time to link him to the murders. When reports of the LaBianca murders came in, Garretson had to be released. Plainly he could not have killed Mr and Mrs LaBianca while in custody.

By this time, Los Angeles was in panic. Poolsides emptied, gun sales soared and security firms were run off their feet. The pressure was on to make a quick arrest.

The most promising lead in the Tate case was drugs. It was well known that celebrity hairdresser Jay Sebring also supplied his clients with marijuana and other drugs. A terrified Polish friend of Voytek Frykowski told the LAPD that he too was setting up as a drugs dealer. However, the Tate case was clearly linked to the LaBianca case, which was also under the LAPD's jurisdiction. They were middle-aged and eminently respectable. There was no drugs connection there. But could there be a mafia connection? Leno LaBianco was a keen gambler and race-horse owner. But this too led nowhere. Sharon Tate's husband Roman Polanski, who had been away filming in Europe at the time, told the police: 'If I'm looking for a motive, I'd look for something that doesn't fit your habitual standard.'

It was prophetic, but unhelpful.

It was not until 15 October, over two months after the murders, that one of the LaBianca team at the LAPD thought of checking out similar cases that might have been handled by the Los Angeles Sheriff's Office. Unlike the Tate team, they were immediately interested in the Hinman killing. However, Whitely and Guenther had not been sitting on their hands. On 16 August 1969, the Los Angeles Sheriff's Office had raided the Spahn Ranch, looking for stolen cars and credit cards.

It became clear to the killers that their senseless slaughter had not set off Helter Skelter, the great revolutionary race war, as they had expected. Instead, it had just provoked a police crack-down. Clearly, the killers were now in danger and the Family began to break up.

'When they catch me, it's going to be like feeding me to the lions,' said Manson, exhibiting, for once, considerable insight. 'They're going to put me far away because I have no family, no one that will help me.'

Some of the Family fled to the Barker Ranch. But that too was raided on 12 October by the local Inyo Country Police looking for stolen cars and illegal firearms. They arrested twenty-four Family members, including Manson himself. It took three days to search the huge ranch properly. When the police approached, Kitty Lutesinger, who was five months pregnant with Bobby Beausoleil's child, and Stephanie Scram stumbled out of a dry gully. They were frightened and begged for police protection. As several of the Family members gave the Spahn Ranch as their address, the Inyo County Police called the Los Angeles Sheriff's Office. Whitely and Guenther had been looking for Kitty Lutesinger in connection with the Hinman murder, so drove up to interview her. Kitty was eager to help. She said that she had heard Manson order Bobby Beausoleil and Susan Atkins to go to Gary Hinman's house and get money from him. This tied Manson to the Hinman case. She also said that she had heard other Family members talking about a man being grabbed by the hair and stabbed in the legs. This was not Hinman, who had no wounds on the legs. But it could have been Frykowski.

Meanwhile Susan Atkins has taken off alone and had turned back to prostitution to support herself. She was already in jail. When interviewed she admitted to being at Hinman's house when he was murdered. She was booked on suspicion of murder and sent to the Sybil Brand Institute.

The police already had one of the murder weapons in their possession. The .22 Bluntline Special had been thrown out of the car by the killers on the way back from the LaBianca murders. It was found on a Los Angeles hillside by ten-year-old Stephen Weiss. But the police just tagged it and filed it away in a manila envelope. Its significance was only recognised after Weiss's father read a description of the gun used in the Tate killings in the *Los Angeles Times*. Meanwhile the LaBianca team were setting their considerable intelligence-gathering team on to gleaning any information they could on Manson and his followers. Eventually, they pulled in Danny de Carlo and Al Springer of the bikers gang Straight Satan. They had a lot of circumstantial and hearsay evidence concerning Manson and the murders. And Terry Melcher told the police that Manson had been to 10050 Cielo Drive when he had lived there. The net was closing.

In jail, Susan Atkins could not keep her mouth shut. She began bragging to her cellmate Ronnie Howard and another prisoner by the name of Virginia Graham about the killings. And she said she planned to do unspeakable things to Elizabeth Taylor, Richard Burton, Frank Sinatra, Tom Jones and Steve McQueen when she got out. They grew frightened and told the authorities. Atkins' so-called hit list was released in the papers. A number of celebrities left Los Angeles. Faced with the jail-cell confessions, Susan Atkins could not back down. On 5 December 1969, she testified to the Grand Jury, describing what had really happened at 10050 Cielo Drive on the night of 8 August. And she blamed Manson.

The Manson trial began on 15 June 1970. It lasted for nine-and-a-half months, the longest murder trial in America at that time. The transcript ran to over eight million words. Throughout the entire trial the jury – seven men and five women – were sequestered. They were kept in a hotel and supervised by bailiffs for 225 days. There was a vast amount of evidence to gather and a huge number of witnesses to locate and interview. Tex Watson had gone home to Texas and fought extradition. Manson had his own line of delaying techniques. First, he said he wanted to defend himself. His request was refused. But the attorneys the court appointed him were rejected one after the other. In the end, he was defended by Irving Kanarek, who was himself a master of delaying tactics. His notorious obstructionism had once stretched a simple case of theft until it took up two years of court time.

The defence began by challenging the right of the judge William Keene to preside over the case. The challenge was successful. He was dismissed and replaced by Judge Charles Older. Then the trial was almost over before it started when the newly elected President Richard Nixon declared that Manson was guilty, overriding the assumption of innocence that is the basis of American law. But as the jury was sequestered it was felt that there was no reason to call a mistrial.

The Manson trial was unique. Never in the history of American jurisprudence had someone been charged with mass murder by proxy. Manson's strategy was to control the entire defence team. As long as he could prevent his followers saying that he had ordered the murders, he stood a chance of getting off scot-free. His female followers were still largely under his thrall. Susan Atkins, who had promised to turn state's evidence and testify against Manson, retracted her earlier statements and faced the charges beside him. And inside court and out, Manson's women pledged to follow him to the end.

On 24 July 1969, Manson appeared in court with a cross carved on his forehead. He had cut it himself with a hacksaw blade. He said nothing, but issued a press statement saying: 'I have Xd myself from your society.' A few days later, his co-defendents appeared with the same mark on their foreheads. And by the end of the week, the Family women who camped outside the court building had done the same. Manson's X later turned into a swastika.

When he turned his back on the judge, so did his followers. Later, he caused uproar by hurling himself at the bench, screaming at the judge that he should have his head cut off.

Prosecution attorneys were given bodyguards and walkie-talkies during the trial for their safety. Family members made no direct attack on them, but they did attempt a raid on a gun store which failed. They were apprehended in a bullet-riddled van after a shoot-out with the police. Their plan had been to use the guns to hijack a plane and demand Manson's release.

During their investigations, the LAPD had spotted the connection between Manson and the Process Church. One former member of the Process Church who was a suspect in two motorcycle murders told them that Manson had used typical Process tactics. They had lost patience with anyone they could not indoctrinate. These were the so-called 'Grey Forces'. Negroes and the rich establishment particularly were their target. Deputy District Attorney Vincent Bugliosi pursued the connection. Two members of the Process Church – calling themselves Brother John and Brother Matthew – visited Bugliosi unannounced during his investigation. They claimed to have been sent by the Church's national headquarters in Cambridge, Massachusetts. They delivered a stack of Process literature and officially denied that Manson had had anything to do with DeGrimston and the Process Church. But when Bugliosi checked, he found that the two men visited Manson in jail the next day. And during his interrogation of Manson, Bugliosi asked whether he knew Robert DeGrimston or Robert Moore – Moore being DeGrimston's last name. Manson answered: 'You're looking at him. Moore and I are one and the same.' Bugliosi later drew parallels between the teachings of Manson and Process – particularly their view that it was their duty to help instigate an imminent and violent Armageddon. They both cultivated connections with motorcycle gangs to promote this. In fact, the only difference that Bugliosi found between them was that Manson had replaced Process's three great gods – Jehovah, Lucifer and Satan – with the traditional Catharite duality of God and Satan, both rolled up in one man.

109

Manson's strategy of letting his acolytes take the rap failed. Linda Kasabian took the stand as a witness for the prosecution. She said she loved Manson, then told the court everything she knew about the murders. She had been outside the house during the Tate murders and heard the other Family members talk about the killing of the La-Biancas. More damningly, from the witness box, she told Manson: 'I am not like you, Charlie. I can't kill anyone.'

Manson's defence had tried to establish Tex Wilson as the evil genius behind the murders. But when he finally arrived from the Texas jailhouse where he had been held during the lengthy extradition battle, the jury saw a good-looking, clean-cut, square-jawed, All-American boy – not an evil genius at all. In his testimony, he too tied Manson to the murders. Watson said: 'Charlie called me over behind a car. He said for me to take the gun and the knife and go up to where Terry Melcher used to live. He said to kill everyone in the house as gruesomely as possible.'

In what amounted to a threat, Manson told the jury: 'You say there are just a few in my Family. There are many, many more, coming in the same direction. They are running in the streets, and they are coming right at you.'

Then he taunted the jury with a simple truth. 'I've killed no one,' he said. 'I've ordered no one to be killed. These children who come to you with their knives, they're your children. I didn't teach them – you did.'

But no one was fooled. They knew who was responsible. Manson, Beausoleil, Atkins, Krenwinkel, Van Houten and Grogan were all sentenced to death in the gas chamber. Charlie was not even afraid.

'My faith in me is stronger than all your armies, government gas chambers or anything you may want to do to me,' he said.

In some ways, he was right. Before the sentence could be carried out, the death penalty was abolished in California. Manson and his followers had their sentences commuted to life imprisonment and they are now eligible for parole. So far, only Steven Grogan has been granted it.

Former Family member Lynette Fromme made a half-hearted attempt to get Manson out. In 1975, she pulled a gun on US President Gerald Ford. But she did not pull the trigger and succeeded only in putting Manson back in the headlines again.

Manson constantly asks for parole. He does it, not because he has a reasonable chance of getting out, but because it gains him publicity. He revels in his image as the baddest man on Earth and boasts that he had been responsible for thirty-five other murders.

Stephen Kay, a Los Angeles County district attorney who worked as Vincent Bugliosi's assistant during the trial, keeps an eye on the parole hearings and turns up to oppose any release. In 1981, at a parole hearing, Manson said that Kay would be murdered in the car park as he left. But he was present again, alive and well, for the next parole board hearing.

The following year, Manson was transferred to a maximum security cell at Vacaville prison after the authorities learned he was planning an escape by hot-air balloon. A ballooning catalogue, a rope, a hacksaw and a container of flammable liquid were found in the jail.

At one parole board hearing, Manson was asked why he unravelled his socks and used the yarn to make into woollen scorpions. He rose from his seat and said quite seriously: 'From the world of darkness I did loose demons and devils in the power of scorpions to torment.'

Parole was refused.

In 1986, Manson's parole request was opposed by California's governor George Deukmejian. In response, Manson read a twenty-page handwritten statement which was described, by those who heard it, as 'bizarre and rambling'. Three years later he refused to appear before the parole board because he was made to wear manacles. These, he said, made the board think he was dangerous.

In 1992, his hearing was held within hours of the first execution held in California for over a decade. Of course, Manson's death sentence cannot be reinstated. Nevertheless,

Manson did not do his chances of getting parole much good when he told the parole board: 'There's no one as bad as me. I am everywhere. I am down in San Diego Zoo. I am in your children. Someone had to be insane. We can't all be good guys. They've tried to kill me thirty or forty times in prison. They've poured fire over me. They haven't found anyone badder than me because there is no one as bad as me – and that's a fact.'

The truth is, Manson will never be allowed out.

His women followers have more chance of being released. Leslie Van Houten, Susan Atkins and Patricia Krenwinkel have all got skilful lawyers working on legal loopholes. Susan Atkins has become a born-again Christian. Like Leslie Van Houten she has become a model prisoner. At the California Institute for Women in Frontera, Van Houten has graduated with degrees in literature and psychology. She can also argue that she did not actually kill anybody. She stabbed Mrs LaBianca, but only after she was dead. Even Vincent Bugliosi concedes that the three women will be released eventually.

Tex Watson is in with less of a chance. He was doing well when he found God and became assistant pastor at the California Men's Colony at San Luis Obispo. He took as his assistant another Family member, Bruce Davis, and Kay suspected he was trying to build himself a powerbase in prison. Watson is now working, inside, as a motor mechanic.

At the time of the trial, Manson's connections to the Process Church became quite well known and Process experienced something of a backlash. Members gave up their distinctive black attire and wore grey leisure suits instead and DeGrimston dropped out of sight. In an effort to save the Church in the US, Mary MacLean changed its name and dropped Lucifer and Satan in favour of Jehovah, then dropped out of sight herself. According to retired Captain Dale Griffis, of the Tiffin, Ohio, Police Department, she changed her name to Circe and opened an occult shop in Toledo, Ohio. She bought a chunk of rural real estate, adjacent to a location said to be the site of satanic rituals involving human sacrifice. In 1985, law enforcement officers dug up the site and, although some ritualistic paraphernalia was found, there was no evidence of human remains. However, the occult shop in Toledo closed and Circe mysteriously disappeared.

Meanwhile, a number of other members of the Process Church have returned to England and, by 1988, they were proselytising their murderous creed as if they had never been away.

7

Son of Sam

At 1 a.m. on 29 July 1976, nineteen-year-old Jody Valente and eighteen-year-old Donna Lauria were sitting in Jody's car outside Donna's home in the Bronx borough of New York. It was a hot summer night and they were discussing their boyfriends. Then Donna said goodnight and opened the door to get out.

A young man was standing a few feet away. He was holding a brown paper sack. As the car door opened, he reached into the sack, pulled out a gun and dropped to a crouching position.

'What does this guy want?' said Donna, rather alarmed.

Before the words were out of her mouth a bullet struck her in the side of the neck. A second bullet smashed the window in the door. A third smashed her elbow as she raised her hands to protect her face. Fatally wounded, she tumbled out of the car on to the sidewalk. The killer then shot Jody in the thigh. She fell forward on to the car's horn which sounded and the killer made off.

Donna's father, Mike Lauria, was taking the family's dog for a walk and was halfway down the stairs when he heard the shots. He ran the rest of the way. Jody was still conscious, though hysterical. In the ambulance, Mike Lauria begged his daughter not to die. It was too late. When Donna reached the hospital, she was pronounced DOA – dead on arrival. Jody was treated for hysteria, but nevertheless gave the police a good description of their assailant. He was a young white male, about thirty years old, clean shaven with dark curly hair. He was not a rejected boyfriend. In fact, Jody had never seen him before. The only other clue to his identity was a yellow car parked near Jody's which was gone by the time the police arrived. But New York is full of yellow cars.

The car in question actually belonged to David Berkowitz. In the days leading up to the murder, he had been looking for a job. But he had spent the nights, he said, 'Looking for a victim, waiting for a signal.' Demon voices inside him told him to kill. Even though the Devil was on his side, he was not sure that he could be successful.

'I never thought I could kill her,' he said of Donna Lauria. 'I just fired the gun, you know, at the car, at the windshield. I never knew she was shot.'

But the police were not looking for a madman driven by demons. They had another theory altogether. As the North Bronx, where the Laurias lived, was a predominantly Italian area, the police immediately suspected Mafia involvement. Perhaps a hit had gone wrong – a case of mistaken identity. However, the Mafia are usually scrupulous when it comes to contract killings. Women and children are out of bounds. Besides, ballistics tests showed that the murder weapon was a Charter Arms five-round .44 Bulldog revolver. It had a powerful recoil and was grossly inaccurate at distances of more than a few metres – hardly a hit man's weapon. But still, it was no Saturday-night special. It is the weapon for a man who seriously wants to kill. A .44 Bulldog can blow a large hole in a door at close range.

The other side of the East River from the Bronx lies the borough of Queens. It is a comfortable middle-class area. Eighteen-year-old student Rosemary Keenan attended Queens College there. Twelve weeks after the murder of Donna Lauria, she went to a bar in Flushing, the area of Queens which has become New York's equivalent of Wimbledon. There she met twenty-year-old record salesman Carl Denaro who was enjoying his last few days of freedom before joining the Air Force. Rosemary and Carl left together in Rosemary's red Volkswagen. They were parked, talking, when a man crept up on them. He had a .44 Bulldog hand-gun tucked in his belt. He may have thought Carl, who was sitting in the passenger seat, was a woman because he had long brown hair. He pulled out his gun and fired five times through the passenger window. But his shooting was wildly inaccurate. Only one bullet found its mark. As Carl threw himself forward to protect himself from flying glass, it clipped the back of his head. It knocked away part of the skull but did not damage the brain. Carl Denaro was lucky. He did not die. After two months in hospital, he had recovered completely. But he now had a metal plate in his head which ended his career in the Air Force before it had begun.

On the evening of 27 November 1976, two school girls, sixteen-year-old Donna DeMasi and her eighteen-year-old friend Joanne Lomino were sitting on the front porch of Joanne's home on 262nd Street in Queens. At the end of the conversation, they said good night and Joanne stood up and reached in her handbag for her front door keys. It was then that the two girls noticed a man walking down the other side of the road. He was acting rather suspiciously. When he saw them he suddenly changed direction. After crossing the street at the corner, he came over to them as if he was going to ask for directions.

'Say, can you tell me how to get to . . .' he said, then he pulled a gun from his waistband and began firing.

The two girls fled toward the front door, Joanne frantically searching for her keys. The first bullet hit Joanne in the back. The second hit Donna in the neck. They stumbled into the bushes as the gunman loosed off the remaining three shots – all of which missed. He ran off down 262nd street and was spotted by a neighbour, gun still in hand.

The two wounded girls were rushed to Long Island Jewish Hospital, where Donna was found not to be badly injured. In three weeks, she made a full recovery. But Joanne was not so lucky. The bullet had smashed her spinal cord. She was paralysed from the waist down and will

116

spend the rest of her life in a wheelchair. The neighbour who had spotted the gunman making his escape gave the police a description. One key feature he mentioned was the young man's dark curly hair. This was strange as the girls themselves claimed that he had long fair hair. Nevertheless, this tied the shooting of Donna DeMasi and Joanne Lomino to the man who had killed Donna Lauria and wounded Jody Valente.

On 29 January 1977, thirty-year-old John Diel and his twenty-six-year old girlfriend, Christine Freund, went to see the movie *Rocky* in Queens. Afterwards they went for dinner at the Wine Gallery in Austin Street, where they discussed their forthcoming engagment. Soon after midnight, the couple walked the several blocks to where their Pontiac Firebird was parked. It was cold outside and their breath fogged the windows. They were eager to get home but stopped for a moment and kissed. Then John turned the key in the ignition. But before he could pull away he heard the blast of gunfire. The passenger window shattered and Christine slumped forward, bleeding. She died a few hours later in St John's hospital of bullet wounds in the right temple and the neck. She had never even seen her killer. But he had seen her – and so had the demons within him. Berkowitz later claimed that he had heard voices commanding him to 'get her, get her and kill her'. After firing three shots and realising that he had hit her, he felt calm again.

'The voices stopped,' he said. 'I satisfied the demon's lust.'

After the murder of Christine Freund, Berkowitz completely gave in to the impulse to kill. After all, he was getting his reward by all the publicity he was getting. 'I had finally convinced myself that I was good to do it, and that the public wanted me to kill,' Berkowitz said later.

However, the New York Police Department were on his trail. Their ballistics lab ascertained that the bullet had come from a .44 Bulldog hand-gun. That, in turn, tied it to the murder of Donna Lauria and the shootings of Jody Valente, Carl Denaro, Donna DeMasi and Joanne

Lomino. However, apart from the mention of dark curly hair by Jody Valente and the neighbour in the DeMasi/Lomino case, the descriptions of the gunman varied so widely that no one in the NYPD had yet concluded that the four shootings were the job of a single individual.

Six weeks later, on 8 March 1977, Virginia Voskerichian, a nineteen-year-old Armenian student, left Columbia University in Manhattan after her day's study and set off home to Forest Hills, Queens. Around 7.30 p.m., she was nearing her home on Exeter Street. A young man was approaching her on the sidewalk and she, politely, stepped out of his way. But he pulled a gun and shoved it in her face. She raised her books in a vain attempt to protect herself. He fired. The bullet tore through them. It entered through her upper lip, smashing out several teeth and lodged in her brain. Virginia Voskerichian collapsed in the bushes at the side of the street and died instantly. A witness saw a young man running away. He was about eighteen and five feet eight inches tall, but there was no dark curly hair to be seen. This killer was wearing a ski mask.

Berkowitz was almost caught that day. Minutes after the murder of Virginia Voskerichian, the police put out a 'Code .44'. Two police officers were assigned to the south end of the Bronx with orders to stop all cars containing a single white man. Berkowitz drove up to the checkpoint with his .44 Bulldog loaded and lying in plain view on the passenger seat of his Ford Galaxie. He was third in line when the police called off the search and he could not believe his luck when he watched the officers walk away.

It was quickly established that the bullet that killed Virginia Voskerichian was a .44 calibre. The riflings matched the marks on the bullet that had killed Christine Freund, six weeks before and just a few miles away. Two days later, it was established that the same gun was responsible for the shooting of seven people.

On the afternoon of 10 March 1977, a press conference was held at One Police Plaza, a thirteen-storey red stone building that is New York's equivalent of London's New

Scotland Yard. Police Commissioner Mike Codd stood with some trepidation before New York's hard-bitten crime reporters. As he read his carefully prepared statement, he began to have an inkling that he was unleashing a wave of hysteria that would engulf the city. He started by saying that the murder of Donna Lauria, nine months before, was linked to the killing of Virginia Voskerichian, a mere two days ago. In both cases, the killer had used a .44 Bulldog revolver. The same gun had also been used in three other incidents. Worse, the killer chose his victims completely at random. Reporters pushed for other information. Commissioner Codd said that the police were looking for a Caucasian male, about six feet tall, medium build, twenty-five to thirty years old, with dark hair. Next day, the .44 killer made the headlines.

The man in charge of the investigation was Deputy Inspector Timothy J. Dowd. He had been one of New York's finest since 1940. By 1973, he had worked his way up to the rank of deputy inspector at a major metropolitan precinct, but the then commissioner, David Crawley, announced a get-tough programme. He said that Dowd and fourteen other senior officers had been underperforming and demoted them. Dowd fought the case and a year later it was Crawley who found himself demoted. Michael Codd took over as police commissioner and Dowd was restored to his former rank. But even then it was not plain sailing. As a test, Dowd was put in charge of an investigation in Chinatown. He was to break a secret society called The Flying Dragon and it was generally thought that no westerner could penetrate the Chinese crime syndicates. However, in 1977, Dowd announced that the leader of The Flying Dragons had been arrested for the murder of the leader of the rival gang, The Ghost Shadows. Under Dowd was Chief of Detectives John Keenan who had a special reason for wanting to capture the .44 killer. His daughter was the girl in the car with Carl Denaro when he was shot in the head.

'I know he was aiming for her,' Keenan said. 'So let's just say I put a little more than I had to into this case.'

The police realised that their chances of catching a lone, seemingly motiveless killer on the streets of New York were remote. So they announced 'Operation Omega' and asked for the help of every New Yorker. Tip-offs jammed the police switchboards. Dowd and the Omega team followed up 250–300 leads a day. There was some speculation that the .44 killer could be the 'Westchester Dartman' who had wounded 23 women in Westchester County just north of the Bronx between 28 February 1975 and May 1976. He prowled the area at night and fired inch-long darts at women through ground floor windows, wounding them in the head, neck or chest. He was never caught.

As the investigation got under way, Berkowitz took pity on the police. He decided he would give them a few clues to juggle with, so he wrote them a letter. It took him two days to complete. Then he had to deliver it. Of course, dropping it in a mail box and letting the postal service handle it was too mundane.

Another young couple went to the movies in New York on the night of 16 April 1977. They were eighteen-year-old Valentina Suriani and her boyfriend twenty-year-old Alexander Esau. After they had seen the film, they went on to a party. Around 3 a.m., they were parked in a borrowed Mercury Montego outside Valentina's apartment building in the North Bronx, only three blocks from where Donna Lauria had been killed. Valentina was sitting on Alexander's lap with her legs stretched out across the passenger seat and they were enjoying a prolonged series of goodnight kisses when bullets shattered the passenger window. Two hit Valentina's head, killing her instantly. Another two hit Alexander Esau in the top of the head as he dived across the seat towards the passenger door. He died two hours later.

When the police arrived, they found a white envelope in the middle of the road by the car. It was addressed to Captain Joe Borelli, Timothy Dowd's second-in-command. The letter was all in capitals and full of spelling mistakes. It appeared to be the work of a madman. The writer claimed that he had been ordered to kill by his father, who was a vampire. His father's name, the writer said, was Sam – hence the killer's macabre sobriquet 'Son of Sam'. In the letter, he professed to love the people of Queens, but said he intended to kill more of them – particularly the women, which he spelt as if it rhymed with 'demon'. The writer signed off with the words:

'I SAY GOODBYE AND GOODNIGHT. POLICE: LET ME HAUNT YOU WITH THESE WORDS; I'LL BE BACK! I'LL BE BACK! TO BE INTER-PRETED AS – BANG BANG, BANG, BANG, BANK, BANG – UGH!! YOURS IN MURDER, MR. MONSTER.'

By the time the letter reached the police labs, eight policemen had handled it. Only tiny traces of the writer's fingerprints remained. He appeared to have held the letter by the tips of his fingers and there was not enough of a print on the paper to identify the sender. Consequently, the police kept the existence of the letter secret. But they showed a copy to celebrated New York columnist Jimmy Breslin, who was so well known at the time that he advertised beer on the television. He dropped hints about the letter in his column in the New York *Daily News*.

On 1 June 1977, Breslin himself received a letter. It had been posted two days before in Englewood, New Jersey, just over the George Washington Bridge from Manhattan. Although the *Daily News* was then the biggest selling newspaper in America – its offices on 42nd Street double as those of the *Daily Planet* in *Superman* films – it held back publication of the full letter for six days as speculation, and circulation, mounted. On 3 June 1977, the *News* ran the front page headline: 'THE .44 CALIBER KILLER – NEW NOTE: CAN'T STOP KILLING'. The next day, they ran: '.44 KILLER: I AM NOT ASLEEP'. By Sunday, they were running: 'BRESLIN TO .44 KILLER: GIVE UP! IT'S THE ONLY WAY OUT'. This edition sold out within an hour of going on sale. So the presses kept rolling. By the end of the day, the *Daily News* had sold 1,116,000 copies – a record beaten only on the day Berkowitz was arrested. The editors assumed that interest had peaked and reproduced the letter in full in the Monday edition. Again it was written all in capital letters and showed the same uncertain grasp of basic spelling. The letter was something of an anticlimax as it was as rambling and incoherent as the letter he had sent before to the police. It signed off:

'NOT KNOWING WHAT THE FUTURE HOLDS I SHALL SAY FAREWELL AND I WILL SEE YOU AT THE NEXT JOB, OR SHOULD I SAY YOU WILL SEE MY HANDIWORK AT THE NEXT JOB? REMEMBER MS. LAURIA. THANK YOU. IN THEIR BLOOD AND FROM THE GUTTER, "SAM'S CREATION" .44.'

Then there was a long postscript:

'HERE ARE SOME NAMES TO HELP YOU ALONG. FORWARD THEM TO THE INSPECTOR FOR USE BY THE NCIC: "THE DUKE OF DEATH". "THE WICKED KING WICKER", "THE TWENTY TWO DISCIPLES OF HELL", JOHN "WHEATIES" – RAPIST AND SUFFOCATER OF YOUNG GIRLS.
  PS: J.B. PLEASE INFORM ALL THE DETECTIVES WORKING THE SLAYINGS TO REMAIN.'

At the police's request, this last page was withheld from publication. The reason they gave was that they did not want the NCIC – the National Crime Information Center – known about. But the .44 killer certainly knew about it. Perhaps the real reason was the satanic undertones in the list of pseudonyms he gives. The 'Wicked King Wicker' is presumably 'wicca'. The 'Twenty Two Disciples of Hell' sounds like some satanic organisation. The name 'Wheaties' was put in inverted commas as if it were a nickname. John 'Wheaties' was supposed to be a 'rapist and suffocater of young girls'. The police could find no trace of him. In fact, none of the names were much help to the Omega team or the NCIC. Nor were they any use to Jimmy Breslin who now began calling the .44 killer, the 'Son of Sam'.

Seventeen-year-old Bronx schoolgirl Judy Placido went to the same school as Valentina Suriani and had been to her funeral. Three weeks after the Breslin letter appeared, on 25 June, she celebrated her graduation from high school at a discotheque called Elephas in Queens. There she met a handsome young man called Salvatore Lupo, who worked in a gas station. They hit it off immediately and went outside to a car for some privacy. As Salvatore slipped his arm around Judy's shoulders, they discussed the Son of Sam killings. At that moment, their lurid speculation turned into murderous reality. A .44 bullet smashed through the passenger window, passed through Salvatore's wrist and into Judy's neck. A second bullet hit her in the head, but miraculously failed to penetrate the skull. A third bullet entered her right shoulder. Terrified, Salvatore threw open the car door and ran back to the discotheque for help. But it was too late. The shooting was over and the attacker had fled. Although she had been hit three times, Judy was quite unaware that she had been shot. She was shocked to see in the rear-view mirror that her face was covered with blood. She too jumped out of the car and headed for the disco, but she only made it a few yards before she collapsed. Salvatore suffered a shattered wrist and cuts from the flying glass. And in hospital, it was found that Judy had unbelievably escaped without serious injury.

Nevertheless, the city was in panic. Takings at discotheques and restaurants – particularly in Queens – fell off, while newspaper circulations soared. Not only did they have the gory details of the latest shooting to relay, they could speculate about the next killing.

123

In the Son of Sam's letter to Jimmy Breslin, he had written: 'TELL ME JIM, WHAT WILL YOU HAVE FOR JULY TWENTY-NINTH?' That was the date of the first murder. Was he planning to celebrate the killing of Donna Lauria with another murder? New York's English-born Mayor Abraham Beame could not wait to find out. He was running for re-election. He quickly announced that even more officers were being seconded to the Omega investigation. Overnight it became the largest single operation in the history of the New York Police Department. Two hundred men were on the case. They recruited from precincts in every borough of the city. The investigation cost more than $90,000 a day to run. Volunteers like Donna Lauria's father, Mike, manned special Son of Sam patrols and the number of calls to Omega's hotline, which started at 250 a day, peaked at 5,000 a day. A team of psychiatrists tried to come up with some sort of profile of the killer. The best they could come up with was that he was 'neurotic, schizophrenic and paranoid'. This description was duly released by the police. It did not help anyone to identify the gunman.

Fortunately, 29 July passed without incident. But two days later, with a sense of relief, two sisters from Brooklyn, fifteen-year-old Ricki Moskowitz and twenty-year-old Stacy, decided to go out. In a Brooklyn restaurant, they were approached by a handsome young man who introduced himself as Bobby Violante. The next day, Bobby and Stacy went to see the movie *New York, New York*. Afterwards, they went to dinner, then headed off to a quiet place where they could be alone. They drove to a secluded spot on Shore Parkway near Coney Island, South Brooklyn, which was used as an urban lovers' lane. They felt safe enough there. So far there had been no Son-of-Sam killings in the borough of Brooklyn and the nearest shooting had taken place 22 miles away in Queens. What they did not know was that, a week before, a man claiming to be the Son of Sam had phoned the Coney Island Precinct and said that he would strike next in that area. Extra patrol cars were assigned to Brooklyn and Coney Island. Shore Parkway was being patrolled regularly.

Bobby Violante and Stacy Moskowitz pulled up under a street lamp, the only available parking spot. And there was a full moon that night. It was not dark enough for what they had in mind, so the two of them went for a walk in the park nearby. They walked over a bridge and spent a few minutes playing on the swings. Near the public toilets they noticed a man in jeans, who they described as a 'hippy type', leaning against a wall. He was not there when they walked back to the car. Back in the car, they kissed. Stacy suggested that they move on, but Bobby wanted one more kiss. It was a mistake. While they were embracing, Bobby Violante took two bullets in the face, blinding him and exploding his eardrums. He could neither see nor hear, but he felt Stacy jerk violently in his arms, then collapsed forward. He feared she was dead. Bobby threw himself against the car horn, fumbled at the car door, cried for help, then collapsed on the pavement.

In the car in front, Tommy Zaino had seen the shooting in his rear-view mirror. He had watched as a man approached the car from behind and pull out a gun. From a crouching position, he had fired four shots through the open passenger window. When his girlfriend, Debbie Crescendo, heard the shooting, she said 'What's that?'

Zaino thought he knew.

'Get down,' he said. 'I think it's the Son of Sam.'

Zaino watched as the gunman ran towards the park. He looked at his watch. It was exactly 2.35 a.m. A patrol car was just five blocks away at the time.

Stacy Moskowitz was still conscious when the ambulance arrived. One bullet had grazed her scalp, but the other had lodged in the back of her brain. She died 38 hours later. Bobby Violante survived, but his sight could not be restored.

Tommy Zaino gave a good description of the killer. He was stocky with stringy, fair hair. This matched with the description given by Donna DeMasi and Joanne Lomino, but not with the dark curly-haired man described by Jody Valente and the neighbour in the DeMasi/Lomino case. The police wondered whether he was wearing a wig. A beautician and her boyfriend were seated by the entrance to the park when they heard the shots. They saw a man wearing a denim jacket and what they took to be a cheap nylon wig. He jumped into a light-coloured car and drove off, like he had just robbed a bank. A young girl on a bicycle identified the car as a yellow Volkswagen. A nurse who looked out of the window when she heard the shots, also said that she had seen a yellow VW. It almost collided with another car at the first intersection and the driver was so incensed that he gave chase, only to lose the car after a couple of blocks. The yellow VW's driver, he said, had stringy brown hair.

But an even more vital witness took a little longer to come forward. She was Mrs Cacilia Davis, a 49-year-old widow, who had been out with a man friend. They had returned to her apartment, two blocks from the park, at around 2 a.m. They sat and talked for a few minutes but, as they had been forced to double park, they kept an eye open for other cars. A little way ahead, Mrs Davis saw a police car and two patrolmen writing out parking tickets. Some way behind was a yellow Ford Galaxie. It was parked by a fire hydrant and a few minutes before an officer from the patrol car had given it a ticket. A young man with dark hair walked up to the Galaxie and irritably pulled the parking ticket from the windscreen.

Mrs Davis invited her friend in for coffee. He declined, saying that it was 2.20 a.m. already. At that moment, the police car pulled off. So did the Galaxie, but it could not get past Mrs Davis' friend's car. The man in the Galaxie impatiently honked the horn. Mrs Davis hurriedly got out and her friend pulled off. The Galaxie followed, passing him quickly and speeding after the police car. Minutes later, Mrs Davis went out to take her dog for a walk in the park. She noticed Tommy Zaino's car, Bobby Violante's car and a VW van. On her way home, she saw a man with dark hair and a blue denim jacket striding across the road from the cars. He glared at her and he was walking with his right arm stiff, as if something was concealed up his sleeve. He also looked rather like the man with the Ford Galaxie she had seen earlier. Mrs Davis did not come forward with this information immediately though. She realised that if the man she had seen was the Son of Sam, she was in danger. He could easily identify her and he knew where she lived. Two days after the shooting, Mrs Davis told two close friends what she had seen. They realised that she might have a vital clue and urged her to call the police. Eventually, her friends called the police on her behalf. Detective Joseph Strano visited her and took her statement. It caused hardly a ripple. Tommy Zaino – the best witness to the shooting – had seen a man with fair hair, not dark. And the driver of the Ford Galaxie had left the scene of the crime before the shooting.

But Mrs Davis now felt that she had risked her life to come forward and would not be ignored. She threatened to go, anonymously, to the newspapers with her story. To humour her, Detective Strano interviewed her again, bringing along a police artist to make a sketch of the man. He also took her on a shopping expedition to see if she could pick out a similar denim jacket. But still nothing got done. The problem with her story was that the local police had not issued any parking tickets in that area that night. But the police cars patrolling the area had been seconded in from other boroughs. It was ten days before four missing tickets turned up. Three of the cars were quickly eliminated. The fourth, a yellow Galaxie, number 561-XLB, belonged to a David Berkowitz of 35 Pine Street, Yonkers, a suburban area just north of the Bronx. Detective James Justus called Yonkers police headquarters. Switchboard operator Wheat Carr answered. Justus said that he was working on the Son-of-Sam case and that he was checking on David Berkowitz. The woman shouted, 'Oh, no.'

Not only did she know David Berkowitz, she had suspected that he was the Son of Sam for some time.

It had begun the previous year when her father began to receive anonymous letters complaining about his dog. In October, a petrol bomb had been thrown through the window of the Carr's house at 316 Warburton Avenue, Yonkers. A neighbour had also been receiving anonymous letters and abusive phone calls. On Christmas Eve 1976, someone had fired a number of shots through their window and killed their Alsatian. Then on 27 April 1977, someone entered the Carr's backyard and shot their black labrador, Harvey. On 10 June 1977, Wheat's father Sam Carr had received a phone call from a man named Jack Cassaras who lived in New Rochelle, out on Long Island Sound. Mr Cassaras wanted to know why Mr Carr had sent him a get well card. The card said that Mr Cassaras had fallen off a roof. He had not, nor had he ever, been on one. Mr Carr had no explanation and invited Mr Cassaras over to discuss the matter. The drive took about twenty minutes. Sam Carr examined the card. Strangely, it had a picture of an Alsatian on it and Mr Carr told Cassaras about the bizarre things that had been happening. Mr Cassaras drove home even more puzzled, but his son thought that he had the answer. The year before, the Cassaras family had rented out a room above their garage to a David Berkowitz. He had complained about the Cassarases' Alsatian. After a few weeks, he had left suddenly without collecting the deposit of $200. When Mrs Cassaras looked David Berkowitz up in the telephone directory, she found that he now lived at 35 Pine Street, Yonkers. She rang Sam Carr and asked him whether Pine Street was near them. It was right around the corner. Mr Carr was convinced that David Berkowitz was responsible for the harassment they had suffered and went to the police. However, the police explained that they could take the matter no further without more concrete evidence.

Another of Berkowitz's neighbours, Craig Glassman, had also been receiving abusive letters. He lived in the apartment underneath Berkowitz. But he was a police officer and when, a week after the Moskowitz murder, rubbish was piled against Glassman's front door and set on fire, he reported it. That was 6 August 1977. He also showed detectives two anonymous letters he had received. They accused Glassman of being a spy planted there by Sam Carr. Glassman and the Carrs were part of a black magic sect out to get him, the author alleged. The detective who examined the letters recognised the handwriting. It belonged to another man he was investigating – David Berkowitz.

However, Berkowitz was not the only suspect in the Son-of-Sam slayings. New York has a rich supply of paranoid schizophrenics. Besides, Berkowitz did not fit the description given by Tommy Zaino. Nor did he drive a yellow VW. So it was not until 10 August 1977 that Omega detectives John Longo and Ed Zigo went to Yonkers to check Berkowitz out. Zigo spotted Berkowitz's Ford Galaxie parked outside the apartment block in Pine Street. There was a bag on the back seat with a rifle butt protruding from it. In New York, possessing a rifle did not even require a licence. Nevertheless, Zigo forced open the car. Inside he found another, more formidable weapon, a Commando Mark III semi-automatic. Then in the glove compartment, he found a letter addressed to the head of Operation Omega, Deputy Inspector Timothy Dowd. It said that the next shooting would be in Long Island. Detective Zigo phoned into Operation Omega and told Sergeant James Shea, 'I think we've got him.'

Police from all over the city were brought in. They staked out the car for six hours until Berkowitz turned up. He was a stocky man with a round cherubic face and dark hair. When he got into the driver's seat, he found himself looking down the barrel of a police revolver.

'Freeze!' yelled Detective William Gardella. 'Police!'

Berkowitz simply smiled.

Detective John Falotico opened the passenger door, held his .38 to Berkowitz's head and told him to get out. When he put his hands on the roof, Falotico asked, 'Who are you?' Berkowitz answered, 'I am Sam.'

At One Police Plaza Berkowitz confessed to the shootings and the anonymous letters. He also admitted that his crime spree had begun on Christmas Eve 1975. About seven o'clock he drove to the Co-op City in the Bronx, where his adoptive father lived. He saw a young Hispanic woman leaving a store and followed her. He pulled a knife and stabbed her in the back. She did not realise what had happened, turned, screamed and grabbed his wrist. He ran away. But on his way home, he followed fifteen-year-old Michelle Forman and stabbed her in the back and head. She fell screaming on the sidewalk. Again Berkowitz fled. Somehow she managed to stagger to the apartment block where her parents lived. They rushed her to hospital where they found that she had a collapsed lung. Her other injuries were superficial and she only spent a week in hospital. His first victim did not even report the attack and was never identified. These early attacks convinced Berkowitz that he needed a gun. A friend called Billy Dan Parka bought him a .44 Bulldog revolver in Houston, Texas, for $130. Under interrogation, Berkowitz explained that he had been ordered to commit the murders by Sam Carr, via Carr's demon dog Harvey. Other demon voices accompanied him when he was stalking his victims. Berkowitz was so forthcoming that his complete confession took only half-an-hour.

Further enquiries revealed that Richard David Berkowitz had been an illegitimate child who had been given up for adoption as a baby. His natural mother, Betty Broder, was Jewish. At nineteen, she married Tony Falco, an Italian American. He left her for another woman six years later. She began an affair with real estate agent Joseph Kleinman, a married man, in 1947. She got pregnant by him, but when she told him that she was going to have a child, he said she had better get rid of it, if she wanted to go on seeing him. The child was born on 1 June 1953 and was adopted immediately by a Jewish couple, Pearl and Nathan Berkowitz, who were unable to have children of their own. They named him David. But in 1967, when David was just fourteen, Pearl Berkowitz succumbed to cancer. He was deeply upset at this new loss.

Two years later, Nathan decided to move to Co-op City in the Bronx, a middle-class suburb. But the area was on the skids and gangs of youths soon began terrorising the neighbourhood. David's school grades plunged and he seemed to lose any sense of direction. He was shy and found himself a victim of bullying, though others saw him as spoilt and something of a bully himself. He was big for his age, strong and an excellent baseball player. But he liked to play with kids younger than himself. His biggest problem was with girls. One friend remembers Berkowitz asking him if he wanted to join the 'girl-haters club'. He only ever dated one girl in Co-op City, Iris Gerhardt. She liked his warm and obliging nature, but the relationship was never consummated. While Berkowitz remained chaste, almost everyone else seemed to be at it.

'After a while, at Co-op City, there wasn't one girl who was a virgin,' he said resentfully.

In prison, Berkowitz wrote: 'I must slay women for revenge purposes to get back at them for all the suffering they caused me.'

His friends also started smoking marijuana but, again, Berkowitz was too inhibited to join in.

Things got worse in 1971 when his father remarried. Berkowitz resented his stepmother and stepsister, and decided to join the army. But that did not last long. Home again in 1974, Berkowitz had rejected Judaism and become a Baptist. Nathan Berkowitz remembers his son standing in front of the mirror beating his head with his fists. Things became so uncomfortable in the Berkowitz household that David moved out to take a drab one-room apartment at 2151 Barnes Avenue in the Bronx. By this time Nathan became convinced that his son needed psychiatric help. But Nathan and his new family were moving to Florida and nothing was done. With his father gone, another door closed for Berkowitz.

He had known that he had been adopted from the age

of seven. Isolated, he tried to trace his real family. It took a year. Through the Bureau of Records, he discovered that his real name was Richard Falco and he came from Brooklyn. Using an old telephone directory, he managed to trace his mother and an elder sister. He dropped a card in his mother's mailbox and, a few days later, she called him. The reunion was emotional. He also met his thirty-seven-year-old sister and became a regular visitor to the house where she lived with her husband and children. At last, he had found a family and, at last, Berkowitz was happy. Or so it seemed.

In the first half of 1976, his visits to his real mother and sister became increasingly rare. He complained of headaches. In February, he moved into the room above the Cassarases' garage out in New Rochelle. Two months later, he moved suddenly to Pine Street, Yonkers. And in July, he killed Donna Lauria.

After a year-long killing spree the police at last had Berkowitz under lock and key. He pleaded guilty to all charges and was sentenced to 365 years in prison. One of the Omega team, Sergeant Joseph Coffey, who had conducted the initial interrogation, said, 'I feel sorry for him. The man is a fucking vegetable.'

However, not everyone was satisfied. Young Yonkers-born investigative journalist Maury Terry spotted a number of inconsistencies in Berkowitz's story. Berkowitz claimed that he had acted alone. But he simply could not have been responsible for the Violante-Moskowitz shooting if Tommy Zaino's description was accurate. Even if he had been wearing a wig, he was not tall enough. And if he was the man Mrs Cacilia Davis had seen outside her apartment building, only minutes before the shootings, he could not have got to Violante's car on Shore Parkway in time. Terry interviewed Zaino and Davis. Both confirmed their original accounts. When Davis went through her story again, Terry realised that it was unlikely that, if Berkowitz had been carrying a .44 Bulldog revolver already connected to a number of murders, he would have sped off after a police car, honking his horn late at night. Maybe, as Berkowitz said, 'The demons were protecting me, I had nothing to fear from the police.' Terry tracked down the witnesses who said that they had seen a fair-haired man in a yellow VW. All of them stuck to their stories. They could have been mistaken. But their descriptions seemed to match those given by the two school girls who had been shot in Queens. Terry concluded that Berkowitz had a fair-haired accomplice.

Another inconsistency was Berkowitz's pseudonym 'Son of Sam'. His real father's name was Tony, and his adoptive father's name was Nathan. The only Sam in the case was Sam Carr, who Berkowitz claimed had given him orders to kill via the demon dog Harvey. However, although the Carr house was visible from Berkowitz's sixth floor apartment, they had never met. Carr confirmed that the first time he had even heard Berkowitz's name was when Mrs Cassaras called and told him about their former lodger. So why was Berkowitz so obsessed with Carr? Sam Carr did, in fact, have two sons, John and Michael. Both of them hated their father. Carr's daughter was called Wheat and John Carr was nicknamed 'Wheaties'. Then Terry remembered 'John "Wheaties", rapist and suffocater of young girls' in the Son of Sam's letter to Jimmy Breslin. John 'Wheaties' Carr was tall, with long stringy fair hair. While Terry tried to trace John Carr, he became interested in some of the satanic clues in the Breslin letter. He was also concerned about Berkowitz's seeming obsession with dogs. He did discover that in Walden, New York, about an hour's drive from Yonkers, eighty-five Dobermans and Alsatians had been found skinned during the year of the Son-of-Sam killings. More dead dogs had been found in a wooded area of Untermeyer Park in Yonkers. A local teenager said that Devil-worshippers held ceremonies there. Could Berkowitz have been involved in a satanic cult? The police dismissed the idea.

In October 1978, when Terry eventually traced John Carr, it was too late to ask him about any of this. He had been shot dead in the small town of Minot, North Dakota. His body had been found in the bedroom of his girlfriend Linda O'Connor, with a bullet through the roof of the mouth and rifle beside the body. The coroner's verdict was suicide, but the police believed he had been murdered.

John Carr had been born in Yonkers, New York, on 12 October 1946 – he shared a birthday with Aleister Crowley. After leaving Catholic school, Carr joined the US Air Force. He was stationed in Korea and served twelve years. In 1972, he returned to the US and was stationed in Minot, North Dakota. He was discharged in 1976, allegedly for drug addiction. In 1976 and 1977, he went to hospital three times with overdoses and had a reputation as a drug dealer and a heavy drinker. He was in New York for probably five of the eight Son-of-Sam attacks, including the shootings of Donna DiMasi and Joanne Lomino, and he closely resembled the descriptions they had given.

In late January 1978, Carr drove the 1,500 miles from Minot to New York, saying he was going to stay for a long time. But within two weeks, he called his girlfriend and told her that the police were after him. On 14 February, he flew back to Minot. He rented a post office box, opened a bank account and enquired about the continued payment of a disability allowance he received for a service injury – hardly the actions of a man contemplating suicide. Two days later he was dead.

Mysteriously, on the skirting board by the body, the letters 'S.S.N.Y.C.' had been scrawled in blood. A man who has blown the top of his head off with a rifle bullet seldom has time to write things in his own blood. Terry deduced that Carr had been beaten to the ground by his assailants, then his killer, or killers, had gone to search for his gun, leaving Carr time to write his message before he was killed. The letters 'S.S.N.Y.C.', Terry concluded, stood for 'Son of Sam, New York City'. Carr also had the figures '666' written in blood on his hand. 666 was the number of the Beast in the Book of Revelations and was used as a satanic pseudonym by Aleister Crowley. The police in Minot had

134

also discovered that Carr was connected with a number of local occult groups and his girlfriend said that when Carr had seen news of Berkowitz's arrest for the Son-of-Sam shootings on the TV, he had said, 'Oh shit'.

Up to this point Terry had been dismissed as a conspiracy theorist. But John Santucci, the District Attorney of Queens, began to believe there was something to Terry's investigation. He re-opened the case. It was soon discovered that, far from being the classic psychotic loner, Berkowitz had a wide circle of friends. Chief among them was John 'Wheaties' Carr's brother Michael. In 1975, the year before the killings started, when Berkowitz was living in his drab one-room apartment in Barnes Avenue, he met Michael, a young drug addict who had been hanging about outside the apartment block. He invited Berkowitz to a party. The guests included John Carr and other members of The Twenty-Two Disciples of Hell, the satanic group Berkowitz referred to in his letter to Breslin. In due course, Berkowitz moved to Yonkers, to within 200 yards of Sam Carr's house where Michael Carr then lived. Michael Carr had since moved out and, by the time he could be traced, he, too, was dead. In the early hours of 4 October 1979, Michael Carr's car ran into a street lamp at 75 miles an hour as he drove towards Manhattan. There were no skid marks and his sister, Wheat, was convinced that he had been forced off the road or that one of his tyres had been shot out.

The most unexpected witness in Santucci's new investigation was Berkowitz himself. In February 1979, he had called a press conference and announced that his story about Sam Carr's dog and demon voices had been concocted in the hope that he would be able to enter a plea of insanity. But court-appointed psychiatrists had passed him sane. Now, a year after being incarcerated in Attica Correctional Facility, he said that he had bought his .44 knowing exactly what he intended to do. He wanted to kill women because of his disappointments with sex.

In prison, Berkowitz had become a prolific letter writer.

In them, he described how he had stage dressed his apartment to back his insanity plea. A week before his arrest, he had stripped his ' apartment of an expensive Japanese stereo system, a dinner service, a bureau, sofa and bed. These had been loaded into a van and dumped in front of a Salvation Army warehouse in Mount Vernon. Berkowitz specified the location of the garage he had rented the van from, the cost of the rental and the location of the warehouse – all of which checked out. He had also vandalised his apartment, knocking a hole in a wall so violently that it had cracked the plaster in a neighbour's flat. He had also covered the walls with ravings. This was all true. In a letter written to a priest in California, Berkowitz wrote:

'I really don't know how to begin this letter, but at one time I was a member of an occult group. Being sworn to secrecy or face death, I cannot reveal the name of this group, nor do I wish to. The group contained a mixture of satanic practices which included the teachings of Aleister Crowley and Eliphaz Levi. It was (and still is) blood orientated, and I am certain you know what I mean. The Coven's doctrines are a blend of ancient Druidism, the teachings of the Secret Order of the Golden Dawn, Black Magick, and a host of other unlawful and obnoxious practices. These people will stop at nothing, including murder. They had no fear of man-made laws or the Ten Commandments.'

None of the other members of The Twenty-Two Disciples of Hell were found. But the postman who delivered letters to the Pine Street district of Yonkers killed himself. He was a young married man named Andrew Dupay. In the month before Berkowitz was arrested, he was noticeably worried. Then on 20 September 1977, five weeks after Berkowitz's arrest, he and his wife were bathing their two baby daughters when Dupay excused himself, went down to the basement and blew his head off with a shotgun. A neighbour said that Dupay had said that he had learned something on his rounds that had frightened him. One of Terry's informants said that Dupay knew both Carr and Berkowitz and had killed himself because threats had been made against his family.

On 7 January 1978, the body of Mary Hirschmann was found in a vacant lot in Queens. She had been strangled and stabbed. Her husband's body had been found the day before, riddled with bullets, in the East Fishkill district of north Yonkers. He had mystical figures tattooed on his body.

On 16 December 1979, abstract painter Howard Green and his girlfriend Carol Marron were found beaten to death over the Hudson River from New York in New Jersey. The year before, both had developed an interest in the occult and had started satanic worship by themselves. Their apartment on DeKalb Avenue in Brooklyn was filled with ritual paraphernalia. Carol had been making enquiries about joining Crowley's OTO.

Berkowitz made other disturbing references in his letters. Shortly after the Son-of-Sam shootings had begun, he applied for a job in a dog pound. The pay was not good, but Berkowitz said that 'there was another way in which I was getting paid. Somebody needed dogs. I guess you understand what I'm trying to say.' Terry's investigation again proved that Berkowitz was telling the truth.

Then Berkowitz dropped a bombshell. He ripped a chapter out of a standard work on Satanism and witchcraft. It concerned the satanic practices of Charles Manson and his Family. Then he wrote a note in the margin, saying: 'Call the Santa Clara Sheriff's office. Please ask the sheriffs what happened to Arlis Perry.' He went on to say that Perry had been 'hunted, stalked and slain. Followed to California. Stanford Univ'.

Stanford University is in Santa Clara County. A nineteen-year-old student called Arlis Perry was horribly murdered in the Church in Stanford University at midnight on October 1974. She had only been in California for a few weeks. Her body was naked from the waist down. Her legs were spread and a thirty-inch altar candle was rammed into her vagina. Her arms were crossed over her chest and another candle was put between her breasts. Her jeans lay inverted over her legs. She had been beaten, strangled and stabbed behind the ear with an ice pick. Little of this was made public until 1988, but Berkowitz knew details about the murder that had been withheld. He even cut out a picture from the paper that he said resembled Arlis Perry. The only picture of her that appeared in the newspapers showed how she looked in her school days. The picture that Berkowitz selected looked much more like Arlis Perry the night she died. At the very least, he had seen a picture of the murder, performed, Terry maintains, by the California satanic group associated with Charles Manson. Berkowitz said that Arlis Perry had once been a member of the group but had tried to leave.

Terry also noted that some of the Son-of-Sam killings had been performed with a ruthless efficiency. Others were inept and bungled. Terry concluded that Berkowitz had only committed three of the Son-of-Sam killings – those of Donna Lauria, Valentina Suriani and Alexander Esau. Donna Lauria had been killed, Terry says, because she knew about the coven. Christine Freund died because she had offended one of the members. Terry believes that the killer in the balaclava was actually a woman, who was a member of the coven. Stacy Moskowitz was killed by John Carr, Terry says. Berkowitz was there because the killing was being filmed as a 'snuff movie'. That is why the killer had picked out the car under the street lamp. Tommy Zaino and his girlfriend Debbie Crescendo were lucky. They had been parked under the street lamp but had moved to a darker spot immediately before Stacy Moskowitz and Bobby Violante drove up.

On 10 July 1979, Berkowitz was slashed with a razor by another inmate in the cell-block reserved for high risk prisoners. The cut ran from the left-hand side of his throat to the back of his neck. It needed fifty-six stitches and nearly killed him. He would not say who had attacked him. He later said that it was an attempt by a satanic group to make him live up to his vow of silence. Maury Terry claimed that the satanic cult was 'a Process offshoot with OTO crossovers' and even named its leader. He was Roy Alexander Radin, a tycoon who earned his money in show business. He moved to California in 1982. But by the time Terry had tracked him down, yet again, it was too late. Radin had been murdered on Friday, 13 May 1983. His body was found dumped in Death Valley – Charles Manson's old stamping ground. A defaced bible was found nearby. Could he have been Grand Chingon of the Four P Movement described by the satanic cannibal Stanley Dean Baker?

Although Roy Rabin and John and Michael Carr are dead and David Berkowitz is locked up, the other members of The Twenty-Two Disciples of Hell are still at large and, Terry reckons, still active.

'I am convinced,' says Terry. 'The evidence is quite clear that organised satanic groups – be they genuine Process, official OTO or subgroups resulting from internal schisms – exist and carry out illegal rituals. It is beyond doubt that some of these involve murder. And this isn't just an American problem. The whole thing started up again in Britain with Aleister Crowley and he exported it to the United States. This is a multinational problem and England isn't exempt.'

8

For the Love of Satan

Satanic slayer Ricky Kasso Jr was another of LaVey's children. Born in Northport, upstate New York, on 29 March 1967, his parents were school teachers and solid, middle-of-the-road Methodists. They had a stable marriage and a two-storey shingled home with white shutters on Seaview Avenue, just two blocks from Main Street. Tall trees shaded it in the summer and provided firewood in winter. There was a swimming pool in the garden and a basketball hoop in the driveway. These were designed to keep Ricky at home. They failed.

The Kassos lived in a small pleasant community, which had been established by English and Scottish settlers in 1653. Handy for the Long Island Railroad, it is something of a dormitory town for New York. Two New York mayors have lived there – James J. Walkers and Fiorello La Guardia. Other famous residents have included William K. Vanderbilt and beat poet Jack Kerouac.

Like many small towns in America, during the 1970s and 1980s, Northport had a problem with its disaffected youth. Drugs were brought in from New York City on the pleasure boats that stopped in at Great Cow Harbour, or dealers sped down the freeway to the Bronx or Harlem. Marijuana, angel dust, mescaline and heroin were traded openly in Cow Park. And Ricky Kasso was the self-styled 'Acid King'.

Ricky started smoking marijuana in fifth grade. By the time he was in eighth grade he was doing little else, getting to school twenty minutes early each day so that he could have a joint before class. His grades slumped to straight 'D's and many felt that he was only passing at all because his parents were teachers. He tried to excel at football, to prove to his father that he was not entirely useless. But his marijuana habit meant that he was easily winded. By the age of thirteen, he was dealing.

At football practice, Ricky met Jimmy Troiano. He was a year older than Ricky and had been adopted at the age of four-and-a-half. He knew nothing of his real parents except that his father had light brown hair and blue eyes, and his mother was of French descent. His adoptive father Vincent Troiano was art director of Fawcett Publishing in New York. Mary Troiano, Jimmy's adoptive mother, was a psychiatric nurse in nearby Huntington Hospital. They too lived a respectable life in an anonymous middle-class development to the East of Northport Village. But Jimmy just did not fit in. School friends called him 'strange'. Even boys twice his size were afraid of him. He was known as Dracula, because of his over-long eye teeth, or Scarface, because of a scar that ran from his eye to the corner of his mouth. This was the result of falling off a swing when he was five, though others made up much more dare-devil explanations.

Ricky and Jimmy became close. After football practice, they would smoke marijuana together and dream of escaping to California.

In 1980, Ricky Kasso first got into trouble with the police. They came round to his home with a warrant for his arrest. He, and five other local boys, were charged with burglary. When his mother searched his room for stolen property, she found a water pipe and other drug paraphernalia. This shocked her more than his arrest. Not only that, he had lied to her. Ricky had told her that he had tried dope once, but didn't like it. As an athlete, he was not going to put poison into his body, he said. The Kassos took their son to therapy to try to wean him off drugs. It did not work. Ricky made it clear to the counsellor that he liked marijuana and had no intention of giving it up.

141

During the summer vacation, bored and high on grass, Ricky dropped into the local public library to look at books on football. Instead he stumbled across *A History of Satanism*. In his drugged state, he felt like the book had sought him out. And when he sat down to read it, it came vividly alive for him. He sat reading it mesmerised for hours until the library shut that night. Afterwards in the wooden gazebo in Cow Park he told Jimmy Troiano about his discovery. The next day Ricky went to an Avitar New Age Book and Record Shop and bought a copy of Anton LaVey's *The Satanic Bible* in paperback. It came highly recommended by the counter clerk. For the rest of the summer vacation, Ricky would smoke marijuana and read his treasured tome in nearby Aztakea Woods. It was a haven for kids up there. Technically it was private property, so even when people did complain about the noise they made, the loud music or the fires they lit, the police simply responded that they could not enter private property without a warrant.

When school started again in autumn, Ricky Kasso was a changed person. He was much more self-assured. And he was a demon on the football field, especially in the tackles. He didn't care who got hurt. Ricky had already taken LSD when he was just twelve years old. Now, at fourteen, he got deeply into acid. He would buy acid and marijuana each day from a contact in the Midway Cafe, a bikers' hangout on Main Street, and sell what he didn't use himself to other kids down on the Loading Dock.

Meanwhile Jimmy Troiano was kicked out of high school and was sent to a special school for problem children. There he had to fight with the other tough cases. At sixteen, he dropped out. By 1982, Jimmy had been kicked out by his parents. They hated to do it, but they could not cope with him openly dealing in drugs from their house.

Ricky also became more of a problem at school. He skipped classes more often than he attended them, spending his time proselytising for Satan among the school's smoking circles and stealing from the teachers. Then, when he was classified 'emotionally crippled', he too was sent to special school. But he ran away from home for seventeen days and that was the end of that. He began to get others involved in his satanic practices. One evening at a friend's house, he drew a pentagram on the floor and said that he was going to hold a seance. In fact, he tried to summon up the Devil. Buoyed by drugs and drink stolen from the cocktail cabinet, Kasso's friends went along with him. But suddenly one of the girls got scared and broke the circle. Kasso passed out.

While Kasso was daubing 'I love Satan' on the gazebo in Cow Park, he was approached by a drunken Vietnam veteran called Pat Pagan. He had a pentagram medallion around his neck and claimed to be a member of a coven. There had been thirteen members in the Nam; he was the only one who had survived. But the veteran passed out from too much booze, so Kasso robbed him of his money and pension cheques. One of Kasso's fellow smokers tried to stop him. His name was Gary Lauwers.

Jimmy Troiano was arrested breaking into a house while high. He was sent to the detoxification centre at South Oaks Hospital in Amityville. There he met and fell in love with another inmate, but they were separated when she tried to commit suicide. Then Kasso turned up in the hospital too. He had been committed by his parents after a suicide attempt just one week before his sixteenth birthday. The first thing Kasso asked his old friend was whether he could get any drugs in there. Troiano said that there were some around but he himself had been clean for almost eight months. When he got out Troiano continued to stay clean. He got himself a job in a MacDonalds and talked about getting married.

One night, Troiano was woken by scratching on his window. It was Kasso. He had escaped from the hospital and said that he was heading for California. Troiano helped his old friend out with $100 – half what he had saved to buy an engagement ring. Later that night Kasso was found by a night-watchman in a lumber yard, semiconscious. He had no money. There were three dots of mescaline in his pocket and he was taken back to South Oaks in handcuffs. He escaped four more times and had to be resuscitated once after another suicide attempt.

Troiano's attempts to stay clean led to a run-in with Gary Lauwers, who was also heavily into drugs by this time. But maintaining the effort to stay clean seemed worthwhile to Troiano when his girlfriend was released from South Oaks and renewed their affair. The Troiano family were pleased to meet her and hoped that his love for her would help him straighten out. But when he went to meet her family, they immediately took against him because of his former drug connections. They threw him out of their house. Troiano was so upset that he drove straight to the Midway Cafe and squandered the rest of the money he had been saving for their engagement ring on drugs.

When Kasso was released from South Oaks, he and Troiano rented a scruffy apartment together. It was just a few yards from the Midway. Kasso and Troiano earned the rent money by selling drugs outside the cafe. Gary Lauwers regularly came round to the apartment and other visitors remember Ricky Kasso experimenting with a Ouija board there. He played loud heavy metal music – Ozzy Osbourne mainly – and lit the apartment with black candles. With their fingertips on a cat's skull, Kasso began to call on Satan. One of the girls present swears that the skull then began to move across the Ouija board by itself. It ended up flying across the room and landing in the lap of a Catholic girl who was already spooked. She screamed the place down.

Troiano and another friend began bringing drugs up from Florida. They were arrested with a bag full of angel dust and were sentenced to eight months in jail. With Troiano inside, Kasso consented to give up the flat and move back in with his parents who took him on vacation up to their summer home in Greenwich, upstate New York. This left Gary Lauwers ruler of the roost in Northport. But he was arrested after branding a local boy with a hot hashish pipe. The pleas of his parents kept him out of jail, but they could not stop him dropping out of school.

Kasso's parents returned to Northport worn out by his belligerent behaviour and his mock suicide attempts. Back home he did not bother them much. He retired to Aztakea Woods where he would take drugs, hold court and compose songs about the Devil. He rarely went home and often slept out. He also began to get close to Pat Pagan, who never twigged that it was Kasso who had stolen his money. Pagan took Kasso back to his apartment one day and showed him the satanic altar he had and the voodoo idols he had collected. His collection included one particularly powerful fetish which he said was made from the pubic hair of nuns. For a regular supply of hash, weed and a little bit of acid, Pagan promised to teach Kasso more about Satanism. How much hash, weed and acid would it take for him to buy the pentagram medallion around Pagan's neck, Kasso asked. 'All the shit in the world,' said Pagan. That medallion had been made for him in the Nam and it was more precious than life itself.

The return of Ricky Kasso caused Gary Lauwers some problems too. There was a growing rivalry between the two of them. To keep up, Lauwers bought himself a book on Satanism and began to study it. But that did not stop Kasso from picking on him. Kasso was in trouble though. He had been sleeping with a girlfriend whose parents were away a lot. But Christmas was coming, they would be home and it was too cold to sleep out. He tried it. But, eventually, like a bedraggled alley cat, he dragged himself back to his parents' home. He had a severe bronchial infection. His parents nursed him and fed him and bought him warm clothes. He agreed to go back to school and they arranged a place in a school for children with special educational needs. He went there a couple of times, but largely to buy drugs. It didn't take him long to get expelled. In the ensuing row, he left home, vowing never to go back. Again.

145

He began big time drug dealing to make money. Another source of income was grave robbing. An occult store in New York City's Greenwich Village would pay $500 each for the skulls of Red Indians and there was a Native American burial ground in Northport. Kasso was caught standing over an open grave with a shovel in his hand. He was out on bail when Troiano got out of jail. Jimmy took a job as a mechanic, but the low wages did not suit him. He went into big-time dealing with Kasso. When his parents found out, they kicked him out of their house again.

Meanwhile Kasso collapsed with double pneumonia and his parents took the opportunity to have him committed to a psychiatric ward. But despite what the doctors described as his 'anti-social behaviour', he was not diagnosed as mentally ill. Nor was he a danger to anyone but himself. So they released him. Shortly after his release, Kasso turned up at a party. He was wearing a swastika earring and an inverted cross around his neck. He was also laden with drugs. He and Troiano had driven down to the Bronx to buy supplies of angel dust and marijuana. They sold some at the party. But when Kasso passed out, Gary Lauwers managed to steal ten hits of angel dust out of his pocket. When Kasso caught up with Lauwers the next day, he only had five left. Kasso took the rest out of his hide in a public beating.

'Nobody steals from the Acid King,' he said and warned Lauwers that he still wanted the money for the other five hits of angel dust.

On 30 April 1984 – Walpurgisnacht – Kasso, Troiano, Pat Pagan and two others from Kasso's circle of drug abusers got together some booze and drugs and drove down to the famous haunted house in Amityville. Outside, Pagan set up his altar. He put five black candles around the points of a pentagram, put a necklace made of snake-skulls in the centre, then poured some of the wine – 'a libation for Satan' – around the makeshift altar. After smoking some marijuana and angel dust, they knelt down around the altar and Pagan lit the candles one by one, calling on Satan to come down to them. He asked for money, food and other material things in exchange for their souls. As Pagan lit the last candle, he asked Satan to slay their enemies. But they could not think of anyone they particularly wanted slaying. Eventually, someone suggested Gary Lauwers, who still owed Kasso $50 for the angel dust he had stolen. So they all solemnly asked Satan to kill him. Pagan was tossing red powder into the flames when the altar was toppled by the kick of a policeman. Pagan cursed him in the name of Satan. The policeman was about to take him in when he learnt that Pagan was a Vietnam veteran. He had been in Vietnam himself and let them off with a warning, urging Pagan to seek psychiatric help.

But it was Kasso who needed help. Now the weather was warmer, he slept out, when he slept at all. He was taking so many drugs that he rarely bothered with sleep. When a young Baptist tried to reach out and recruit him for the local church, he threw the offer back in the young man's face.

'Christ can't help me,' he said, 'Do you know who I am? I am Satan. He is my main man. Satan is going to burn your precious Christ. Satan will destroy your God and take his rightful place as ruler of this planet.'

Those who heard the outburst were terrified.

A little later, Pat Pagan approached Kasso in the park. He had been ill and he needed $90 to pay his rent and get some food. Kasso refused. But he said he would give Pagan $90 for the medallion around his neck.

'No way,' said Pagan. 'This is my pride. This is what keeps me going.'

And he walked away. Kasso sprang after him. He tripped Pagan and leapt on top of him. He beat Pagan and abused him. Pagan had been his teacher, but he had graduated.

'I'm Satan now,' Kasso said as he ripped the medallion from Pagan's neck.

He left the once-proud Vietnam veteran sobbing on the ground and walked away. When Pagan got the strength together he went to the police station on Main Street and reported that Ricky Kasso had beaten him up and stolen his medallion. The police did nothing about it.

Later that afternoon, Kasso and Troiano caught up with Lauwers again. They took him round the back of Trinity Church and beat him up. This was the fifth time he had beaten up Lauwers, but Lauwers had still not paid him the $50 he owed him. Kasso swore that this was the last time he was going to beat up Lauwers. If he did not get his money, next time he would do much worse. Lauwers also swore that he had taken his last beating and began carrying a knife.

Kasso began an affair with a girl which offered the serious possibility of reform. But when her parents discovered that she had been seen in the company of a notorious drug dealer they got the police to warn him off. Meanwhile Troiano was arrested once again for burglary.

On the night of 16 June 1984, the local kids met at the gazebo before going on to their friend Randy's birthday party. Everyone knew that Randy's parents had specifically barred Ricky Kasso and Jimmy Troiano. Gary Lauwers was among the crowd at the gazebo. Kasso pretended not to be mad at him. He even gave Lauwers a free hit of mescaline and everyone assumed that Lauwers had paid Kasso the $50 he owed him. But he hadn't. When the crowd took off to the party, Lauwers and a boy named Albert Quinones stayed behind with Kasso and Troiano. The four of them decided to go up to Aztakea Woods and take more drugs. On the way, Gary suggested they stop for doughnuts and orange juice, which they did. For all the world they looked like four ordinary kids out to enjoy a warm Saturday night in summer. It was pitch black as they started up the trail to Aztakea Woods. But they did not need a torch. Kasso knew the way like the back of his hand. A little way up the trail, there was a noise, a rustling. It came from the trees above them. Then there was a scratching sound nearer the ground, first in one place, then in another.

'It must be a squirrel,' said Gary.

'No,' said Kasso. 'It's Satan. That's Satan up there and he is giving me a sign. He says everything is going to be all right, everything's going to be cool.'

Up in a clearing, Kasso had already piled up some brushwood for a fire. While Quinones lit it, Kasso dug up another stash of mescaline he had buried in an old mayonnaise jar and handed the dots round. Troiano had lost count of how many he had taken at least six. He reckoned Kasso had had eight or nine. They put on a Black Sabbath tape. Quinones was so out of it he began to study the way the trees were swaying, but Kasso was in a more sinister mood. Troiano sat down next to Lauwers. The fire was not burning well, so Lauwers peeled off his socks and threw them on.

'What else have you got that will catch fire?' asked Kasso as he sat down on the other side of Lauwers.

He pulled at Lauwers' jacket. Lauwers protested.

'My mother bought me this.'

'Maybe just the sleeves then,' said Troiano.

Kasso agreed and pulled a pocket knife from his jeans. He opened it up.

'That's a beauty, Rick,' said Quinones, looking at the knife.

'I bought it at Midway's today,' Kasso said. 'It is guaranteed for life.'

'Whose life?' asked Troiano.

'Anybody's,' said Kasso hacking off Lauwers' sleeves. Lauwers threw them on the fire himself and seemed pleased when they flared up. Quinones turned his attention back to the sway of the trees, while Kasso wanted to feed the fire some more.

'You can't have my trees,' said Quinones. 'They're green.' Kasso tousled Lauwers' hair.

'Hey, man, this is dry,' he said.

'No, man, find something else,' said Lauwers, jumping to his feet.

Kasso jumped up too, pushed Lauwers down again and held him. He told Troiano to take his knife and ordered him to cut off Lauwers' hair. While Lauwers squirmed, Troiano grabbed a handful of his hair and hacked it off. It sizzled on the fire. Then he came back for another hunk. Kasso let go and took his knife back. Lauwers began to howl. Then he said: 'What are you thinking, Ricky? I am getting some strange vibes.'

'What kind of vibes?' said Kasso.

'Like you want to hurt me.'

'Shit no, man. I don't want to hurt you,' said Kasso. 'I want to kill you.'

Then they began arguing about the money that Lauwers owed Kasso. Lauwers protested that he thought they were friends now. But Kasso brought up his knee, slamming it into Lauwers' groin. Lauwers crumpled, grabbing Pat Pagan's pentagram medallion as he slid to the ground. Then Kasso kicked him again, and again.

'I'll teach you to mess with me, you scumbag,' screamed Kasso. He raised the knife and plunged it into Lauwers' flesh.

Lauwers looked in shock at the handle sticking out of him. Kasso grabbed it, pulled out the knife and stabbed him again.

'Say you love Satan,' yelled Kasso as he stabbed Lauwers a third time.

'No,' howled Lauwers as Kasso stabbed him again.

'I am going to keep this up until you do,' he said.

'I love my mother,' sobbed Lauwers.

'Satan!' yelled Kasso wielding the knife again. 'I won't stop until you say you love Satan.'

Suddenly Troiano interjected: 'Ricky, enough, you're killing him.'

'He's got to say he loves Satan,' insisted Kasso.

With the next blow, the knife hit bone and went flying off. Troiano retrieved the knife and gave it back to Kasso.

Quinones was barely conscious by this time. But Kasso and Troiano got him to his feet. He helped them drag Lauwers' body away from the fire, some thirty metres into the woods where they began digging a shallow grave under the bushes. They were hard about their work when, suddenly, Lauwers sat up. Some macabre reflex made him bend at the waist. The boys screamed. Kasso began to babble. He grabbed his knife and frantically stabbed at the eyesockets, dislodging the eyeballs. He slashed at them, cutting the nerves and muscles that held them in place and they rolled down Lauwers' cheeks. Then Kasso slashed at the mouth and nose. And he repeatedly stabbed at the body until gradually he became calmer. Terrified, Quinones ran off blindly into the woods and somehow stumbled home. Kasso and Troiano left Lauwers' body where it was and stood by the fire. A crow cawed overhead and Kasso said that it was a good sign.

'Satan is with us,' he said. 'It is a sign he approves of what we have done in his name.'

Then he said with some satisfaction: 'I did it, man. I made my first sacrifice for Satan.'

The Black Sabbath tape was playing 'Bark at the Moon'.

Around 2.30 p.m., a local resident called Northport Police Station and reported a disturbance in Aztakea Woods. There was a fire up there and loud music. And they had heard screaming. It was just kids, the police said. They repeated the old excuse – the woods were private property and they would need a warrant to go up there. Best thing to do, the police told the complainant, was to go back to sleep.

Kasso went to Quinones' house and washed the blood off his hands. He threw away his blood-splattered T-shirt. Quinones gave him a clean one of his. Kasso's jeans were already so dirty and stained that they did not show the blood. When he was cleaned up, Quinones urged Kasso to go. He was coming down off his mescaline high and Kasso's presence reminded him of the terrible thing that had happened in Aztakea Woods. Kasso strolled over to the home of a fourteen-year-old girlfriend. She let him sleep in the living room. He was up and gone by the time her parents woke. As he walked down by the harbour, he felt in his pockets for another hit of mescaline and found his pocket knife. His fingerprints were etched in Lauwers' blood that had dried on the handle. That would never do. He threw the knife into the clear water of Long Island Sound.

It was Sunday morning and the church bells were ringing. He smoked a couple of joints to steady his nerves then called his father. On Monday Kasso was due in court on grave robbing charges. His father was coming too. They arranged to meet in front of the Midway Cafe at 9 a.m.

In fact, Kasso turned up at home at 7.30 the next morning. He was so dishevelled that his mother reeled from him. His body stank and there were leaves and earth in his hair. He had tried to sleep in the open ground behind the Midway, but he was so worried about his court appearance the next morning that he could not get to sleep. But when he appeared in court – still filthy – he found that the grave robbing charges had been dropped. He had been disturbed before he had actually stolen a skull or any of the bones. Instead, he was charged with the lesser offence of endangering the public health by disturbing a grave, granted legal aid and the hearing was adjourned until he had consulted an attorney.

Afterwards, when Kasso's father dropped him off in front of the Midway, father and son had one final row. Kasso had asked for a quarter to buy a bagel. His father said they had a whole fridge full of bagels at home. If he came home and had a shower, he could have as many as he wanted. Kasso complained to friends that his father was so tight he would not even give him a quarter.

The next day, Kasso and Troiano went over to their friend Billy Evans' house. They drank some booze from Evans' father's cocktail cabinet. Kasso pulled a strip of mescaline dots from his pocket and they took some. Kasso fell asleep. Billy innocently picked up the strip of mescaline and said to Troiano: 'I'm going to borrow one of these. You want one?'

Troiano jumped to his feet, grabbed the mescaline and snatched it away from him.

'You stupid son of a bitch. Don't ever steal from him,' he yelled. 'He killed Gary Lauwers for doing that.'

Troiano hardly ever drank, but he took a stiff shot and told the friend what had happened.

Kasso slept soundly that afternoon. But it was the last time he would sleep at all. Soon, his conscience began to bother him. Every time he closed his eyes he saw a bloody face coming towards him. He decided that maybe it was time to ease up on the drugs.

Everyone in Northport was asking: 'Where is Gary Lauwers?' His parents were particularly worried, but Gary had taken off before and they were sure he would come back. They did not report him as a missing person to the police. When Kasso was asked what had happened to Lauwers, he said he did not know – to start with. Then a rumour began to spread that Lauwers had been sacrificed to Satan. Kasso was eager to take the credit for that. He openly boasted that he was the one who had made the sacrifice and took a fifteen-year-old friend called Tyler up to see the mutilated corpse.

'It smelt like fifty guys had taken a crap and left it cooking in the sun,' Tyler said. The body was black and bloated. There were no eyes. The nose had been sliced off. The lips were gone and maggots were crawling in and out of the face. Tyler puked. But, shocked though he was, he did not tell his parents. After all, Kasso had already killed once.

A week after Lauwers had been murdered, Kasso took three more kids up to see his body. By then, the maggots had practically picked him clean. Kasso and Troiano discussed cremating the remains and burning down the woods so that no one would ever find it. They discussed how much gasoline they would need and which way the wind should be blowing. But they did nothing about it.

Troiano did not go up into the woods again, but he could not keep his mouth shut. He began telling people that Kasso had killed Lauwers in self-defence.

Eventually Kasso called in an old friend called Russell,

who Troiano had met in prison, to help dispose of the body. He bought a spade and Kasso dug a shallow trench, four foot long and two foot deep beside the body. He thought that would be deep enough if they covered the grave with leaves. Then the two of them carefully dragged the corpse into the trench, afraid that one of the rotting limbs would come off in their hands, and tipped it in. They were just about to cover it over when Russell spotted something shining. It was Pat Pagan's satanic medallion that Lauwers had snatched from Kasso's neck during the final struggle. And it was stuck in Lauwers' rotting flesh. Russell picked it out.

'Hey, look at this, man,' he said.

Kasso shuddered in horror for the first time.

'No, man, put it back. Satan has taken it for his own,' he said as he threw the medallion back in the shallow grave. He grabbed the spade and, with the first spadeful of earth, he made sure he covered it.

Later that day, Kasso heard that his girlfriend, the only one he ever loved, had overdosed. She was dead.

Troiano, Kasso and the other kids spent the next Saturday night with an old woman who read the cards – ordinary playing cards, not the tarot. She predicted that Troiano would be going away and that he would be reconciled with his adoptive parents, though they would not be living together again. In Kasso's cards, she saw a fire and a stopped clock with liquid – blood maybe – running out of it. Then she dealt again. The first card was the King of Clubs – this stood for a figure of authority, she said, the police maybe. Next came the King of Spades which symbolised death.

One of the girls that Troiano told about the murder called the police anonymously. Then she plucked up the courage to tell her parents what Troiano had said. They called their attorney who handled liaison with the police from then on. Sniffer dogs were brought in and the police organised a search of the woods, but were hampered by torrential rain.

Meanwhile Kasso and Troiano had left Northport, making their long-awaited trip to California. They stole $200 from a student who gave them a lift, bought a broken down Pontiac for $50 and spent another $150 on mescaline – aiming to sell it for a profit on the way. They soon found that this was not as easy as they had hoped. In a truckstop where they had tried to market their wares, they were warned by the waitress that the owner had called the police. So they decided to return to Newport, where they knew they had a ready market, borrow as much money as they could and head off again.

By the time their maroon Pontiac turned off the Long Island Expressway, the police had found the body and shovelled the maggot-riddled remains into plastic autopsy bags. They had photographed the area and called the Lauwers family, asking for someone to come and perform the gruesome task of identifying the body. The police were out looking for Troiano and Kasso, who were innocently speeding down Woodbine Avenue into Northport. Suddenly, they screeched to a halt. A black cat had walked out into the road in front of them. It just sat there looking at them. Kasso sounded the horn and the cat darted off the way it had come.

'A black cat means bad luck,' said Troiano

'No, man,' Kasso said. 'A black cat is Satan's favourite animal. It's mine too. No, a black cat means good luck – lots of good luck for both of us.'

Troiano and Kasso were not at home when the police called their parents' houses. But Albert Quinones was. He says that the police beat him up. They deny it. But he told them everything that had happened that night.

Troiano and Kasso intended to be in and out of Northport before anyone realised they were there. They sold their entire stash of mescaline at a friend's 4 July cookout, much to the disapproval of her dad. Then they were back on the road to California again. But before they left Northport, they decided to wash up. They stopped at the Northport Yacht Club – parking by a sign that said 'No parking at any time – Police Department' – and went in for a shower. They smoked a joint on the balcony, then went back to the car – only to find that the ignition key had snapped in two.

'See, I told you so,' said Troiano. 'That black cat was bad luck.'

As it was 4 July, the Independence Day holiday, they could not call anyone out to make them a new key. They would have to wait until the next day. So they had a couple more joints, some laced with angel dust, and settled down to sleep in the car. But they had chosen the wrong area to sleep in. The Northport Yacht Club is in a smart part of town. People who spend half-a-million dollars on their homes do not take kindly to vagrants sleeping in wrecked cars at the end of their driveways. The following morning, one of them complained to the police.

Troiano and Kasso were woken at 7.30 a.m. by the single word 'Freeze!' They opened their eyes to look down the barrel of a gun. The police flung open the front door and dragged Troiano out by the foot. Moments later, he was spreadeagled against the side of the car. When they tried the same thing on Kasso, he pulled a knife. But a drug-addled hung-over teenager was no match for a fully trained wide-awake law enforcement officer. Kasso was handcuffed and the knife was waved under his nose.

'Is this what you used to kill that boy in the woods?' asked the policeman.

'I didn't kill nobody,' said Kasso. But no one believed him.

The two of them were taken to Northport Police Station where they were booked. Then they were hustled into separate police cars and transported to the Suffolk County station at nearby Yaphank. Although Troiano signed away his rights to be represented by an attorney, he tried to remain silent. Then the police told him that Quinones had said he had held Lauwers down while Kasso stabbed him. So Troiano trotted out his story that Kasso had killed Lauwers in a fight over some angel dust. It was self-defence, he said. After Troiano had made a statement to that effect, he was put in a room with Kasso and the two of them were left alone. Kasso told Troiano that he had already admitted to killing Lauwers deliberately. He had also said that Troiano had held Lauwers down. The police had typed all this up in a statement, which Kasso signed. And after he had signed the statement, he turned it over and wrote on the back: 'Gary Lauwers deserved everything I gave him.'

'Neat, huh?' Kasso said to Troiano.

When Troiano was taken back in for more questioning, he changed his statement, implicating himself in the murder – saying that Quinones had told him Kasso was going to kill Lauwers and that he had held Lauwers down while Kasso stabbed him. Up to that point, the police admitted later, Troiano was not even a suspect. He was just eighteen years old.

The Long Island newspaper *Newsday* broke the story. The press immediately seized on the satanic elements of the murder. They found Kasso's 'I love Satan' daub on the gazebo. They also found Gary Lauwers' name there, surrounded by 'X's and the number '666', the number of the Beast. And Ricky Kasso played up to the image by wearing a satanic AC/DC T-shirt to the arraignment.

Afterwards, back in the jailhouse at Riverhead, Long Island, Kasso was allowed to watch a little TV. He was delighted when he saw himself on the news. But when the newscaster mispronounced his name he got up and shook his fist at the TV set.

'A guy finally makes the grade and they fuck it up,' he said.

That night, at 12.30 a.m., the guard looked in at Kasso in his cell. At 1 a.m., the seventeen-year-old self-styled satanist was found dead. He had hanged himself from the cell door with a bedsheet.

Troiano cursed when he heard. This dropped him right in it. He considered Kasso the murderer and himself as nothing but a witness. But he knew that somebody had to pay for the murder of Gary Lauwers. He was the only one they had. Ironically, Troiano could not even take the same cop-out route as Kasso. The prison psychiatrists had found Troiano, not Kasso, had suicidal tendencies and he had been placed under special supervision, while Kasso had been left with the prison's general population.

Kasso's parents identified his body. He was taken to the Brueggeman Funeral Home in East Northport where he was cremated. No family members attended. No words were said. There was no ceremony, Christian or satanic. His ashes went unclaimed.

Despite Gary Lauwers' satanic leanings, he was given a Christian funeral. The whole town turned out. Later, the kids took buckets of water and bleach down to the gazebo and scrubbed off Kasso's satanic daubs. It did not stay clean for long. The new graffiti saying 'Gary Lauwers lives in our hearts' and 'Death to Troiano' appeared. And someone began selling T-shirts that said, bizarrely, 'Ricky Kasso lives.'

On the same day as Lauwers' funeral, Troiano was indicted for murder in the second degree. Albert Quinones was not charged and agreed to testify for the prosecution. Things looked bleak for Troiano. But then the magazine *Rolling Stone* dropped a bomb. It quoted Albert Quinones alleging that the police had beaten him up. If this was true, it would destroy Quinones' credibility as a witness for the prosecution. Quinones found himself increasingly unpopular in Northport. The other kids refused to speak to him and his parents received threatening phone calls. After the grand jury hearing, he was beaten up – not for testifying against Troiano but for not preventing Kasso killing Lauwers.

When the trial got under way on 4 April 1984, prosecution attorney William J. Keahon tried to blacken Troiano's character by producing witnesses who said he was a drug dealer. The coroner testified that there were thirty-two stab wounds in the body. On other points the medical evidence was equivocal though, but it allowed the possibility that Lauwers was already dead when Troiano picked up the knife and gave it back to Kasso, as the defence contested. But Albert Quinones' testimony implicated Troiano far more heavily than the defence had been expecting. Quinones said that Lauwers initially thought that Troiano, not Kasso, was going to kill him. But during cross-examination, Quinones admitted to kicking Lauwers in the face. He made several other significant deviations from his original statement. When asked to explain them, he said that the police had beaten him up and he had told them what they had wanted to hear. He admitted quite candidly that he had lied in his statement. After all, he said, the police wanted Kasso and Troiano not him. The defence also contended that Quinones was burnt out on drugs, making his testimony so unreliable as to be useless. Law students who attended the trial thought it was quite wrong that Quinones had been granted immunity from prosecution. They thought that he should be standing trial alongside Troiano. The defence then began to chisel away at the credibility of Troiano's second statement, the one where he had implicated himself. The police officer who had taken the second statement admitted taking unnecessary pictures of Troiano at the murder scene in an attempt to smear him, falsifying the sequence of events in the statement and leaving vital information out.

Despite the fact that the prosecution case was crumbling, public opinion was running heavily against Troiano. A seventeen-year-old boy had been killed and people wanted someone to blame.

The defence called just three witnesses. One was the local mailman who fixed the time Troiano and the others had gone up to Aztakea Woods, showing the time stated in some of the statements was wrong. The other two were experts on drug abuse who testified that not only were the memories of drug users highly unreliable, but that they were highly suggestible – especially when suggestions came from authority figures like the police. This further discredited Quinones' testimony and cast even more doubt on Troiano's second, incriminating, statement.

159

In his summing up, the defence council Eric Naiburg showed that Troiano had no motive to kill Lauwers, that much of the evidence must be discounted because it had been given by unreliable and highly suggestive drug abusers, and that the police had, essentially, fitted Troiano up in a second statement after Kasso had implicated him.

The prosecutor William Keahon told the jury that the facts of the case were simple. Troiano was a depraved individual. Troiano and Kasso had killed Lauwers together. Troiano had lied in his first statement, blaming Kasso for everything. Then, when he had learned that Kasso had told the police everything, he had tried to repair the damage in his second, incriminating statement.

The night before the jury returned their verdict, Troiano says he saw Kasso in his cell. He was not frightened because he knew Kasso was dead. Troiano says he told the vision that he was going to get out of there and go to California – like they had always planned. Kasso laughed.

'They got me and they are going to get you too,' he said. 'It is all planned. They are going to sling your ass in the penitentiary and a guy with a big knife is going to get you. You won't last six weeks.'

The following day, the jury returned a verdict. They founded Troiano not guilty of murder in the second degree. Although they had spent a long time on their deliberations, not one of them had ever voted for conviction. Later they said that they would have convicted him for assault, concealing a body or any other lesser charge. They just did not feel that the prosecution had proved Troiano had contributed to Lauwers' death.

The good people of Northport were not pleased. They had tried and convicted Troiano in their own minds long before. The kids were more forgiving though. They commemorated Ricky Kasso in a little song:

'Hey, Ricky, you're so fine,
Why don't you stab me one more time?

160

Hey, Ricky, you're a nice guy,
Why don't you stab me in the eye?
Hey, Ricky, you're so swell,
Why are you hanging in your prison cell?'

They sing it down at the gazebo.

Satanism and the all-pervading influence of Anton LaVey is only one aspect of the murder of Gary Lauwers in Northport, New York. But around the same time, a far more sinister satanic sect started work in Chicago, Illinois. It began with a series of Ripper-style murders. In May 1981, Linda Sutton was abducted, gang raped and stabbed to death. When her body was found she had been horribly mutilated and her left breast was missing.

The following year, two young women, Shui Mak and Lorraine Borowski, were taken from their homes. Their bodies were found similarly mutilated. Then the body of Sandra Delaware was found in a tributary of the Chicago River. She had been strangled and she too had her left breast missing.

Next, Mrs Rose Beck Davis was found. Her body was left in the Gold Coast district of the city, between two apartment blocks. She had been raped, beaten, stabbed, strangled, bludgeoned, hacked about with an axe and, again, the killer or killers had paid special attention to the mutilation of her breasts.

Then, in September 1982, the police got lucky. They found a live witness, but only just. An eighteen-year-old prostitute was found dumped by the North Western railway tracks. She had been raped, hacked about and left for dead. Somehow she had survived the ordeal and, in hospital, she told the police that she had been picked up by a man in a red van. She also gave a good description of the driver.

A few days later, the police stopped a red van driven by a man answering the prostitute's description. The driver was twenty-one-year-old Edward Spreitzer. With him was

161

nineteen-year-old Andrew Kokoraleis, who admitted a random shooting earlier that year. The van's owner was Spreitzer's employer Robin Grecht. He, in turn, had worked for the infamous homosexual serial killer John Wayne Gacy, who killed over twenty-nine children. Grecht had a string of convictions for violence and sexual assault. The police then discovered that Grecht had a satanic temple where they took the abducted women. There they were repeatedly raped and tortured. One breast was severed with a cheese wire. It was passed around and eaten. The victim was then sacrificed to Satan.

Spreitzer was found guilty of the murder of Linda Sutton and sentenced to death. Andrew Kokoraleis and his brother Thomas were sentenced to death for the murder of Lorraine Borowski. But on appeal, Thomas Kokoraleis won a reversal. His sentence has been reduced to 70 years in jail.

Grecht managed to dodge the murder charges. But convictions for rape and attempted murder earned him 120 years inside.

But even seemingly harmless kooks can turn into murderers under the influence of Satan. In 1989, twenty-eight-year-old Texas-born Daniel Rakowitz provided New York's East Village with some unnecessary local colour. He would wander around with a cockerel perched on his shoulder. He ran his own satanic sect and claimed that Crowley had got it all wrong. The number of the Beast of the Apocalypse was not 666 but 966. It would have been better if he had called 911.

His girlfriend, a Swiss immigrant who was studying at the Martha Graham School of Contemporary Dance, was not convinced by his reasoning and flung him out. He responded by murdering her. Then he cut her body up and boiled the flesh off her bones. He put her skull and bones in a bucket which he carried around with him.

Naturally, he did not keep quiet about what he had done. He told his acolytes in the Church of 966 all about it. One of them went to the police and they found all the evidence they needed in Rakowitz's handy bucket.

On 14 September 1990, he was found guilty of murder. He was sentenced to life.

9

Lesbian Vampires

Vampires are things of myth and legend. But they also exist in real life. George Haigh, the infamous 'Acid Bath Murderer' of the 1940s, claimed that he killed his victims to drink their blood. But as he dissolved the rest of their earthly remains in a bath of acid, the jury preferred to believe the more mundane motive that he wanted to purloin the money and belongings of his victims.

Tracy Wigginton, a convent-educated Catholic, grew up believing that she was a vampire. She went out only at night and avoided sunlight and mirrors. Six feet tall and seventeen stone, she was never seen to eat. Her only sustenance came from drinking blood which she collected from the local butchers' shops.

In Brisbane in 1989, Wigginton, a committed lesbian, gathered around her a group of girls called the Swampies. They wore black clothes and heavy boots, and surrounded themselves with occult imagery. Wigginton's lover, former heroin user Lisa Ptaschinski, would use a tourniquet to pump up the veins in her arm, then nick her wrist so that Wigginton could suck her blood. But this was not enough. Wigginton craved more human blood and was willing to kill to get it.

Wigginton, Ptaschinski, Acid House Swampy Kim Jervis and her lover, unemployed secretary Tracey Waugh, planned to commit the perfect murder to satisfy Wigginton's bizarre lust. Meeting in gay clubs, they discussed how they could stalk, trap and kill a human victim so that Wigginton could drink their blood.

One night at Jervis's flat, which was hung with pictures of cemeteries and had a stolen headstone as a centre-piece, they came up with what they thought was the perfect plan. Waugh and Ptaschinski would pose as prostitutes and lure the victim into one of the inner city parks. In a secluded spot, Wigginton and Jervis would kill him and drink his blood. The women would then take his body to a cemetery and dump his body in a freshly dug grave and cover it over. When the funeral party arrived the following day, a coffin would be lowered on top of the body, the grave would be filled in and the victim would be buried without anyone realising it. There would be no witnesses, no clues and no corpse.

On the night of Friday 20 October 1989, the four women met at the Club Lewmors, a lesbian dive, where they sipped champagne. Wigginton and Jervis were carrying knives – but Wigginton bragged that she would kill with her bare hands if she had to. Around 11.30 p.m., they left the club and began cruising the streets in Wigginton's green Holden sedan looking for a likely victim. On River Terrace, they spotted forty-seven-year-old Edward Baldock, clinging drunkenly to a lamp post. He had been out for a few beers and a game of darts with his mates in the Caledonia Club and was now slowly making his way home to his wife of twenty-five years. The women stopped and asked him if he wanted a lift home. He thought it was his lucky night, accepted and climbed in the back with Wigginton. They held hands. Wigginton instructed Ptaschinski to drive down to Orleigh Park, which was near Baldock's home. Ptaschinski parked under a fig tree near the deserted South Brisbane Sailing Club. Wigginton asked Baldock whether he wanted a good time. He was all for it. They got out of the car and walked down to the river bank, where they both undressed. A few minutes later Wigginton returned to the car, complaining that Baldock was too strong. Ptaschinski said she would help and Jervis handed her her knife. The two lesbian lovers walked back down to the river where Baldock sat, naked except for his socks. Wigginton urged Ptaschinski to creep up on him and stab him, but she did not have the nerve. She could not kill a poor old drunk. Instead, she collapsed in the sand in front of him and began to gabble. Wigginton had no such qualms. She stabbed Baldock repeatedly in the neck and throat until his head was nearly severed, then she drank his blood. She returned to the car satisfied and the women drove back to Jervis's flat elated, convinced that they had committed the perfect murder. It was only when they arrived at the macabre apartment that Wigginton realised that she had lost her bankers card. She had dropped it while she was undressing.

Panicked, the women drove back to Orleigh Park and scoured the area, but they could not find the card. They decided that Wigginton must have lost it elsewhere. On the way back to Jervis's flat, they were stopped for a routine check by a patrol car and Ptaschinski was breathalysed. The breath test was negative, but she had come out without her driving licence and the police took down the details of the car.

Next morning, Baldock's naked body was discovered by two women out on an early morning walk. They called the police. Within minutes of their arrival, detectives found Wigginton's bankers card in Baldock's shoe. They quickly discovered that the green Holden that had been stopped by a patrol car in the area was also registered to a Tracey Wigginton and put two and two together. At this point, they assumed that Wigginton was Baldock's mistress and she had murdered him in an argument over money.

In the morning, the four women realised that their perfect crime might not be so perfect after all. The loss of Wigginton's bankers card began to worry them more and more. If the card was found and any of them were questioned, they decided to say that they had been out fooling about in that area earlier the day before. That's when Wigginton must have lost the card. However, the story had one major flaw. It did not take into account that they had been stopped in that same area by a patrol car that night.

Acting on the theory that Wigginton was Baldock's aggrieved mistress, the police picked her up. But under questioning, she began to change her story from the one that they had agreed. She began to elaborate on it, mentioning that they had seen a suspicious-looking couple in the park – then, later, she said that she had gone to the park in the evening and had fallen over a dead body in the dark, but had been too frightened to report it.

Ptaschinski's nerve had gone the night before. With Wigginton in custody, it went again. She could not stand the waiting. She left the flat and began walking about in a confused state. As she wandered about aimlessly, the guilt gradually ate into her. She turned herself in at a nearby police station. Jervis and Waugh were arrested the next day.

Under relentless questioning, Tracey Wigginton admitted that she was a 'vampire'. She was sent for detailed psychological examination. The doctors discovered that Tracey had been abandoned by her father and mother when she was a baby and was brought up by her grandparents George and Avril Wigginton. George was a profligate womaniser and Avril took out her hatred of her unfaithful husband on the children in her care. She beat Tracey mercilessly and poisoned her mind against men. Tracey turned to her genial grandfather for affection, but claimed that he demanded sex with her after she had turned eight. At Catholic school, she became a notorious lesbian and was known for her strange and evil behaviour. When she left school in 1982, she began calling herself Bobby and she went round to beat her grandmother up. She had a sado-masochistic relationship with a woman called Jamie who beat her with a strap and demanded total submission. She later underwent a lesbian 'wedding' performed by a member of the Hare Krishna sect and became a bouncer at a gay night club.

After the 'marriage' broke up, she asked the club's owner, a man named John O'Hara, to help her have a baby. They had sex in front of six close friends. Tracey fell pregnant, but later miscarried. She began a stormy relationship with a woman named Donna Staib. They lived together but both were enormously promiscuous with other women. Around that time, Tracey dyed her hair 'midnight blue' and had her body tattooed with mystical signs. She and Staib shared a taste for horror videos. The night before Baldock's murder they had watched a sequence of a man being shot in the forehead and his skull exploding over and over again in slow motion.

The police feared that Wigginton's warped upbringing might be used in an insanity plea. But Wigginton, twenty-four, took responsibility for her acts and was aware of their consequences. She pleaded guilty and was sentenced to life imprisonment.

The other three women pleaded not guilty. They claimed that they had not thought that Wigginton was serious when she talked of killing and drinking people's blood. But they had been forced to go along with her by her overbearing personality. Under cross-examination though, Ptaschinski admitted that she had been fascinated by the 'thrilling and chilling' plan to murder a man to drink his blood. In court, the three women claimed that Wigginton had occult powers. They said that she claimed to be the Devil's wife and practised mind control. The cross around Kim Jervis's neck had been broken by her diabolical power, and she could disappear leaving only the eyes of a cat.

Ptaschinski, twenty-four, was found guilty of murder and sentenced to life. Jervis, twenty-three, got eighteen years for manslaughter. Only Waugh, twenty-three, walked free from the court. Although she was the brightest of the four women, the jury decided that she was completely under the evil sway of Tracey Wigginton.

Wigginton is certainly not the only woman who killed for occult reasons. In 1973, a thirty-six-year-old Irish tinker named Eric Willmot went to have his fortune told. In the clairvoyant's caravan, he found not an old crone, but an attractive young gypsy woman. He fell for her and ended up in her bed. What he did not know was that the gypsy,

Phoebe Brady, was no ordinary fortune teller. She was the High Priestess of the Devil Worshippers, a position she had inherited when her mother died.

Phoebe had about thirty followers and insisted that, now he had bedded her, Willmot must marry her. She already had the ring and Willmot reluctantly underwent a satanist wedding ceremony under 'an arch of cross clubs' and 'with the sanction of the Devil'.

Willmot soon found that satisfying Phoebe's formidable libido was an exhausting task and tried to run away. Each time he was caught by Phoebe's cohorts and given a good beating. Once they broke his arm and cracked three of his ribs. The only way to get away for good, he thought, was to go abroad. He began saving the money to emigrate to Canada and sold the wedding ring Phoebe had given him to buy the ticket. Unwisely, Willmot let this fact slip in his cups in the pubs of Cork. Phoebe heard about it. She gave local hard man Michael Harmsworth £800 to teach Willmot a lesson, she said. He was to deliver her feckless husband, bound and gagged, to the moor outside of town. Harmsworth coshed Willmot in an alley in Cork. Pretending that Willmot was a drunken friend, Harmsworth carried him out of the city to a spot on the moors Phoebe had specified. For good measure, Harmsworth went through Willmot's pockets and stole his money. He left him bound and gagged and ran off.

Phoebe and her Assistant High Priestess, her daughter Verren, beat Willmot with a dog whip on the buttocks and back. Then they set about him with iron bars.

In December 1979, a motorist saw a foot protruding from a shallow grave on the moorland between Cork and Dublin. The police dug up Willmot's body. His testicles were bruised. His ribs were smashed and several internal organs ruptured. His skull was fractured and his face smashed in.

Harmsworth, Phoebe and Verren were sentenced to life imprisonment.

* * *

Earlier, in 1952, Ben Lyles, the husband of Anjette Lyles, a well-known devotee of Satanism and voodoo in Macon, Georgia, died suddenly. His wife took the $3,000 she got from his life assurance and used it to open a restaurant named, aptly, The Gay Widow. One of the regulars there was Joe Neal Gabbert, an airline pilot. In June 1955, he married Anjette. But three months later he became ill and died. The insurance money was, naturally, ploughed back into the business. If that was not coincidence enough, Anjette's mother-in-law from her first marriage, Julia Young Lyles, passed away, followed by Anjette's daughter, nine-year-old Marcia Elaine Lyles.

This time however, things did not go so smoothly. The pathologist at the hospital where the child died did a thorough autopsy and discovered a fatal dose of arsenic in her system. When the police searched Anjette Lyles' home, they found a number of bottles of rat poison, several of which were empty. Anjette claimed that Marcia must have swallowed some by accident while playing doctors and nurses. But then it was established that the documents allowing Anjette to inherit the estate of Julia Young Lyles, after the death of Marcia, were forged.

In all Anjette Lyles had netted nearly $50,000 from her career as a poisoner. She had squandered it on men and satanic paraphernalia.

She was convicted and sent to death row. But she has escaped the electric chair by being declared insane. She now languishes in the State Hospital at Milledgeville, Georgia.

In 1982, in Dusseldorf, another satanic priestess killed her lover. He was found naked sitting on a sofa in his scruffy flat in the run-down Metzer Street district of the city. There was a butcher's knife in his heart and his fingers were curled around its handle.

The man was Spanish immigrant Jose Luis Mato Fernandez and the police thought at first he had committed suicide. However, in the apartment, they found a notebook cover with satanic symbols – pentagrams and inverted crosses. Inside there was a curse on anyone reading the contents. The police read on. The book called on 'O Lucifer, Prince of Darkness'. The author promised to sell the Devil their soul. It begged for a sign, saying: 'I want to be possessed by you totally. Come to me when Mato is sleeping.'

Enquiries revealed that Mato Fernandez had been living with twenty-two-year-old Sylvia Brakel for nine months. But he had a string of other girlfriends and she had a teenage lesbian lover who lived nearby. However, Mato had grown jealous, accusing Brakel of taking another lover – the Devil perhaps – and she had stabbed him.

The police already had a substantial file on Sylvia Brakel. She had been sexually abused by her grandfather when she was eight. At sixteen, she had been gang raped by nine boys. This turned her to crime and she spent a year in a juvenile prison. When she left, she found herself a boyfriend, a baker's apprentice who introduced her to bisexuality and Satanism. In exchange, she stabbed him.

The police traced a member of Brakel's satanic coven who said Brakel had confessed to the murder within hours of committing it. She was caught and sentenced to life imprisonment.

Also in 1982, Nadia Kasprzak lost her husband. Twenty-two-year-old Serge Pognon, a slow-witted army deserter, shot Henri Kasprzak. The police were puzzled. Pognon had little connection with Kasprzak. Then they discovered that Pognon and his lover Agnes Bouvier had shared a holiday flat with Madame Kasprzak in Saint Raphael. Pognon said that he came under her spell and, although she did not tell him to, her satanic influence forced him to attack her husband. When the bullets were removed from Henri's corpse, it was found that they were each inscribed with the number seven. Three sevens has an occult significance and Madame Kasprzak had more than a passing interest in the occult. It was enough to earn her a twelve-year sentence, while Pognon got fifteen.

Strangely, the judge who handed down the sentences died of a heart attack soon after at seven o'clock on the seventh of July – the seventh month of the year.

During her childhood in Scotland, Sheena McLauchlan had dabbled in the occult. And when she fell pregnant in the early 1980s, she claimed it was an immaculate conception. A spirit had entered her while she was walking on Salisbury Plain, she said. She named the child Kether, a name redolent with associations to the Rosicrucians.

Soon after she gave birth, Sheena met Alan Porter who, at twenty-six, was five years her senior. She moved out from her mother's house, taking the baby, and went to live with Porter. When three-month-old Kether suddenly disappeared, Sheena said she had been a victim of a mysterious cot death. But two years later, she told her mother that Kether had been killed and was buried near Loch Lomond.

The police were called and they searched the area. They found the pram and the baby's clothes, but there was no body. It was assumed that it had been taken by scavengers.

In Glasgow's High Court, Sheena McLauchlan explained that a saffron-robed Tibetan monk, who was her spirit guide, had instructed her to strangle her daughter as a sacrifice. Sheena could not go through with it and Porter admitted that he had stepped in and helped her murder the child. Sheena McLauchlan pleaded diminished responsibility. Porter had no such excuse and was sentenced to life for murder.

10

Cannibal Cults

In June 1970, twenty-year-old Steven Hurd, a barbiturate addict and self-confessed satanist, was arrested along with four friends for the cannibalistic slaying of a schoolteacher in Orange County, California. Hurd and his friends did not have the money for hotel rooms and lived under bridges and in fields. They had forced their way into the teacher's car and driven her to a nearby orange grove, where they stabbed her to death. The body was dismembered, offered up to Satan, then consumed. The night before, the group had murdered a petrol station attendant with an axe for $20 and a can of STP.

Hurd was diagnosed as a paranoid schizophrenic and sent to the Atascadero State Hospital for the criminally insane. There he claims to have been visited by 'Father Satan', who he says is a 'man wearing a gold helmet, with the skin of a pine cone'.

Nineteen years later, a full-blown satanic cannibal cult went to work in Mexico. After sacrificing and eating a number of Mexicans, they decided that stronger magic was needed. Their leader decided that they needed to kill and eat an Anglo – a white man. The college spring break presented them with the perfect opportunity.

The spring break is an enduring institution of American college life. After long winter months of study and examinations, students enjoy a frantic week of partying. Those in Texas often pop across the border into Mexico. No visa is required and they can return to the safety and sanitation of the 'good ole US of A' to sleep at night. The beach

173

resorts are particularly popular. There, vacationing students can enjoy the sun, surf, sand and, if they are lucky, sex during the day, and the bawdy pleasures of the clubs and cantinas after dark. And while many of the students are too young to drink in the Lone Star State, Mexican bars are only too happy to take their money. In fact, the border towns depend on this daily cross-border traffic.

One such town is Matamoros. In March 1989, it was packed with revellers from the Texas colleges, letting their hair down. One of them was Mark Kilroy, a handsome twenty-one-year-old pre-med student at the University of Texas. He had driven down from Santa Fe to South Padre Island, a beach resort on the US side of the border, on 11 March with his best friend, Bill Huddleston, and two other students, Brent Martin and Bradley Moore. From there, they could walk over the border to Matamoros.

On the evening of Tuesday 15 March 1989, Mark seemed to be having some success chatting up a pretty contestant from the 'Miss Tanline' competition which had been held earlier that day at South Padre Island. Around two o'clock in the morning the crowd began to disperse. Mark Kilroy and his three friends decided they had drunk enough for one night. They went outside into the cool night air and began following the crowds of students making their way up main street to the bridge over the Rio Grande, back into the US. In the crowd, the boys got separated. Brent Martin and Bradley Moore went on ahead. Bill Huddleston ducked into a dark alley to relieve himself. When he emerged, he saw Mark talking to a Mexican. He saw Brent and Bradley up ahead, and he turned and followed them.

Spring-breakers usually steer clear of the tough streetwise Mexicans of their own age, but this one had come up and addressed Mark out of the blue.

'Do you want a ride?' he said.

There was a pick-up truck alongside him with another Mexican at the wheel. Mark was tired and his reactions were dulled by alcohol. He hesitated for a second. But that

174

was long enough. The two Mexicans grabbed him and bundled him into the pick-up. The truck took off at high speed, away from the bustling highway, into the quiet back streets of Matamoros. Mark Kilroy must have realised he was in grave danger. When the driver pulled up in a side street to take a leak, Mark dived out of the truck and ran back down the street. But he had not noticed the Chevrolet station-wagon that had been following them. As he passed it, two Mexicans leaned out and grabbed him. They pulled him in and held him at knifepoint as the vehicle sped away.

Mark's three friends soon became concerned. They waited for him on the other side of the bridge, but he did not appear. After a while, they walked back over into Mexico and searched the streets and bars. By the time it got light, they were dead on their feet. Perhaps they had missed him somehow. So they returned to their hotel room in South Padre Island. But Mark wasn't there either. They fell asleep for a few hours while they thought about what to do. And when they woke, they went to the police and filed a missing person's report.

Meanwhile, Mark had been on a high-speed cross-country drive through the Mexican night. Eventually, the station-wagon and the pick-up slowed on a dirt track by a huddle of flimsy farm buildings. Mark was taken out of the station-wagon and forced to sit on a hammock slung between two spindly trees. He must have thought about trying to escape again, but when a group of men turned up with automatic weapons, he would have realised it was impossible.

A couple of the Mexicans told him that he would be okay, there was nothing to worry about. At dawn, an old caretaker gave him some water and cooked him a pan of scrambled eggs. At noon, Mark was still sitting in the hammock. Early in the afternoon, he was taken for a walk for about three-quarters of a mile to a board and tar-paper shack. The smell inside was foul and flies swarmed noisily over something putrid in the darkness. The Mexicans bound him hand and foot. They forced him to kneel while

175

a wide band of tape was stuck over his mouth. Then an order was given. Mark was brought outside. A little way from the shack, a tarpaulin was laid on the earth.

Mark Kilroy may just have heard the swish as a machete swung through the air. It was aimed at the back of his neck and killed him instantly. Mark Kilroy's parents, devout Catholics, believe he spent his last few hours in silent prayer.

The police in Texas did not hold out much hope of finding out what had happened to Mark Kilroy. Cross-border investigations were notoriously difficult because of the number of competing law enforcement agencies in Mexico. There were the local police, the state police, the Federal Judicial Police and the Mexican Army. They were all fiercely protective of their own territory and their own *mordida* – institutionalised bribes. As police salaries were only the equivalent of $2,400 a year in 1989, there was a strong temptation to take a percentage from criminal profits rather than make an arrest. In the three years up to 1989, two hundred local and state policemen had been prosecuted for drug-running offences and another 1,200 were fired for corruption.

If Mark Kilroy had been a Mexican, nobody would have looked any further for him. But his family had a connection with the Mayor of San Antonio, who had been at college with the new President of Mexico. Chance played its part too. The DEA – America's Drug Enforcement Agency – had been putting pressure on the new Mexican administration to crack down on drugs being smuggled over the border. In a joint operation, the Federal Judicial Police and the Mexican Army began putting road blocks on the border roads. In just a few weeks, they made huge hauls of marijuana and cocaine, worth millions of dollars in the USA.

Then, on the night of 5 April 1989, a Chevrolet Silverado with Texas registration plates driven by David Serna Valdez – a homosexual known as 'El Coqueto' (the Flirt) – crashed through an Army road block. The *Federales* gave chase and followed the Chevrolet along the dirt roads to a farm called Santa Elena Ranch. There they cornered Valdez and arrested him. He seemed insanely self-confident and taunted the police that their bullets could not hurt him. The police found a large amount of marijuana and cocaine, and a whole arsenal of guns. At the farm, there were eleven brand new automobiles, all equipped with the latest cellular phones and two-way radios. The *Federales* also picked up an old caretaker and, as the pressure was on to find Mark Kilroy, as a matter of routine, they showed him his picture. The caretaker recognised him immediately and said that he had made a meal for him a couple of months back.

A computer search was made on the cellular phones. They belonged to Serafin Hernandez Junior, Elio – 'Little Elio' – Hernandez Riveria and Sergio Martinez, also known as 'La Mariposa' (the Butterfly). These men were members of a well known drugs gang who operated on both sides of the border. They were picked up and subjected to intense and, allegedly, violent interrogation – and came up with similar stories. All three talked of a man called 'El Padrino' (the Godfather), who was a Cuban black magic sorcerer, and his accomplice, a beautiful Mexican woman with a college education, called 'La Padrona' (the Godmother) or sometimes 'La Bruja' (the Witch). El Padrino and La Padrona had initiated the gang members into a cult in a series of ceremonies that involved brutal human sacrifices and torture. They were told that these rituals would make them immune to arrest and even to the bullets of the police. They could not be killed, they said, because their souls were already dead.

On Tuesday 11 April 1989, the police returned to Rancho Santa Elena and went out to the tar-paper shack. Inside they discovered the paraphernalia of a black-magic cult. There was a breeze-block altar against one wall. It was decorated with strings of hot green peppers and garlic. There were ritual objects, including coins and beads, in small pots. Others contained the intestines of goats and sacrificed chickens. And a goat's head was impaled on a trident. Cigar butts, sweet wrappers and empty cane liquor bottles littered the floor. But there were also cases of candles decorated with pictures of Mexico's Indian Madonna and the Virgin of Guadeloupe stacked inside the door.

The Mexican police realised that they were dealing with a gang using the ritual of Santeria, a cult practised by millions throughout Latin America. The word 'Santeria' means the worship of the saints. In fact, it is a religion similar to Voodoo in Haiti. Both are so-called syncratic religions where belief in the African gods brought over by the slaves were concealed from the white slave-owners by giving them Christian counterparts. Over the centuries, the distinction has become blurred and a good Catholic can be a follower of Voodoo or Santeria as well. The origin of 'Voodoo' is the word 'vodun' in the Fon language. It means spirit and Voodoo is concerned with the spirits of the passions and the elements. Usually it has little to do with zombies and sticking pins in dolls. While Voodoo is mainly associated with Haiti, Santeria is centred on Cuba, though it is also practised throughout the Hispanic islands of the Caribbean and Latin America. The ritual regalia of Santeria is freely available in shops called 'botanicos' in the Hispanic areas of cities throughout the US and Canada. Santero priests and priestesses are consulted for help with life's problems. A present is given in exchange for a spell. However, there are sometimes full-blown festivals with hundreds of people, dancing for hours and, occasionally, swooning into religious trances. Blood sacrifices are part of these rituals. Usually a live chicken is decapitated during the ceremony.

But, as with Voodoo, Santeria has a darker side. This is known as *Palo Mayombe*. An adherent of this secretive sect seeks closer ties with the spirit world through the ritual use of human body parts stolen from graves. The priest or 'palero' puts these in a ritual cauldron or 'nganga' along with magical herbs. He can increase the magical power of the cauldron's brew by adding his own blood. However,

178

sometimes it is said the 'nganga' develop a strong thirst and demands human sacrifice and cannibalism. This seems to have been what had happened at Rancho Santa Elena.

At the back of the shack was a small iron cauldron about thirty inches in diameter. It was about two-thirds full of a vile soup. This was the source of the terrible stench and it was crawling with flies. There were half a dozen mesquite stirring sticks stuck in the half-congealed mixture. On analysis, the brew was found to contain boiled blood, a horseshoe, human bones including segments of spine, human brain tissue, animal organs, pieces of turtle and a goat's head.

The police started excavating the area around the shack. They found Mark Kilroy in a shallow grave about three feet down. They dug him up using a mechanical digger and identified his body from his dental records. He had been brutally mutilated. His head had been removed and his brain scooped out. His spinal column had been ripped out of his back. His legs were amputated at the knee. And his fingers and genitals were missing.

However, Mark Kilroy was not the only victim of the sect. Gang members pointed out nine other graves containing thirteen bodies in all. All had been similarly mutilated. Some had had the skin stripped from their bodies, possibly while they were still alive. The TV cameras were there when the thirteenth body was dug up. The suspect Sergio Martinez had been brought from his prison cell to do the digging. It took him an hour in the hot midday sun. When the body was unearthed, it could clearly be seen that the chest had been hacked open, the ribs prised outwards and the heart was missing. The victim was just fourteen years old. There were more victims, Martinez said. But Chief of Police Benitez Ayala had stopped the excavation. A believer of Santeria himself – he kept Santeria charms on his desk in police headquarters – he called in his own 'curandero' (sorcerer) to sprinkle holy water around the shack and recite spells. A white dove was held under an upturned cardboard box. The shack was doused in petrol and the curandero lit it. When it had disappeared in a cloud of flames and black smoke, he released the dove.

In jail, the gang members continued to sing like canaries and soon the police were on the trail of the gang's ringleader, Adolfo de Jesus Constanzo.

Constanzo was born on 1 November 1962 in Miami, Florida. His parents were Cubans who had recently fled their home country after Castro's communist revolution. When he was just a year old, his father left and his mother and his grandmother took him to live in Puerto Rico, where his mother married a wealthy businessman. Adolfo got on well with his stepfather. He was a very serious little boy, well behaved, meticulously neat and an assiduous churchgoer. But when he was ten, his stepfather died. His mother moved back to Miami and married again. But the marriage was short-lived.

In Miami's Cuban expatriate community it was openly acknowledged that Constanzo's mother was a priestess of Palo Mayombe. She performed rituals and cast spells for neighbours. She had been trained by her mother who had been a Palo Mayombe priestess back in Cuba. In turn, she trained her son. She soon recognised that her son was a powerful sorcerer. His clientele quickly grew. It was said that he was a potent medium, an infallible oracle and a magician capable of astral projection. He was also a handsome boy and from an early age he exhibited an irresistible sexual magnetism towards both sexes. At the age of fourteen, he fathered a child.

In 1983, Constanzo was offered a modelling job in Mexico City. He moved there with his mother. Quickly he established himself as a fashionable figure in Mexican high society and immersed himself in the homosexual subculture. He continued to practise as a Santero priest. He was reputed to be a curandero, or sorcerer, with powers of purification and prophecy. Even the police consulted him. His influence spread far beyond his immediate followers and a number of very influential people were rattled when Constanzo came under investigation. Not least among these were the drug barons who sought his help to secure the success of their smuggling operations.

To further enhance his powers, Constanzo's mother sent him away to study under a major Santero she called 'The Great One'. When he returned, he began making human sacrifices.

The police also discovered the identity of his priestess 'La Bruja'. She was Sara Maria Aldrete, born 6 September 1964 in Matamoros. Married at eighteen, she was divorced at twenty. At twenty-one, she enrolled in a two-year physical education course at Texas Southmost College across the bridge in Brownsville, Texas. A beautiful girl, she was six feet tall, with the body of an athlete and big brown eyes. She was voted 'top cheer-leader' and was a straight-A student. The school's *Who's Who* lists her as one of the most popular and active students.

While she was a student, Sara would drive across the Rio Grande back into Mexico at weekends. One day in late 1986, she was forced over by a Mercedes. It belonged to Adolfo Constanzo. But while his friends came on to her in a macho way, Constanzo asked her quietly whether she would accompany him to a cafe. When she did, he read her tarot cards for her. He told her that someone very close to her would come to her with a problem she would not be able to handle. Sara's boyfriend at the time was Serafin Hernandez Junior. The Hernandez family were well-known drugs smugglers. Two weeks after the tarot reading, Serafin told Sara that the family was in serious trouble. It had split in two. Serafin's father – Serafin Hernandez Senior – was operating north of the border, but was soon arrested. Meanwhile, Serafin Junior was working with his uncle Little Elio. They were based in Matamoros and had expanded their business into gun-running, car theft and muscling in on the drug operations of other gangs. This was dangerous work though. Not all of the remaining Hernandez family wanted a part of it and the gang was falling apart.

Sara contacted Constanzo and told him that his tarot

prediction was right. She explained her boyfriend's problem. Constanzo said he could help. He had seen how the drugs lords lived in Mexico City and wanted a piece of the action. First, he took Sara as his lover. Although jealous at first, Hernandez began to accept this as he was also beginning to fall under the spell of the magnetic curandero. Perhaps he knew of Constanzo's real sexual leanings. He had two boyfriends. One, Omar Orea Ochoa, he referred to as his 'lady'. The other, his flatmate Martin Rodriguez, was his 'man'. Sara was so besotted with Constanzo that she accepted his bizarre arrangement and seems to have become genuine friends with Ochoa and Rodriguez. Constanzo started training her in the ways of Palo Mayombo and the four of them participated in ritual sacrifices. Ochoa and Rodriguez would lure victims along to the ceremonies and Sara would take an active part in their torture.

In early 1988, Constanzo made further demands on her. She was to sleep with Hernandez' uncle, the drugs boss Little Elio. She got Serafin Junior to introduce her and, after she had seduced him, she told him that what he needed to restore the fortunes of the Hernandez family was the help of a powerful sorcerer. She introduced Little Elio to Constanzo, who persuaded him he was a natural for the priesthood. To initiate him, Constanzo cut Santeria symbols into the flesh of his chest, back and shoulders. Other members of the family were also marked according to rank. Pimps were marked with a five-spotted dice, enforcers with tridents and executioners with a pierced heart. The price for Constanzo's help was half the Hernandez family's drugs profits. In exchange, Constanzo would carry out human sacrifices which would give Little Elio's gang magical powers. The remaining gang members north of the border wanted no part of this, so Little Elio was deprived of the rich Texan markets and his US distribution network. This put him more in the power of Constanzo, who introduced him to his own drug connections in Mexico City. Little Elio became involved in more human sacrifices.

Ochoa and Rodriguez would pick up homosexuals and bring them back to Constanzo's white-carpeted, white-furnished house. There, he and Little Elio would torture and murder victims on Constanzo's altar.

Despite the sacrifices, business did not go well. In June 1988, a major drug deal went wrong. The police seized a $20-million drugs shipment in Houston, Texas. Constanzo and the rest of the gang only just managed to escape in time. They left behind them an altar complete with herbs and candles. What they needed was stronger magic.

Cesare Sauceda, a former Matamoros cop, had been telling rival gangs that Little Elio had been cheating them. So Sauceda was kidnapped and taken out to Rancho Santa Elena, which belonged to the Hernandez family. Constanzo had set up his altar in a shack on the property and set about sacrificing Sauceda. But Little Elio lost his cool. Sauceda had been causing the family big problems and he killed him with a burst of automatic fire. Other victims were seized and ritually murdered. And slowly the drugs business began to pick up again. But to prevent any further mishaps north of the border, it was decided that even more powerful magic was needed. They needed to kill an Anglo. This would give them control over other living whites.

While the bodies of Constanzo's victims were still being dug up at the Rancho Santa Elena, the police raided Sara Aldrete's home. Her father let them into her apartment. In the living room, they found an altar with candles depicting Santa Barbara – or Chango in Santeria – on it. It was caked with blood. And in the corner of the room, there was a pile of blood-stained children's clothes.

At the same time, the *Federales* broke into Constanzo's white-carpeted apartment in Mexico City. They seized a number of notebooks containing the names of Constanzo's clients. Soon all the law enforcement agencies were racing to catch Constanzo. A lot of very important people wanted him dead.

Sara and Constanzo were in Brownsville at the time. They flew to Mexico City where they collected a car and

183

some money. Then they headed for Cuernavaca, a resort area some fifty miles south of Mexico City, where they met up with the rest of the Matamoros gang who were still at large. They travelled around for about three weeks, collecting more money by extortion. Then they returned to Mexico City where they holed up in a friend's flat.

A woman phoned the police anonymously and said that she had been forced to help the gang. Then on 5 May 1989, a police informer called in to say that he had seen a woman make several large purchases at a grocery store and pay with cash. The next day the *Federales* located the flat and surrounded it. But there was no way that Constanzo was going to be taken alive. As he had acted as a curandero to the police themselves, if he was still in a position to talk when he was arrested it would be far too embarrassing.

Just before noon on 6 May 1989, one of Constanzo's look-outs spotted a plain-clothes policeman in an unmarked car prowling the area. Constanzo looked out of the window to see heavily armed *Federales* moving into position. One of the gang, Alvaro de Leo Valdez – alias 'El Dubi' (the Wild Man) – loosed a burst of AK47 fire at them. The *Federales* responded with machine-gun fire. But, single-handedly, El Dubi held them off.

When it was plain that they were surrounded, Constanzo went crazy. He piled money over the gas stove and set fire to it, shouting: 'Let us all die.' Constanzo then embraced his lover Martin Quintana, led him into a walk-in wardrobe and told El Dubi to shoot them. El Dubi could not understand what he was being ordered to do. Constanzo had to slap his face to get through to him. But eventually, the wild man sprayed the two lovers with bullets, then, along with Ochoa, he gave himself up.

El Dubi was sentenced to thirty years for killing Constanzo and Quintana. Sara Aldrete, Omar Ochoa and other gang members were charged with offences including murders, gun-running, drug smuggling, conspiracy and criminal association – though they all claim that confessions were tortured out of them. They all face long prison terms.

184

Little Elio lives in high style in jail on the proceeds of his drugs operations. But on 7 February 1990, Omar Orea Ochoa – Constanzo's 'lady' – died of a heart attack, said to be AIDS related, in a prison hospital. After they have finished their sentences in Mexico, they can expect to spend the rest of their lives in an American jail. A US Grand Jury has already indicted them and arrest warrants have been issued.

Constanzo's death cult was by no means unique in the history of Mexico. In 1962, two other Hernandez brothers, Santos and Cayetano, had their own variation on the satanic cult which they called Yerba Buena. It was largely a way to extort money out of the local farmers around Monterrey in north-east Mexico. The Hernandez brothers were gay and to purge themselves of the demons that were ruining their crops the devotees of the cult were forced to submit themselves to humiliating sexual rites. Things were going swimmingly and the Hernandez brothers thought the time was ripe to expand. They found Magdalane Solis, a young prostitute, and her brother Eleazor, a homosexual who acted as her pimp, and made them high priest and priestess of the cult.

Magdalena added lesbian rites to their religious menu, but times were hard for farmers and the popularity of Yerba Buena began to drop off. Magdalena came up with a solution: they would add human sacrifice to their services. She had two men stoned to death and their blood collected for the purpose of drinking it. Soon eight members of the cult had been killed off. Magdalena even gave up her own lesbian lover as a sacrifice. Then things started to go wrong. A teenage boy accidently witnessed one of the human sacrifices. He ran to fetch a policeman and returned with Officer Martinez. The two of them were then hacked to death.

The mysterious disappearance of a policeman while he is on duty is not something that goes unnoticed by the authorities. The *Federales* rode in and surrounded the cult's headquarters. Cayetano Hernandez was killed by a disaffected member of the cult for getting them into that position in the first place. And Santos Hernandez was killed in the shoot-out with the police.

Magdalena and Eleazor Solis were arrested along with twelve other members of the cult. They were found guilty of multiple murder and sentenced to thirty years.

Belief in Santeria, Yerba Buena and Voodoo is not confined to Latin America and the Caribbean. It was responsible for the death of four-year-old Stacey Kavanagh and seven-year-old Tina Beechock in the Rotherhithe district of London's docklands in 1985.

Around 4.20 p.m., on the afternoon of 18 September, Lynn Kavanagh let her daughter leave their flat in a tower block on the Swan Lane estate and go down to play in the central area between the buildings. There, theoretically, she could keep an eye on her. She warned her daughter, once again, not to talk to strangers. Only five days before, a young girl had been abducted in Great Yarmouth. Soon after 6 p.m., there was a frantic knocking on the front door. It was twenty-five-year-old Mirella Beechock, a neighbour and the mother of Stacey's best friend, Tina. Mrs Beechock was so upset that she could barely speak. But in her hand she held one of Stacey's shoes. When she composed herself, Mrs Beechock told Mrs Kavanagh that she had taken Tina and Stacey to the nearby shops. They had waited outside for her. But when she came out, they had gone. She supposed that they were bored and had run back to the play area. But they were not there. Then, when she walked back down Rotherhithe Street to the shops again, she had found Stacey's shoe.

Naturally, both mothers assumed the worst. Soon neighbours, relatives and other friends were combing the area. The police called in a helicopter and tracker dogs and, just before midnight, Stacey Kavanagh's body was found in the undergrowth in nearby Southwark Park. She had been strangled. The search for seven-year-old Tina Beechock became desperate.

By dawn, Scotland Yard issued a statement saying that

they were growing more fearful with every minute that passed and Mrs Beechock appeared on television, appealing for the safe return of her daughter.

But the police began to have their suspicions. When they visited Mrs Beechock's flat, they found that it was practically a shrine to the Voodoo god Baron Samedi, the Lord of the Graveyard.

Mrs Beechock had been born in Mauritius in 1960 to a family who followed Voodoo fanatically. When she came to England at the age of fourteen, she got involved in an off-shoot of Voodoo called Gris-Gris. In 1977, she married Ravi Beechock and the following year she gave birth to Tina. But Ravi was not a very dependable husband and would often wander off, sometimes for long periods. When he returned he would find a pin sticking through his head in a photograph or an effigy stuck with pins and needles on the doorstep.

Their second daughter, Sabrina, was born in October 1979. At less than a month old Sabrina was hospitalised with stomach trouble. Nurses became concerned about her drowsiness and, after one of her mother's visits, found a tablet of Mogadon – a powerful adult sleeping pill – under the child's cot. Blood tests revealed a seriously high level of the drug in her system. Charged with endangering the child's life, Mirella claimed that the evil eye had made her harm her baby. But a psychiatric examination found that she was not seriously mentally ill and she was put on probation. However, the children were taken into care. Sabrina was adopted, but Tina was returned to her mother in 1980.

In 1985, Mirella Beechock was found guilty of shoplifting and sentenced to three months. When she was released, she was arrested again for the same offence. This was less than a week before the two children went missing.

The police kept a close watch on 7 Sandwich House, the flat where Mirella Beechock lived. On the morning of 21 September, Ravi Beechock turned up. He talked with his wife on the doorstep for a little while, then they took a

walk down to the area where the children had been playing. Suddenly, Ravi broke away and ran back towards the
flat. The police intercepted him. He was barely able to tell
them what his wife had just told him – that Tina was dead.

Police officers searched 7 Sandwich House and found
that he was right. Tina's body had been tied up in a bag
and stuffed under her mother's bed.

At the Old Bailey, Mirella pleaded guilty to manslaughter on the grounds of diminished responsibility. The
jury disagreed. They found her guilty of murder. Mirella
claimed that voices in her head had forced her to kill the
children; they had been sacrificed to Baron Samedi, Lord
of the Graveyard.

Such occult murders are not uncommon in the Caribbean. On St Kitts, St Clair Daniel's family thought that he
might be Satan even before he went on a murder spree on
the nearby island of St Thomas.

Daniel was brought up as a fierce adherent of Voodoo.
At 7 a.m., on the morning of 2 March 1988, he was seen
on the beach dismembering a body with a machete. When
the police reached the beach, they found the badly mutilated corpse of Genevieve Lewis, a fifty-three-year-old
tourist from Newfoundland who had come to St Thomas
to recuperate after a serious operation. She had been decapitated, disembowelled and her body hacked to pieces.
The small dog she had taken with her for a walk on the
beach had also been killed and mutilated.

The body of a second victim, Steven Cornish from Lans-
ing, Michigan, was found in Vessup Bay. He too had been
decapitated and dismembered. Witnesses had seen a
machete-wielding black man in his thirties with dreadlocks
and a beard. They had fled. From the safety of boats out
to sea, others had seen him hacking up the dead bodies and
washing himself in the waves.

The police found a man answering that description. He
was naked and covered in blood. There was no doubt that
they had found the culprit.

Charged with carrying a dangerous weapon, mayhem

and two counts of first-degree murder, Daniel argued that he had killed Genevieve Lewis, Steven Cornish and Mrs Lewis's dog in self-defence. He had dismembered them according to the precepts of Voodoo, which he described as a 'beautiful and strict' religion. They had to be decapitated and cut up to prevent them turning into zombies.

His plea of insanity was allowed in the case of Steven Cornish, who was an enthusiastic gardener and was carrying a pair of shears with him. It was thought that Daniel could possibly have mistaken these for a weapon in his deluded state. But the court ruled that faith in Voodoo and zombism was a cultural belief rather than a proof of insanity. It in no way explained his slaughter of Mrs Lewis. St Clair Daniel was sentenced to life without the possibility of parole.

But mitigating pleas *are* sometimes entertained in satanic killings. In 1953, Juana Catrilaf, a Mapuche Indian in Chile, was charged with killing her grandmother. She admitted that she had killed the old woman, but said she had no choice. Her grandmother was possessed by the Devil and Juana blamed her evil influence for the death of her child and her own epilepsy. She bludgeoned the old woman to death, then slashed her across the forehead and sucked the blood from the wound. She also said that she saw a fiery spirit rise from the old woman's corpse. She was acquitted on the grounds that she was 'compelled by an irresistible psychic force'.

The Zulu equivalent of Voodoo or Palo Mayombo is a belief in the 'tokoloshe'. This is an evil spirit whose favour can be curried with blood sacrifice.

In Richmond, Natal, in 1953, a witch doctor named Elifasi Msomi was down on his luck and he figured that he needed a little help from the tokoloshe. He abducted a young girl and, in the presence of his girlfriend, raped and stabbed the child. His girlfriend was horrified and reported him to the police. Msomi was arrested but managed to escape.

Plainly, as his fortunes had declined still further, more

blood sacrifices were needed. So he went to an outlying village and posed as an agent who could get children well-paid jobs as servants for whites. He left the village, taking with him five children. Then he stabbed and killed them all. Later he went back to the village, assured the parents that the children were happy and asked for a little extra money that the children needed to make their stay happier. Msomi went round remote villages and continued this practice until he was arrested in 1955. The police found on him a knife which he had used for the murder, and some of the property of the victims. Msomi then took the police to the place where he had buried some of the children.

In court, Msomi argued that he was not responsible for the children's deaths. It was the tokoloshe, he said. Despite the plea, Msomi was found guilty and hanged. The local people were so afraid that the tokoloshe might arrange for him to cheat the hangman that the authorities allowed village elders to examine the body after the execution to check that he was dead.

11

The Devil Made Me Do It

Richard Ramirez, the Night Stalker who terrorised Los Angeles for two years, was a devil-worshipper. A scrawled pentagram – a satanic symbol – was his calling card and he made his rape victims declare their love of Satan before he slaughtered them. He had met Anton LaVey and had read a great deal about black magic and Satanism.

The Night Stalker's murder career began ordinarily enough. On the night of 28 June 1984, the mutilated body of seventy-nine-year-old Jennie Vincow was found spread-eagled on the bed of her one-bedroom apartment in the Eagle Rock district of Los Angeles. She had been raped and her throat had been slashed so violently that she had almost been decapitated. There was blood up the walls of the bedroom and bathroom and her flat had been ransacked. But in LA it was just another murder.

Nine months later, Maria Hernandez had just parked her car in her garage in Los Angeles' Rosemeade suburb and was walking towards her apartment when she heard footsteps behind her. She turned to be confronted by a man with a gun. He shot her but, miraculously, the bullet ricocheted off her car keys and hit her only a glancing blow. Even so, the impact of the bullet was enough to knock her to the ground. The gunman stepped over her, giving her a vicious kicking, and made his way into her apartment. From inside, Maria heard a gunshot. She staggered to her feet, only to be confronted again by the gunman running from the house.

'Please don't shoot me again,' she begged. The gunman

froze, then took to his heels. Inside the apartment Maria Hernandez found her boyfriend, thirty-four-year-old Hawaii-born traffic manager Dayle Okazaki lying on the kitchen floor, dead. He had been shot through the head.

There was only one clue to the murder. Maria said that the gunman had worn a baseball cap with the AC/DC logo on the front. AC/DC had recently released an album called *Highway to Hell*. On it, there was track called 'Night Prowler'. This was the *nom d'assassin* Ramirez preferred. He was annoyed that the newspapers insisted on calling him the 'Night Stalker'.

That night though, his lust for blood had not been nearly satisfied. Less than an hour later, on his way home, Ramirez pulled thirty-year-old Taiwanese law student Tsai Lian Yu from her car and shot her repeatedly. She died before the ambulance arrived.

Ten days later, Ramirez entered the home of Vincent and Maxine Zazzara, half a mile from the San Gabriel freeway. Maxine was a successful lawyer and Vincent had just fulfilled a lifetime ambition, opening his own pizzeria. Both of them were shot at point blank range and Maxine Zazzara's naked body was mutilated after death. Ramirez stabbed her repeatedly. The wounds made a pattern of a large ragged T. He also gouged her eyes out. The bodies were found by their son Peter, who dropped by the house the next day.

On 14 May, Ramirez broke into the home of William and Lillie Doi. He shot sixty-six-year-old William in the head while he lay sleeping. His wife, sixty-three-year-old Lillie, who was lying in the bed next to him, was beaten repeatedly around the head until she told the intruder where the valuables were hidden. Then he handcuffed her and ransacked the house. Later he returned to rape her.

A fortnight later, Carol Kyle was awoken in her Burbank flat by a torch shining in her eyes. A man pointed a gun at her and dragged her out of bed. In the next room, Carol's terrified twelve-year-old son was handcuffed and locked in a cupboard. His mother was then raped. Even then, she was sympathetic.

'You must have had a very unhappy life to have done this to me,' she said.

Ramirez shrugged off her sympathy.

'I don't know why I'm letting you live,' he said. 'I've killed people before.'

He ransacked the apartment for valuables. Satisfied with the jewellery he found, he went away leaving both Carol and her son alive.

Around the same time, two elderly women, eighty-three-year-old Mabel Bell and her eighty-year-old sister Florence Long, an invalid, were attacked in their home in the suburb of Monrovia. On 1 June, Carlos Venezuela, a gardener who did chores for the sisters, dropped round. The house was unusually silent and he let himself in. He found Florence lying on her bed in a coma. There was a huge wound over her ear and a bloodstained hammer was lying on the dressing table. Mabel was lying barely conscious on her bedroom floor in a pool of her own blood. Both women had been beaten with the hammer. They had been cut and tortured. There were even signs that Ramirez had tried to rape the older sister Mabel. The police concluded that the two sisters had been left that way for two days. The house had been ransacked but, this time, the attacker had left some clues. Along with the hammer, he had left a half-eaten banana on the dining table. He had also left what was to become his trade mark – an inverted penta-gram. One was scrawled in lipstick on Mabel's thigh. Another was drawn on Florence's bedroom wall.

Six weeks after the attack Mabel Bell died. But Florence eventually regained consciousness and survived.

Then the Night Stalker's onslaught began in earnest. On the night of 27 June 1985, Ramirez slashed the throat of thirty-two-year-old Patty Elaine Higgins in her home in Arcadia. The same fate befell Mary Louise Cannon five days later. In that same suburb, Arcadia, three days later, Ramirez savagely beat sixteen-year-old Whitney Bennett with a crowbar. She survived.

On 7 July, Ramirez turned his attention back to Monterey

Park, where Tsai Lian Yu and the Dois had been attacked. Sixty-one-year-old Joyce Lucille Nelson was found beaten to death in her home and sixty-three-year-old Sophie Dickmann was raped and robbed in her apartment.

On 20 July, Ramirez murdered sixty-six-year-old Maxson Kneiding and his sixty-four-year-old wife Lela in their Glendale home, then went on to murder thirty-two-year-old Chainarong Khovananth at his home in Sun Valley. After shooting Chainarong while he was still asleep in his bed, Ramirez raped and beat Chainarong's twenty-nine-year-old wife Somkid. He forced her to perform oral sex on him and stole $30,000 in cash and jewellery. Then he forced her to swear in Satan's name that she would not cry out while he raped her eight-year-old son.

The police had concluded long ago that they had a serial killer on their hands. The problem was that he had no clear *modus operandi*. He killed with guns, hammers and knives. He raped orally, anally and genitally both children and women, young and old. Sometimes he mutilated the bodies after death and sometimes he didn't. The LAPD quipped that he was an equal opportunity monster.

But some patterns *were* emerging. The killer stalked quiet suburbs away from the city's main centres of crime where home-owners were less security conscious. He tended to pick houses painted in beige or pastel yellow. They were usually close to a freeway, making his escape easier. Entry was through an open window or an unlocked door. Although burglary was one of his motives, rape and sheer brutality seemed also to figure highly. Pentagrams and other satanic symbols were also commonly left by the killer.

On the night of 5 August, postal worker Virginia Petersen was awoken by the sound of an intruder. She sat up in bed and cried out: 'Who are you? What do you want?' The burglar laughed, then shot her in the face. The bullet entered the cheek just below her eye and went clean through the back of her head. Miraculously, she survived. Her husband Christopher, who was lying beside her, was woken by

194

the shot. He leapt to his wife's defence. This earned him a bullet in the temple. But Christopher Petersen was a tough guy, a truck driver. It took more than one small-calibre bullet to put him down. He dived out of bed and chased his attacker. The intruder was unprepared for this. He panicked and ran.

Christopher Petersen also survived the ordeal, though he has suffered partial memory loss and has had to live ever since with a bullet lodged in his brain. But, for the first time the Night Stalker had been put to flight.

It did not end his violent rampage though. Three days later, he shot another thirty-five-year-old Asian man and beat and raped his twenty-eight-year-old wife. Again she was forced to swear by Satan that she would not cry out, but this time he left their two young children unharmed, though their three-year-old son Amez was tied up.

By this time, public opinion was at fever pitch in Los Angeles. In the affluent suburbs, locksmiths and burglar alarm salesmen were doing a roaring trade. Gun shops quickly sold out and local residents set up neighbourhood watch committees.

So Ramirez took a vacation. He travelled north to San Francisco. There on the night of 17 August, he attacked sixty-six-year-old Asian accountant Peter Pan and his sixty-four-year-old wife Barbara in their home in the suburb of Lake Merced. Both were shot through the head. An inverted pentagram was painted in lipstick on the bedroom wall and, under it, Ramirez wrote 'Jack the Knife'. At first, the police thought it was a copy-cat killing. But the bullets with which he killed the couple matched the small-calibre rounds found in the Los Angeles murders.

A week later, Ramirez travelled 50 miles south of Los Angeles to the small town of Mission Viego. He shot twenty-nine-year-old computer engineer William Carns three times in the head and raped his fiancée Inez Erickson, also twenty-nine, twice.

'You know who I am, don't you,' Ramirez taunted. 'I'm the one they're writing about in the newspapers and on TV.'

He also forced Inez to say 'I love Satan' during her ordeal.

William Carns survived the shooting, but suffered permanent brain damage. The couple never married. But Inez managed to spot Ramirez' rusty old orange Toyota after he left the house. This proved to be the vital clue that put an end to the reign of the Night Stalker.

A sharp-eyed kid, James Romero III, had also spotted the orange Toyota as it cruised the area and had noted down its licence-plate number. The police put out an all-points bulletin. Two days later, the car was found in a parking lot in Los Angeles' Rampart suburb.

Forensic scientists used a radical new technique when examining the car. They put a dab of superglue in a saucer in the car and sealed the doors and windows. Fumes from the superglue would react with moisture in any fingerprints and turn them white. The interior of the car was then scanned using a laser beam. This technique should pick up any fingerprints, including those that the culprit had tried to wipe off. The scan yielded one fingerprint. It was computer matched to that of twenty-five-year-old Ricardo Ramirez, who had been arrested three times for marijuana possession in El Paso. Soon Ramirez' photograph was on the front page of every newspaper in California.

Ramirez was quite unaware of this when he stepped down from the Greyhound bus at Los Angeles main bus station. He had been out in Phoenix, Arizona, to score some cocaine and was high. He had killed thirteen people so far and felt good. Surely by now he must be Satan's favourite son. He went to a drug store to buy himself a Pepsi. Then at the check-out desk he saw his own face splashed across the Spanish language paper *La Opinion*. The check-out clerk recognised him too, as did the other customers. Ramirez made a run for it.

In the street, someone cried out: 'It's the Night Stalker.' Soon he heard the wail of police sirens behind him. He knocked on a door. Bonnie Navarro opened it. Ramirez shouted 'Help me' in Spanish. She slammed the door in his

196

face. On the next block, he tried to pull a woman from her car, but bystanders rushed to her rescue. Ramirez jumped a fence into a backyard where Luis Muñoz was cooking a barbecue. He hit Ramirez with his tongs. In the next garden, he tried to steal a red 1966 Mustang, but fifty-six-year-old Faustino Pinon, who was working on the transmission, grabbed him in a headlock. Ramirez broke free, but across the street fifty-five-year-old construction worker José Burgoin heard Pinon's shouts. He picked up a steel rod and hit Ramirez with it. Ramirez stumbled on but Burgoin soon caught up with him. This time he clubbed him to the ground. In the nick of time, deputy sheriff Andres Ramirez pulled up in a patrol car.

'Save me!' yelled the Night Stalker.

As his namesake handcuffed him, Ramirez said: 'Thank God you came. I am the one you want. Save me before they kill me.'

Only the arrival of more police patrol cars prevented the angry mob taking the law into their own hands. Even at the police station, a crowd gathered calling for him to be lynched.

Ramirez showed no contrition. He told the police: 'I love to kill people. I love watching them die. I would shoot them in the head and they would wiggle and squirm all over the place, and then just stop. Or I would cut them with a knife and watch their faces turn real white. I love all that blood. I told one lady one time to give me all her money. She said no. So I cut her and pulled her eyes out.'

In court, Ramirez made satanic signs and even appeared with the inverted pentagram scratched in his palm. He told the judge: 'You maggots make me sick. Hypocrites one and all. You don't understand me. You are not expected to. You are not capable of it. I am beyond your experience. I am beyond good and evil.'

Ramirez was found guilty on sixty-three counts, including thirteen murders. He was sentenced to twelve death penalties and over a hundred years' imprisonment. Automatic appeals make it unlikely that he will go to the gas chamber this century. But curiously, while many urge his execution, many women write to him sending provocative pictures, pledging undying love and proposing marriage. When Ramirez accepted divorcée Christine Lee over nude model Kelly Marquez, it made headlines.

Christine, the mother of two, bombarded Ramirez with pin-up pictures of herself and has visited him over a hundred and fifty times. She is undaunted by the fact that her husband-to-be is a satanic killer.

'We really love each other and that's all that matters,' she says. 'From the moment I saw him in prison, I knew he was special. I couldn't believe he was the evil monster people were calling him. He's always been sweet and kind to me.'

Ramirez carved the inverted pentagram on his hand after he had been caught. But Rodney Dale, a twenty-six-year-old Australian carved the satanic number '666' on the palms of his hands before he went on the rampage.

On the afternoon of 17 April 1990, he shot eight people – one of whom died – in just thirty minutes in the Burleigh Heads district of Australia's Gold Coast. And the '666' in the palm of his hands earned him the sobriquet 'Satan's laughing hitman' in the Australian press.

With no warning at all, Dale went out on the balcony of his flat overlooking Tweed Street which was packed with Saturday afternoon shoppers at around 4 p.m. He was wearing a balaclava and carrying a rifle and a pump-action shotgun, and he started shooting.

By the time the first police car arrived, one woman was lying badly wounded on the Gold Coast Highway and the gunman was out on the road shooting randomly at anything that moved. A bridal party happened to be driving through the area at the time. A bridesmaid was hit in the leg and the driver of the bride's car was hit in the right hand, left arm and the shoulder. But he managed to drive his passenger out of the area before he was rushed to hospital. The wedding went ahead, but the shooting, it is said, did put something of a damper on the proceedings.

Seven more police cars and five ambulances rushed to the area. But another six women were wounded before thirty-eight-year-old Sergeant Bob Baker from Burleigh Police Station took decisive action. He pulled his Magnum pistol and walked straight across the road at the crazed gunman.

'Police, put your gun down,' he shouted.

In response, Dale turned his gun on the courageous policeman and started firing. What followed was something out of a western. The gunman loosed off bullet after bullet, but none found their mark. Sergeant Baker stood his ground and responded in kind. His fourth shot hit the gunman in the arm. He dropped his gun and surrendered.

In Dale's flat was a note for his girlfriend saying he was 'going out hunting'. Neighbours described him as friendly, nice and happy. There were rumours that he was involved with a satanic cult. He never explained why '666' – the number of the Beast – was carved in his palms.

12

The Hand of Death

America's most prolific serial killer, Henry Lee Lucas, and his partner in crime, Ottis Toole, confessed to over 360 murders – 157 of these have been checked out by the authorities and proved to be true. They claimed to be part of a satanic group called the Hand of Death.

Lucas's mother was half-Chippawa. She was drunk most of the time on corn liquor which she bought with the proceeds of prostitution. She was known to be 'as mean as a rattle snake' and packed the seven children from her first marriage off to a foster home. Lucas's father worked on the railways and lost both legs in an accident, but the boy was brought up by another of his mother's bizarre lovers, Andrew Lucas, who gave him his surname.

Lucas's mother beat the children constantly. She also made Henry grow his hair long and wear a dress. After one beating he was unconscious for three days and suffered damage to his brain. Another accident left him with a glass eye.

At the age of ten, Henry Lucas was introduced to sex by Bernard Dowdy, yet another of his mother's lovers. Dowdy was mentally retarded. He would slit the throat of a calf and have sex with the carcass, and would encourage the boy to do the same. Lucas enjoyed this and, from his childhood on, he associated sex and death. Throughout his childhood he continued to have sex with animals, sometimes skinning them alive for sexual pleasure. At fourteen, he turned his perverted attention to women. He beat a seventeen-year-old girl unconscious at a bus stop and raped her. When she came to and started screaming, he choked the life out of her.

At fifteen, he was sent to reformatory for burglary. Two years of hard labour on a prison farm did nothing to reform him. When he was released, he returned to housebreaking. He was caught again and sent back to jail. He escaped and met and fell in love with a girl called Stella. They stayed together for four years and she agreed to marry him. But then his mother turned up on his doorstep and demanded that he take care of her. After a violent row, Lucas killed her. This time he got forty years.

By 1970, the authorities considered Lucas a reformed character and released him. He killed a woman within hours of getting out. In 1971, he was arrested for attempting to rape two teenage girls at gunpoint. His only excuse was that he craved women all the time.

Released in 1975, he married a woman called Betty Crawford. The marriage broke up when Betty discovered that he was having sex with her nine-year-old daughter and trying to force himself on her seven-year-old. Lucas then moved in with his sister, but was thrown out when he started having sex with her daughter too.

In 1978, he met another sex murder freak called Ottis Toole in a soup kitchen in Jacksonville, Florida. He was a sadist with homosexual tendencies. He often dressed as a woman and picked up men in bars. He even started a course of female hormones as part of his ambition to have a sex change. Toole was also a pyromaniac, getting an orgasm at the sight of a burning building.

Lucas and Toole became lovers and together they began a series of violent robberies which frequently involved murder – often for the sheer pleasure of it. In Toole's confession, he admitted that around that time they saw a teenage couple walking along a road after their car had run out of petrol. Toole shot the boy, while Lucas forced the girl into the back of the car. After he had finished with her, he shot her six times and they dumped her body on the roadside. This was one of the cases the police could

201

confirm. Another murder occurred outside Oklahoma City. There they had picked up a girl called Tina Williams when her car broke down. Lucas shot her twice and had sex with her dead body.

In 1978, Lucas and Toole were in Maryland when a man asked them whether they would help him transport stolen cars. This was too tame a sport for such hardened criminals, they explained. So he asked them whether they were interested in becoming professional killers. They said that they were. The one proviso was that they had to join an international satanist cult.

Lucas and Toole claimed to have been inducted into the Hand of Death sect in Florida by a man named Don Meteric. As part of the initiation Lucas had to kill a man. He lured the victim to a beach and gave him a bottle of whiskey. When the man threw his head back to take a swig, Lucas cut his throat.

The cult had a training camp in the Everglades, Florida. They practised animal sacrifice, drinking the blood of decapitated victims and cannibalism. As part of cult activity, Lucas and Toole kidnapped young prostitutes who were forced to perform in pornographic videos which often turned out to be 'snuff movies'. They also abducted children who were used in paedophile movies. They took some children across the border into Mexico where they were sold or used as sacrifices in satanic ceremonies.

Around that time, Toole introduced Lucas to his eleven-year-old niece, Becky Powell, who was slightly mentally retarded. She lived in Toole's mother's house in Florida where they were staying. Toole had been seduced by his elder sister Druscilla, before he became homosexual, and he enjoyed watching his pick-ups make love to Becky or her older sister Sarah. When Druscilla committed suicide, Becky and her brother Frank were put in care. Lucas decided to rescue them. By January 1982, they were on the run together, living off the money they stole from small grocery stores. Becky called Lucas 'Daddy'. But one night, when he was tickling her innocently at bedtime, they began to kiss. Lucas undressed her, then stripped off himself. Becky was only twelve, he said, but she looked eighteen.

During his time with Becky, Lucas continued his murderous rampage with Toole. Lucas outlined a typical two weeks in Georgia. In that short space of time, they kidnapped, murdered, then raped the dead body of a sixteen-year-old girl and abducted, raped and mutilated a blonde woman. Another woman was abducted from a parking lot and stabbed to death in front of her children. In the course of one robbery, the store owner was shot. Another man died in a second robbery. In a third, the store owner was stabbed. And in a fourth, a woman was tied up before being stabbed to death. Toole also tried to force his sexual attentions on a young man. When he spurned him, Toole shot him. Becky and her brother Frank were often in on the robberies and witnessed several of the murders.

Eventually, Lucas and Toole parted company. Toole took Frank back to Florida, while Lucas and Becky got a job with a couple named Smart who ran an antique shop in California. After five months, the Smarts sent Lucas and Becky to Texas to look after Mrs Smart's eighty-year-old mother, Kate Rich. A few weeks later, Mrs Smart's sister visited her mother to find the place filthy. Lucas had been taking money to buy beer and cigarettes. She found him drunk in bed with Becky and the two of them were fired. They were hitch-hiking out of town when they were picked up by the Reverend Rueben Moore, who had started a religious community called the House of Prayer nearby. Lucas and his fifteen-year-old common law wife quickly became converts and lived in a converted chicken barn.

While they were staying at the House of Prayer, Becky seems to have had a genuine change of heart. She was homesick and she wanted to go back to Florida. Reluctantly, Lucas agreed and they set off hitch-hiking. At nightfall, they settled down with their blankets in a field. It was a warm June night. A row broke out about Becky's decision to return home. She struck him in the face. Lucas grabbed a knife and stabbed her through the heart. Then he had sex with her corpse, cut her body up and scattered its dismembered pieces in the woods.

After killing Becky, who Lucas later described as the only woman he had ever loved, he returned to the House of Prayer. He too seems to have had some sort of change of heart. One Sunday, he dropped around to Mrs Rich's house to offer her a lift to church. She accepted. But during the journey, she began to question him about the whereabouts of Becky. Lucas pulled a knife and stabbed it into her side. She died immediately. He drove her to a piece of waste ground where he undressed and raped her corpse. He stuffed her naked body into a drainage pipe that ran under the road. Later he collected it in a garbage bag and burnt it in the stove at the House of Prayer.

Sheriff Bill F. 'Hound Dog' Conway of Montague County, Texas, had begun to have his suspicions about Lucas when he reappeared without Becky. Now he was linked to the disappearance of another woman, Mrs Rich. Lucas was hauled in for questioning. Lucas was a chain smoker and caffeine addict. Conway deprived him of both cigarettes and coffee, but still Lucas refused to break. Lucas maintained that he knew nothing about the disappearance of Kate Rich, and that Becky had run off with a truck driver who promised to take her back to Florida. Finally, Sheriff Conway had to release him.

Soon after, Lucas told the Reverend Moore that he was going off to look for Becky. He headed for Missouri, where he saw a young woman standing beside her car in a petrol station. He stuck a knife in her ribs and forced her back into the car. They drove south towards Texas. When she dozed off, Lucas pulled off the road with the intention of raping her. She awoke suddenly to find a knife at her neck. He stabbed her in the throat, pushed her out on to the ground and cut her clothes off. After he raped her dead body, he dragged it into a copse and took the money from her handbag. He abandoned her car in Fredericksburg, Texas, and returned to the House of Prayer.

While he had been away, the Reverend Moore had told

Sheriff Conway that Lucas had given Becky a gun for safe-keeping. Lucas was a convicted felon and had, consequently, forfeited his right to carry a gun. It was enough to put him back in the slammer. Sheriff Conway again deprived the little tramp of coffee and cigarettes. This time he began to crack. He was found hanging in his cell with his wrists slashed. After being patched up in the prison hospital, Lucas was put in a special observation cell in the women's wing. The next night, he cracked completely. In the early hours of the morning, he started yelling. When the jailer arrived, Lucas claimed that there was a light in his cell and it was talking to him. The night man, Joe Don Weaver knew that Lucas had already smashed the bulb in his cell and told him to get some sleep. Later in the night, Lucas called the jailer again and confessed that he had done some pretty bad things. Joe Don advised him to get down on his knees and pray. Instead, Lucas asked Joe Don for a pencil and paper. Lucas spent the next half-hour writing a note to Sheriff Conway. It read:

> I have tried to get help for so long, and no one will believe me. I have killed for the past ten years and no one will believe me. I cannot go on doing this. I have killed the only girl I ever loved.

When the confession was finished, Lucas pushed it out of the cell door's peep hole. Joe Don read it and called Sheriff Conway. He knew the Sheriff would not mind being awoken in the middle of the night. When Sheriff Conway arrived, he plied Lucas with coffee and cigarettes – and asked about the murders. Lucas said that he had seen a light in his cell and it had told him to confess his sins. Then he told the Sheriff that he had killed Kate Rich. Later, Sheriff Conway and Texas Ranger Phil Ryan asked Lucas what had happened to Becky Powell. Tears flowed from his one good eye as Lucas told how he had stabbed, raped and dismembered her. The story left the two hardened law officers sick and wretched.

'Is that all?' asked Ryan wearily, half-hoping it was.

'Not by a long way,' said Lucas. 'I reckon I killed more than a hundred.'

The next day, Montague County police began to check out Lucas's story. Near the drainage pipe where Lucas had temporarily hidden Mrs Rich's body, they found some of her underclothes and her glasses, broken. At the House of Prayer, they found some burnt fragments of human flesh and some charred human bones. Lucas took them to the field where he had killed Becky. They found her suitcase, full of women's clothing and make-up. Her skull, pelvis and other parts of her body were found in the woodland nearby, in an advanced stage of decomposition.

Lucas began to confess to other murders too – often in breathtaking detail. These too checked out. A week after he had begun to confess, Lucas appeared in court, charged with the murders of Kate Rich and Becky Powell. When asked whether he understood the seriousness of the charges against him, Lucas said he did and confessed to about a hundred other murders. The judge, shocked, could scarcely credit this and asked Lucas whether he had ever had a psychiatric examination. Lucas said he had, but 'they didn't want to do anything about it . . . I know it ain't normal for a person to go out and kill girls just to have sex.'

Lucas's sensational testimony made huge headlines and the news wires carried the story to every paper in the country. Police departments in every state in the country began checking their records and Lucas's confessions were run through the computer at the newly formed National Center for the Analysis of Violent Crime.

Toole, it was discovered, was already in prison. He had been sentenced to fifteen years for arson in Springfield. In jail he was regaling a cell mate with the tale of how he had raped, murdered, beheaded, barbecued and eaten a child named Adam Walsh. Suddenly, the police were taking his stories seriously. Lucas and Toole began to confess freely. They admitted to a series of robberies of convenience stores. At one, they had tied up a young girl. She had wriggled free, so Lucas had shot her in the head and Toole had sex with her dead body.

Lucas went on a 1,000-mile tour of murder sites. In Duval County, Florida, Lucas admitted to eight unsolved murders. The victims had been women ranging in age from seventeen to eighty. Some had been beaten, some strangled, some stabbed and some shot. Lucas said that the Hand of Death had told him that he should vary the M.O. Near Austin, Texas, Lucas pointed out a building and asked whether it had been a liquor store once. It had. Lucas confessed to murdering the former owners during a robbery in 1979. In the same county, Lucas led them to a field where he had murdered and mutilated a girl called Sandra Dubbs. He even pointed out where her car had been found.

Lucas and Toole had cruised Interstate 35, murdering tramps, hitch-hikers, men who were robbed of their money and old women who were abducted from their homes. They had killed more than twenty people up and down that highway alone, over five years. One was a young women who was found naked except for a pair of orange socks near Austin, Texas. She had been hitch-hiking on Interstate 35 when Lucas had picked her up. She refused to have sex with him, so Lucas strangled her and took what he wanted. She was never identified but Lucas was sentenced to death for her murder. Although he withdrew his confession in the Becky Powell murder and pleaded not guilty, he was found guilty anyway and sentenced to life. On top of that he received four more life sentences, two sentences of seventy-five years each and one of sixty-six years, all for murder.

During his confessions, Lucas told the police that Toole had poured petrol over a sixty-five-year-old man and set him alight. They had hidden so that they could watch the fire engines arrive. The police identified the man as George Sonenberg. He had died four days later. Until then, they had assumed that the fire was an accident. Toole freely admitted the murder and claimed to have started hundreds of other fires. But it was for this particularly horrific murder that Toole, as well, was sentenced to death.

Both Lucas and Toole enjoyed their brief celebrity and took a certain relish in revealing the ghoulish details of their shocking crimes. But the FBI have not been able to unearth any more information on the Hand of Death.

13

The Zodiac Killer

On a chilly, moonlit night around Christmas in 1968, a teenage couple pulled up in an open space next to a pump house on Lake Herman road in the Vallejo hills overlooking San Francisco. This was the local lovers' lane and David Faraday and Bettilou Jensen were indifferent to the cold. They were so wrapped up in each other that they did not even notice when another car pulled up about ten feet away. They were rudely awoken from their amorous reverie by gunfire. One bullet smashed through the back window, showering them with glass. Another thudded into the bodywork. Bettilou threw open the passenger door and leapt out. David tried to follow. He had his hand on the door handle when the gunman leant in through the driver's window and shot him in the head. His body slumped across the front seat. Bettilou's attempt at flight was futile. As she ran screaming into the night, the gunman ran after her. She had run just thirty feet when he fired five shots into her. She collapsed and died. Then the gunman calmly walked back to his car and drove away.

A few minutes later, another car came down the quiet road. Its driver, a woman, saw Bettilou's body sprawled on the ground, but did not stop. Instead, she sped on towards the next town, Benica, to get help. On the way, she saw a blue flashing light coming towards her. It was a patrol car and she flashed her lights frantically to attract the driver's attention. The car stopped and she told the patrolmen what she had seen. They followed her back to the pump station, arriving there about three minutes later. They found Bettilou Jensen dead, but David Faraday was still alive. He was unconscious and could not help them with their enquiries. They rushed him to hospital, but he died shortly after arriving there.

There was little to go on. The victims had not been sexually assaulted, nor was anything missing. The money in David Faraday's wallet was untouched. Detective Sergeant Les Lundblatt of the Vallejo county police investigated the possibility that they had been murdered by a jealous rival. But there were no jilted lovers, no other amorous entanglements. The two teenagers were ordinary students. Their lives were an open book. And six months later, Bettilou Jensen and David Faraday had just become two more of the huge number of files of unsolved murders in the state of California.

Then, on 4 July 1969, their killer struck again. Around midnight, at Blue Rock Park, another romantic spot just two miles from where Jensen and Faraday were slain, Mike Mageau was parked with his girlfriend, twenty-two-year-old waitress Darlene Ferrin. They were not alone. Other cars of other courting couples were parked up there. Again Mike and Darlene were too engrossed in each other to notice when a white car pulled up beside them. It stayed there just a few minutes, then drove away. But it returned and parked on the other side of the road.

Suddenly, a powerful spotlight shone on Mike Mageau's car. A figure approached. Thinking it was the police, Mike reached for his driver's licence. As he did so, he heard gunfire and Darlene slumped down in her seat. Seconds later, a bullet tore into Mike's neck. The gunman walked calmly back to the white car, paused to fire another four or five shots at them, then sped off, leaving the smell of cordite and burning rubber behind him.

A few minutes later, a man called the Vallejo county police and reported a murder up on Columbus Parkway. He told the switchboard operator: 'You will find the kids in a brown car. They are shot with a 9 mm Luger. I also killed those kids last year. Goodbye.'

When the police arrived, Darlene Ferrin was dead. Mike Mageau was still alive, but the bullet had passed through his tongue and he was unable to talk. However, there were some other leads. Four months earlier, Darlene's baby-sitter had spotted a white car parked outside Darlene's apartment. Suspicious, she asked Darlene about it. It was plain that the young waitress knew the driver. 'He's checking up on me again,' she told the baby-sitter. 'He doesn't want anyone to know what I saw him do. I saw him murder someone.'

The baby-sitter had had a good look at the man in the white car. She told the police that he was middle-aged with brown wavy hair and a round face. When Mike Mageau could talk again, he confirmed that the gunman had brown hair and a round face. But after that clues petered out.

Then, on 1 August 1969, almost two months after the shooting of Ferrin and Mageau, three local papers received handwritten letters. These began; 'DEAR EDITOR, THIS IS THE MURDERER OF THE 2 TEENAGERS LAST CHRISTMAS AT LAKE HERMAN & THE GIRL ON THE 4TH OF JULY ...' Like Berkowitz's letters, they were printed and contained basic errors in spelling and syntax. But the author gave details of the ammunition used and left no doubt that he was the gunman. Each letter also contained a third of a sheet of paper covered with a strange code. The killer demanded that the papers print this on the front page otherwise, the writer said, he would go on 'killing lone people in the night'. The letter was signed with another cipher – a circle with a cross inside it which looked ominously like a gunsight. All three newspapers complied and the full text of the coded message was sent to Mare Island Naval Yard where cryptographers tried to crack it. Although it was a simple substitution code, the US Navy's experts could not break it. But Dale Harden, a teacher at Alisal High School, Salinas, could. He had the simple idea of looking for a group of ciphers that might spell the word 'kill'. He found them and, after ten hours' intense work, he and his wife decoded the whole of the message.

It read: 'I like killing people because it is so much more fun than killing wild game in the forrest [sic] because man is the most dangerous of all to kill ...' The killer went on to boast that he had already murdered five people in the San Francisco Bay area. He said that when he was born again in paradise, his victims would be his slaves.

The killer's cryptic message brought with it a tidal wave of information from the public. Over a thousand calls were received by the police. None of them led anywhere. So the killer volunteered more help. This time he gave them a name – or, at least, a nickname that would attract the attention of the headline writers. He wrote again to the newspapers, beginning: 'DEAR EDITOR, THIS IS ZODIAC SPEAKING ...' Again he gave details of the slaying of Darlene Ferrin that only the killer could have known. But although this increased the killer's publicity profile, the police were no nearer to catching him.

On 27 September 1969, twenty-year-old Bryan Hartnell and twenty-two-year-old Cecelia Ann Shepard – both students at the Seventh Day Adventist's Pacific Union College nearby – went for a picnic on the shores of Lake Berryessa, some thirteen miles north of Vallejo. It was a warm day. They had finished eating and were lying on a blanket kissing at around 4.30 p.m. when they noticed a man coming across the clearing towards them. He was stocky and had brown hair. He disappeared for a moment into a copse. When he emerged he was wearing a mask and carrying a gun. As he came closer, Bryan Hartnell saw that the mask had a symbol on it. It was a circle with a white cross in it. The man was not particularly threatening in his manner. His voice was soft.

'I want your money and your car keys,' he said.

Bryan Hartnell explained that he only had 76 cents, but the hooded man was welcome to that. The gunman then began to chat. He explained that he was an escaped convict and that he was going to have to tie them up. He had some clothes-line with him and got Cecelia to tie up Bryan. Then he tied Cecelia up himself.

The gunman talked some more then calmly announced: 'I am going to have to stab you people.'

Bryan Hartnell begged to be stabbed first.

'I couldn't bear to see her stabbed,' he said.

The gunman calmly agreed, sank to his knees and stabbed Hartnell in the back repeatedly with a hunting knife. Hartnell was dizzy and sick, but still conscious when the masked man turned his attention to Cecelia. He was calm at first, but after the first stab he seemed to go berserk. He plunged the hunting knife into her defenceless body again and again, while she twisted and turned frantically under him in a futile attempt to escape the blows. When she finally lay still, the man grew calm again. He got up and walked over to their car. He pulled a felt-tip pen from his pocket and drew something on the door. Then he walked away.

A fisherman heard their screams and came running. Bryan and Cecelia were both still alive. The Napa Valley Police were already on their way, alerted by an anonymous phone call. A gruff man's voice had said: 'I want to report a double murder.'

He gave a precise location for where the bodies were to be found, then left the phone hanging.

Cecelia Shepard was in a coma when the police arrived. She died two days later in hospital without regaining consciousness. Bryan Hartnell recovered slowly and was able to give a full description of their attacker. But the police had already guessed who he was. The sign he had drawn on the door of their car was a circle with a cross in it. The police found the phone that the man with the gruff voice had left hanging. It was in a call box less than six blocks from the headquarters of the Napa Valley Police Department. And they managed to get three good fingerprints off it. Unfortunately, they were not on record.

Two weeks after the stabbing, on 11 October 1969, a fourteen-year-old girl was looking out of the window of her home in San Francisco and witnessed a crime in progress. A cab was parked on the corner of Washington and

Cherry Street and a stocky man, in the front passenger seat, was going through the pockets of the driver. She called her brothers over to watch what was happening. The man got out of the taxi, leaving the cab driver slumped across the seat. He wiped the door handle with a piece of cloth, then walked off in a northerly direction. The children called the police, but they did not give their evidence clearly enough. The telephone operator who took the call, logged at 10 p.m., noted that the suspect was an 'NMA' – negro male adult. An all-points bulletin was put out and a patrolman actually stopped a stocky man nearby and asked whether he had seen anything unusual. But as he was white, the police officer let him go.

Later a stocky man was seen running into the nearby Presidio – a military compound that contains housing and a park area. The floodlights were switched on and the area was searched by patrolmen with dogs. In the cab, the police found the taxi-driver, twenty-nine-year-old Paul Stine, dead from a gunshot wound to the head. The motive, they thought, was robbery.

Then, three days later, the *San Francisco Chronicle* received a Zodiac letter.

'THIS IS THE ZODIAC SPEAKING,' it said. 'I AM THE MURDERER OF THE TAXI DRIVER OVER BY WASHINGTON ST AND MAPLE ST [sic] LAST NIGHT, TO PROVE IT HERE IS A BLOOD STAINED PIECE OF HIS SHIRT.'

San Francisco criminologists managed to match the piece of cloth in the letter exactly with the shirt of the murdered taxi driver. And the bullet that had killed Stine was a .22 and fired from the same gun that had been used in the murder of Bettilou Jensen and David Faraday.

The letter went on to say: 'I AM THE SAME MAN WHO DID IN THE PEOPLE IN THE NORTH BAY AREA.

'THE S.F. POLICE COULD HAVE CAUGHT ME LAST NIGHT,' it taunted, concluding, 'SCHOOL CHILDREN MAKE NICE TARGETS. I THINK I

SHALL WIPE OUT A SCHOOL BUS SOME MORN-
ING. JUST SHOOT OUT THE TYRES AND THEN
PICK OFF ALL THE KIDDIES AS THEY COME
BOUNCING OUT.'

The letter was signed with a circle with a cross in it.

The description given by the children and the policeman
who had stopped a stocky white male leaving the scene of
the crime matched those given by Darlene Ferrin's baby-
sitter, Mike Mageau and Bryan Hartnell. A new composite
of the Zodiac killer was drawn up and issued to the public
by San Francisco Chief of Police Thomas J. Cahill. It
showed a white male, thirty-five to forty-five years old with
short brown hair, possibly with a red tint. He was around
five feet eight inches tall, heavily built and wore glasses.
The wanted poster was plastered around town.

But the Zodiac killer's appetite for publicity seems to
have been endless. At 2 a.m. on 22 October 1969, eleven
days after the murder of Paul Stine, a man with a gruff
voice called the police department in Oakland, which is
just across the bay from San Francisco. He introduced
himself as the Zodiac and said: 'I want to get in touch
with F. Lee Bailey. If you can't come up with Bailey, I'll
settle for Mel Belli. I want one or other of them to appear
on the Channel 7 talk show. I'll make contact by telephone.'

The men he was asking for were the two top criminal
lawyers in America. F. Lee Bailey has been more recently
defending O. J. Simpson. But he was not available on such
short notice and Melvin Belli agreed to appear on the Jim
Dunbar talk show at 6.30 the next morning. The show's
ratings soared as people throughout the Bay area got up
the next morning and tuned in. At around 7.20 a man
called in and told Belli that he was the Zodiac, though he
preferred to be called Sam. He said: 'I'm sick. I have headaches.'

But the two police switchboard operators who talked to
the Zodiac when he reported the murders said his voice was
that of an older man. The mystery caller was eventually

215

traced to Napa State Hospital and proved to be a mental patient.

The real Zodiac continued his correspondence. He wrote to Inspector David Toschi of the San Francisco homicide squad threatening to commit more murders. In another letter, he claimed to have killed seven people – two more than the official Zodiac body count so far. Later he claimed to have killed ten, taunting the San Francisco Police Department with the scoreline: 'ZODIAC 10, SFPD 0.' He gave cryptic clues to his name and fantasised about blowing up school children with a bomb.

The following Christmas, Melvin Belli received a card saying: 'DEAR MELVIN, THIS IS THE ZODIAC SPEAKING. I WISH YOU A HAPPY CHRISTMAS. THE ONE THING I ASK OF YOU IS THIS, PLEASE HELP ME ... I AM AFRAID I WILL LOSE CONTROL AND TAKE MY NINTH AND POSSIBLE TENTH VICTIM.' Another piece of Paul Stine's bloodstained shirt was enclosed and forensic handwriting experts feared that the Zodiac's mental state was deteriorating.

On 24 July 1970, the Zodiac killer wrote a letter which spoke of 'THE WOEMAN [sic] AND HER BABY THAT I GAVE A RATHER INTERESTING RIDE FOR A COUPLE OF HOWERS ONE EVENING A FEW MONTHS BACK THAT ENDED IN MY BURNING HER CAR WHERE I FOUND THEM.' The woman was Kathleen Johns of Vallejo. On the evening of 17 March 1970, she had been driving in the area when a white Chevrolet pulled alongside her. The driver indicated that there was something wrong with her rear wheel. She pulled over and the other driver stopped. He was a 'clean-shaven and neatly dressed man'. He said that the wheel had been wobbling and offered to tighten the wheel nuts for her. But when she pulled away, the wheel he had said he had fixed came off altogether. The driver of the Chevrolet then offered her a lift to a nearby service station, but drove straight past it. When she pointed this out, the man said, in a chillingly calm voice: 'You know I am going to kill you.'

But Kathleen Jones kept her head. When he slowed on the curve of a freeway ramp, she jumped from the car with her baby in her arms. Then she ran and hid in an irrigation ditch. He stopped and, with a flashlight from the trunk of his car, started searching for her. He was approaching the ditch when he was caught in the headlights of a truck and made off. An hour later, she made her way to a police station to report what had happened to her. When she looked up and saw the Zodiac's wanted poster, she identified him as the man who had threatened to kill her. And when the police drove her back to her car, they found it burnt out. It seemed he had returned and set it alight.

Despite the new leads Kathleen Johns provided, the police got no nearer to catching the Zodiac killer. Police in Vallejo believed that the man they were after was now the driver of a new green Ford. He had stopped and watched a Highway Patrolman across the freeway. When the Highway Patrolman decided to ask him what he was doing and cut around through an underpass, he found the green Ford was gone. It was now sitting on the other side of the freeway where the squad car had been moments before. This cat and mouse game was played every day for two weeks.

Detective Sergeant Les Lundblatt became convinced that the Zodiac killer was a man named Andy Walker. He had known Darlene Ferrin and Darlene's sister identified him as the man who had waited outside Darlene's apartment in a white car. He also bore a resemblance to the description of the man seen near Lake Berryessa when Cecelia Shepard was stabbed to death. And he had studied codes in the military. However, his fingerprints did not match the one left in Paul Stine's cab and his handwriting did not match the Zodiac's notes. But the police discovered that Walker was ambidextrous and believed that the murder of Paul Stine had been planned so meticulously that the Zodiac may have used the severed finger of a victim they did not know about. He was also known to suffer from bad headaches and he got on badly with women at work.

The police decided that they had to get his palm prints

217

to see if they matched those on the telephone that had been left dangling after the Paul Stine killing. An undercover policeman asked Walker to help him carry a goldfish bowl. Walker obliged, but the palm prints he left were smudged. Walker realised what was going on and a judge issued a court order forcing the police to stop harassing him.

Zodiac letters threatening more murders were sent. Some of them have been authenticated, but rendered few new clues. The only thing that detectives could be sure of was that the Zodiac was a fan of Gilbert & Sullivan. He taunted with a parody of 'The Lord High Executioner' – listing those people he intended to kill – and used the refrain 'titwillo, titwillo, titwillo'. And there were no letters or criminal activity that could have been ascribed to the Zodiac killer during the entire run of the *Mikado* in San Francisco's Presentation Theatre.

There may have been more Zodiac murders, too. On 21 May 1970, the naked body of Marie Antoinette Anstey was found just off a quiet country road in Lake County. Traces of mescaline were found in her body. She had been hit over the head and drowned. Her clothes were never found. The murder of Marie Antoinette Anstey followed the pattern of the Zodiac killings. It took place at a weekend, in the same general area around Vallejo, and near a body of water. Although she was naked, there were no signs that she had been sexually molested.

The Zodiac had some curious connection with the water. All the names of all murder scenes had some association with water – even *Wash*ington Street. In one of the Zodiac letters, he claimed that the body count would have been higher if he had not been 'swamped by the rain we had a while back'. The police deduced that he lived in a low-lying area, susceptible to flooding. Perhaps he had a basement where he kept the equipment to make the long-threatened bomb.

A K-Mart store in Santa Rosa, California, was evacuated after a bomb threat by a man identifying himself as the Zodiac killer. Two months later, the Zodiac wrote

218

another letter to the San Francisco *Chronicle* claiming to have killed twelve people and enclosing the map with an X marking the peak of Mount Diablo – the Devil's Mountain – in Contra Costa Country across the bay from San Francisco. From there, an observer could see the entire panorama of the area where the murders had taken place. But when detectives checked it out more closely, the spot marked was within the compound of a Naval Relay Station, where only service personnel with security clearance could go.

The letters continued, demanding that people in the San Francisco area wear lapel badges with the Zodiac symbol on it. When they did not, he threatened Paul Avery, the *Chronicle*'s crime writer who had been investigating the story. Journalists, including Paul Avery, began wearing badges saying 'I am not Paul Avery'. But Avery, who was a licensed private eye and a former war correspondent in Vietnam, took to carrying a .38 and put in regular practice at the police firing range.

An anonymous correspondent tied the Zodiac slayings to the unsolved murder of Cheri Jo Bates, a college girl in Riverside, California, on Hallowe'en 1966. The police could not rule out a connection, but could not prove a concrete link either. But when crime writer Paul Avery checked it out he discovered that the police had received what they considered to be a crank letter about the murder, five months after the killing. It was signed with the letter Z.

Cheri Jo Bates was an eighteen-year-old freshman, who had been stabbed to death after leaving the college library one evening. In a series of typewritten letters, the killer gave details of the murder only he could have known. He also said that there would be more and talked of a 'game' he was playing. But there were also handwritten letters, where the handwriting matched the Zodiac's and Avery managed to persuade the police to re-open the Bates case in the light of the Zodiac murders.

During 1971, there were a number of murders that could

have been committed by the Zodiac. Letters purporting to come from him confessed to them. But he could easily have been claiming credit for other people's handiwork. However, on 7 April 1972, thirty-three-year-old Isobel Watson, who worked as a legal secretary in San Francisco, alighted from the bus at around 9 p.m. in Tamalpais Valley and began walking home up Pine Hill. Seemingly out of nowhere, a white Chevrolet swerved across the road at her. The car stopped. The driver apologised and offered to give her a lift home. When Mrs Watson declined, he pulled a knife on her and stabbed her in the back. Her screams alerted the neighbours. The man ran back to his car and sped off. Mrs Watson recovered and gave a description. Her assailant was a white man in his early forties, around five foot nine inches and he wore black-rimmed reading glasses. The police said that there was a better than fifty-fifty chance that this was the Zodiac killer.

As time went on, other detectives dropped out of the case, leaving only Inspector David Toschi. The FBI looked at the files, but even they could take the case no further.

The correspondence from the Zodiac ceased for nearly four years. Though psychologists believed that he was the type who might commit suicide, Toschi did not believe he was dead. Toschi reasoned that the Zodiac got his kicks from the publicity surrounding the killings, rather than the killings themselves. Surely he would have left a note, or some clue in his room, that he was the Zodiac. Then on 25 April 1978, Toschi got confirmation. The *Chronicle* received a new letter from him. This time it mentioned Toschi by name. And the author wanted the people of San Francisco to know he was back. This gave the police a new opportunity to catch him.

Robert Graysmith, author of the book *Zodiac*, deduced that he was a movie buff. In one of his cryptograms he mentions 'the most dangerous game' which is the title of a film. In another, he calls himself 'the Red Phantom', the title of another movie. And he frequently mentions going to the movies to see *The Exorcist* or *Badlands*, a fictionalised account of the murderous spree of Nebraskan killer Charles Starkweather. The police used this information and the Zodiac killer's obvious love of publicity to try and trap him. When a movie about the Zodiac killings was shown in San Francisco a suggestions box was left in the lobby of the cinema. The audience were asked to drop a note of any information or theories they may have in it. The box was huge and a detective was hidden inside it. He read every entry by torchlight as it fell through the slot. If any looked like they came from the Zodiac killer, he was to raise the alarm. None did.

The Oakland police thought that they had captured the Zodiac killer. He was a Vietnam veteran who had seen the movie three times and had been apprehended in the lavatory at the cinema masturbating after a particularly violent scene. The Oakland PD was soon proved wrong. His handwriting did not match the Zodiac's. Soon there was a welter of recrimination. Toschi was transferred out of homicide after baseless accusations that he had forged the Zodiac letters for self-promotion. The police in the Bay area began to believe that the Zodiac killer was either dead or in prison outside the state for another crime. Or it could have been, after the close call with the killing of Paul Stine, that he figured that his luck was running out.

But Robert Graysmith was not convinced. He managed to connect the Zodiac killings with the unsolved murder of fourteen young girls, usually students or hitch-hikers in the Santa Rosa area in the early 1970s. Most of them were found nude, their clothes were missing but largely they had not been sexually molested. Each of them had been killed in different ways, as if the murderer was experimenting to find out which way was best. Graysmith reckons that the Zodiac's body count could be as high as forty.

The Zodiac's symbol, a cross in a circle, Graysmith believes, is not a stylised gunsight but the projectionist's guide seen on the lead-in to a movie. Through a cinema in San Francisco which has the constellations painted on the ceiling he traced a promising suspect. The man, Graysmith was told, filmed some of the murders and kept the film in a booby-trapped film can.

Another Graysmith suspect was a former boyfriend of Darlene Ferrin's. He had also been a resident of Riverside when Cheri Jo Bates had been murdered. He lived with his mother, who he loathed, and dissected small mammals as a hobby. During the crucial 1975–78 period when the Zodiac killer was quiet, he was in a mental hospital after being charged with child molesting at a school where he worked.

Although he had two promising candidates Graysmith could not pin the Zodiac murders on either of them. He published the story of his investigation in 1985.

But then, in 1990, a series of strange murders began in New York. The perpetrator claimed to be the Zodiac. The killer's description does not match those given by the witnesses in California. But a man can change a lot in twenty years.

14

Apocalypse Now

The Process Church, Charles Manson and other murderous sects turned to Satan because of their belief in the Apocalypse. They believed that the world was about to end in a cataclysm and that Satan would rule the earth for a period before the great battle of Armageddon. A number of religious cults believe the same thing. These apocalyptic cults believe in Satan, though they do not follow him. They are on the side of God, but they believe that Satan is abroad in the world and that the final battle is on its way.

It seems that believing in Satan, whether you worship him or you oppose him, can result in the same thing – the random taking of life. The only difference between Charles Manson and the Reverend Jim Jones, say, is that Jones killed more people. Manson was responsible for the death of just eight people. At the mass suicide in Jonestown, Guyana, Jones killed nearly a thousand. When fanatics start talking of Armageddon, the water gets murky. Though killers use the name of God to justify their acts, it is often difficult to work out just whose side they are on.

Jim Jones began his religious career at the age of twelve, delivering hellfire-and-damnation speeches at mock funerals for dead cats. But some saw a more sinister side to his interest in animals.

'Some of the neighbours would have cats missing and we always thought he was using them for sacrifices,' a contemporary recalled.

There may have been something to this. Jones' mother

believed in spells, omens, black magic and the transmigration of souls.

Jones was brought up in the small town of Lynn in Indiana. It depended for its livelihood on one thriving local industry – coffin-making. Jones's father had been gassed in France during World War I. Back in Lynn, he became the local barfly. He was a dyed-in-the-wool redneck racist and a lifelong member of the Ku-Klux-Klan. His mother was far more unconventional though. She shocked small-town Indiana by wearing trousers and smoking in the street. She subscribed to *National Geographic* and made up bedtime stories for her son, featuring her imaginary journeys up the Amazon and her times with the headhunters there. She also believed that dreams were visions of the future and predicted that her son would one day help the poor and the weak. He was destined to be a man who left his mark on the world, she said.

While his contemporaries made their way in the white world of banking, business, farming or teaching, Jones worked in a hospital in Indianapolis where his colleagues were mainly poor and black. There he met and married a pale student nurse, five years his senior. Jones was intent on becoming a doctor and enrolled at the University of Indiana in Bloomington. After a year he dropped out, now intent on becoming a preacher. He began as a door-to-door recruiter for a Methodist mission, then he became an unordained supply preacher. But his ministry was not a success. The largely white congregation did not like the blacks that Jones was bringing in. They did not like his fire-and-brimstone sermons – and they did not like being told that Jones had met God on the train to Philadelphia one day. He was thrown out and the church was closed down as if it had been desecrated.

At the age of 22, unfinanced and unordained, Jim Jones founded the Community National Church in a run-down section of Indianapolis. Although the Community National sounds like a savings bank, it was very much a shoestring operation. Jones supported it by importing and selling monkeys – at $29 each.

But Jones was not the prototype American tele-evangelist who preached God, the Flag and the American way. In 1953, he joined the Communist Party. That year, he also conceived the idea of 'revolutionary death' when atom spies Julius and Ethel Rosenberg were executed. Their deaths, he concluded, shattered the illusion that America was the 'last best hope of mankind'. Jones described himself privately as a 'socialist' though his political philosophy seems to owe more to Robin Hood than to Karl Marx. The poorer and the weaker his followers, the more attention he lavished on them. One early member of his church recalls: 'He had a lot of them, the kind of people most folks don't want to have nothing to do with. Fat, ugly old ladies who didn't have nobody in the world. He'd pass around hugs and kisses like he really loved them, and you could see on their faces what he meant to them.'

His success at building a truly multi-racial congregation – one of the first in America – attracted unwelcome attention. Segregationalists called him a 'nigger-lover' and threw dead cats into his church. His windows were broken and explosives went off in his yard. But the more opposition he faced, the harder he tried. He even adopted eight Korean and black children. His unwavering stand against racism led to his appointment to the newly created City Human Rights Commission, reporting directly to the mayor, in 1961.

In 1957, Jones and his wife had collected $50,000 and established the first People's Temple in a lavishly converted synagogue on North Delaware Street, Indianapolis. Around that time, Jones made several pilgrimages to the Peace Mission of Father Divine, the most successful ministry to the urban poor in the country. He learnt at the master's feet. The keys to Father Divine's success were his absolute insistence on his own divinity and extravagant demonstrations of the power of faith. Jones quickly learned the lesson and began putting on his own displays of healing. In carefully contrived theatrical settings, he got believers to spew up chicken livers claiming they were

225

cancers. He raised perfectly fit young people made up to look like paralysed ancients from their wheelchairs and astounded his congregation with his mind reading powers. This was a trick too. He had a photographic memory and kept detailed files on all his followers.

Jones also noted that Father Divine, though black with an exclusively black following, surrounded himself with an inner circle of attractive, middle-class white women. But Jones did not follow his mentor's example of compensating himself for long days at the ministry with Cadillacs and forty-room mansions. Instead, Jones took his young family off for two years' missionary work in the favelas of Belo Horizonte in Brazil. There he met hardened Marxists for the first time and added a fresh dollop of communist philosophy to his gospel of social change through Christian love. On the way back to America, he stopped in British Guiana, soon to become the independent country of Guyana.

Back in the USA, everything was changing. His fight to unite black and white was no longer a single-handed struggle. For the first time, he heard Martin Luther King expound his vision of future America where racism would no longer be an issue. But what made a more powerful impact were the words of Malcolm Little, aka Malcolm X, an ex-junkie and street pimp who asked: 'What has Christianity done for black people – except oppress them?'

The Vietnam war, civil rights marches in the South and race riots across the USA convinced Jones that he must take his followers to a 'promised land'. He decided that Redwood Valley near Ukiah, California, was the place and relocated the People's Temple there, bussing hundreds of followers across the country. Some stayed behind. But those who went had to sell their property and became totally dependent on Jim Jones and the Temple. From Redwood Valley, the Temple spread into San Francisco and Los Angeles. Jones opened food kitchens and day-care centres. Soon he was wielding considerable political power.

Jones could deliver the several thousand members of his

Temple as a block vote. Virtually every liberal office-holder – from lieutenant governor of the state of California down to district attorney – was offered the chance to address the congregation. They quickly became beholden to Jones. In gratitude San Francisco mayor George Moscone appointed Jones chairman of the city's Housing Authority. Even national politicians cultivated him. During the 1976 presidential campaign, he had dinner with Rosalynn Carter. For his part, Jones used his influence to secure preferential treatment for his congregation with welfare agencies, housing authorities or even in court.

In affluent Redwood Valley, California, he attracted an educated white middle-class congregation, which he installed as the upper echelon to organise the church's activities.

In California, Jones met an ambitious young lawyer named Tim Stoen. He had just married his young wife Grace. Stoen had been disillusioned by the assassination of President Kennedy and was searching for a revolutionary way ahead. Jones promised just that. His multi-racial congregation and free-wheeling Christian/Marxist philosophy seemed to represent the wave of the future. Jones's growing political influence also secured Stoen the plum job of Assistant District Attorney in San Francisco. The price of Stoen's participation was the body of his wife. In January 1972, she gave birth to a son, John-John. The birth certificate listed the father as Tim Stoen. But in an affidavit, Stoen stated that he requested Jones to sire a child by his wife 'with the steadfast hope that said child will become the devoted follower of Jesus Christ and be instrumental in bringing God's kingdom here on earth, as has been his wonderful natural father'. Jim Jones, Tim Stoen said, was the 'most compassionate, honest and courageous human being on earth'. The affidavit was witnessed by Marceline, Jones's wife. Grace Stoen's feelings were not recorded.

Jones was also using his congregation as a harem and his young women followers seemed to consider it a privilege to satisfy his sexual cravings. It was the least they could do for the great man. Jones's secretaries kept a separate appointments book for these liaisons. Jones boasted of his sexual prowess. He claimed that he had an almost superhuman endurance, technique and potency. He even asked for psychiatric advice on how to bring his libido under control at one time. Jones used sex, not just for pleasure, but for power. It corroded the bond between couples and bound each partner closer to him and to the Temple. Jones banned all sex with outsiders. Any relationship inside the congregation needed the Temple's specific approval, in advance. It was seldom forthcoming. One woman had an abortion rather than bear his child, but at least three of Jones's children were carried to term by members of the congregation.

Sex was a frequent topic of discussion at the all-important Planning Commission. This was an inner circle of around a hundred members, largely the better-educated middle-class whites. Meetings would drag on to the early hours with Jones railing against bourgeois sexual attitudes. He would force members to publicly confess their sexual fears and fantasies. Sometimes Jones would sentence those less than forthcoming to long periods of celibacy. They should follow his example, Jones said. He took no sensual pleasure in sex. For him, he said, it was a revolutionary tool. During one meeting, Jones forced one white man to perform cunnilingus on a black woman in front of everyone to prove he harboured no racial prejudice. Sexual candour and public urination, Jones maintained, were symbolic representations of the Temple's openness. But Jones, it seemed to some, took an unhealthy pleasure in exhibiting himself.

Jones did not just sleep with the women. The men were encouraged to have sex with him too. It was, Jones contended, a revolutionary act. Again, Jones entered into the spirit of the thing with a little too much relish. In 1973, he was picked up for making flagrant homosexual overtures to an undercover policeman in the toilet of a cinema during a matinée of *Jesus Christ Superstar*. Jones said it was part of a police vendetta against him and the Temple. If it was, it failed. Jones had enough political influence not only to get the charges dropped but also have the arrest record sealed by a Los Angeles judge.

While things were becoming more open inside the community, Jones began to take a more paranoid view of the outside world. He believed that his phone was being tapped by the FBI and he was being followed by government agents. Ex-members' houses were watched to make sure they were not talking to government agents or hostile journalists. Their private lives – and sometimes even their garbage – were combed for potential blackmail material. The Mertle family were typical victims.

In 1968, newly-weds Elmer and Deanna Mertle were invited to visit the People's Temple in Redwood Valley. They found there a friendship and community they had not experienced before. Both came from fatherless homes and found a convenient father figure in Jim Jones – who was already styling himself 'Dad'. Deanna found her Seventh Day Adventist beliefs challenged. She was told that Christianity was a 'slave religion' and the bible was full of logical contradictions. She read her bible again and found that it was. Elmer was more attracted by Jones's politics. And he liked the way, after their first visit, everyone greeted them by name. They and their children were fussed over like they really belonged.

One night Deanna had a dream. She and Elmer were being threatened by a terrible monster. Jones saved them. Soon after, they sold their home and moved into a farm Jones had found for them nearby. Within a few weeks, he had also found them jobs. By 1975, the Mertles were members of the Planning Commission, but were becoming increasingly disturbed by Jones's bizarre behaviour. And when their sixteen-year-old daughter was spanked for a minor infraction, they decided to leave.

This was not as easy as they thought. Two of their children lived in the homes of other Temple members and felt more commitment to Jones than to their natural parents. Their home and everything they owned belonged to the Temple. It was also their only source of income. They had been completely supported by – and surrounded by – the Temple for five years and they had little or no contact with the outside world.

The Mertles were lucky though. Elmer's mother gave them a profitable rest home she owned in Berkeley and the money to buy a house. But when Deanna Mertle called one of Jones's aides to tell him they were leaving all hell broke loose. A delegation came round and tried to persuade them to change their minds. Others searched for stolen documents. Jones threatened to smear Elmer as a child molester. The Mertles responded by threatening to take lurid tales of the meetings of the Planning Commission to the press. Eventually they had to change their names and deposited documents damaging to the Temple and sworn affidavits charging Jones with all manner of indecent behaviour in a safe-deposit box to ensure their safety.

After they had left, Jones denounced the Mertles as traitors who abandoned building up a better world for worldly pleasures. They had sold out their brothers and sisters, Jones told his followers, 'for a pocketful of credit cards and a fancy car'.

That same year, Jones was named 'Humanitarian of the Year' by the *Los Angeles Herald-Examiner* and the Foundation for Religion in America picked him as one of their '100 Outstanding Clergymen in America'. On Memorial Day 1977, Jim Jones was invited to speak at an anti-suicide rally in San Francisco. The purpose of the rally was to get the city fathers to construct an anti-suicide barrier along the Golden Gate Bridge – a favourite jumping off point for the depressed and disturbed. Although Jones's speech began with stern moral disapproval of suicide – suddenly, half-way through, he changed course. His condemnation of suicide became a blanket endorsement for it.

Jones had first mentioned the idea of 'revolutionary suicide' to Grace Stoen in 1973. At that time, he only planned for his followers to die. He said he would stay alive to explain why they had done it. In 1976, he began to put his plan into practice. On New Year's Day, he coerced his followers into drinking what he told them was poison. He railed against the 'traitors' who had left the Temple and told the congregation that, if they loved him, they could only prove it by drinking the poison. Some became hysterical. But after the mock shooting of a member who tried to run away, Jones's followers meekly did what they were told. Forty-five minutes later, he told them that the 'poison' was innocuous. They thanked him for testing them. This was the first of a series of suicide rehearsals that Jones called 'white nights'. Each time the congregation were told they were swallowing poison – and they could never be sure that they were not. But gradually they got used to the idea of laying down their life for 'Dad' – who by now was claiming to be God, or at the very least from another planet like Superman. At the same time, Jones gave up all belief in Christianity, even hurling his bible to the ground during a sermon to reinforce his point.

Then things started going wrong for the Temple. *New West* magazine published an article attacking Jones. Once free, the Mertles dedicated themselves to fighting the Temple. They told the *New West* reporter about the sexual and physical abuse they had witnessed. The magazine unearthed evidence of extortion, embezzlement and blackmail. Jones had begun diverting into off-shore investments. The article also outlined Grace Stoen's relationship with Jones.

Grace had run away from the Temple some time before. Now she began suing for the return of her son. Jones was determined she should not have him – he was one of the new breed that Jones was determined would inherit the earth. Tim Stoen was still Jones's legal adviser. He told Jones that there was no point in fighting Grace through the courts. They were bound to return John-John to his natural mother – especially when Grace and the Mertles outlined Jones's bizarre sexual practices from the witness box. There was only one way that Jones could hold on to John-John. That was to take him abroad. Fighting for custody in a foreign court could be strung out for years – perhaps forever. Jones knew exactly where to go.

231

Seven years after his first fleeting visit to Guyana in 1963, Jones went back with his plans of building a Utopia there. The Guyanese government were immediately receptive. An underdeveloped country, they welcomed any scheme that would bring in foreign capital – especially from a source as politically sympathetic as Jim Jones. Jones's proposal of clearing the jungle and turning the virgin land over to agriculture also coincided with Guyanese development aims. The land they leased him was along the Venezuelan border in an area that had long been disputed. Establishing a large colony of Americans there would prevent the Venezuelan army annexing the region and would provide the Guyanese government with documentation establishing that it belonged to them. Guyana was also perfect from Jones's perspective. Although the majority of the people in the country are ethnically East Indian, Guyana has had a socialist government run by blacks of African origin ever since it was granted independence by Britain in 1966.

In 1974, Jones paid $1 million for 27,000 acres of jungle in Guyana. In 1976, it was still an experimental agricultural outpost, but in 1977 large amounts of building materials were shipped up the river to nearby Port Kaituma. Some 380 Templars applied for visas and headed for Guyana. John-John was among them. The next year, another 700 set off. The entry fee to Jones's Utopia was everything they owned or earned. Many chose to pay it. Others had no choice. An unknown number of children – perhaps as many as 150 – were handed over to the Temple, along with their welfare cheques, by probation officers and the welfare agencies in Ukiah and San Francisco. Briefly free from the discipline of Jones, Templars went wild. They got drunk in the grog shops of Georgetown. The party continued on the boat up river. One teenage girl, full of rum, had a brief fling with one of the Guyanese boatmen. Jones was furious. Once inside the compound at Jonestown, iron discipline was enforced. Casual sexual encounters were banned – and the Relationship Committee enforced three months' celibacy on any couple applying to have a serious relationship. Such prohibitions did not apply to Jones himself of course. He moved into a hut with two of his mistresses while his wife lived nearby. One young girl who refused his advances was forcibly drugged and taken from the Jonestown hospital to Jones's hut each night. And when one member, Debbie Blakely, left, Jones confessed that her defection was his fault – it was because he refused to have sex with her. She wanted bourgeois sex – for pleasure! For him, sex was a political act.

Those who found favour with Jones were given special privileges. The Jonestown doctor who supported Jones's claim that non-revolutionary sex caused cancer was indulged with a succession of teenage girls. Beatings were commonplace for minor offences or simply because Jones thought the offender's 'head was between their legs' – that is, they were thinking of sex rather than socialist work. He was especially hard on any male who was interested in a girl he fancied. Adults were caned, or forced to fight each other until 'right triumphed', or simply beaten into bloody submission. Children were especially harshly treated, even for minor breaches of discipline. They were taken before a microphone at 2 a.m. and beaten – as many as seventy-five times – with a board while their cries echoed from the PA system around the compound. One was buried in a metal box for twenty-four hours. Others were lowered down a well, where they were pulled into the water by a waiting assistant.

Meanwhile, Jones became increasingly paranoid. He claimed to have killed a burglar breaking into his hut and served the man's flesh up in a stew for his followers. While his followers toiled in the fields from sun-up to sundown, Jones stayed in his hut taking drugs and monitoring the news from San Francisco and the Temple's outpost in Georgetown. He controlled the Templars' listening and doctored all news from the outside world. He claimed that Jonestown was about to be attacked by a force of mercenaries trained by the CIA who were mustering in a staging area across the Brazilian border. Armed guards were posted around the compound, ostensibly to protect the Templars from attack. In fact, they were to stop disaffected Templars escaping.

However, the members who had left the People's Temple in America – traitors, Jones called them – could not be controlled. They had told the press bizarre tales of the goings-on in Guyana. The bisexual Jones sexually dominated his flock, they claimed. He had forced them into gruelling manual labour in appalling physical conditions. They were disciplined in humiliating rituals and were not allowed to leave. A support group, the Committee of Concerned Relatives, had been formed. One of these relatives, Sam Houston, a journalist with Associated Press, accused the cult of murdering his son. He had left the Temple after a violent argument with Jones. The next day he had died in a grisly railroad accident near the waterfront in San Francisco. One of Houston's drinking buddies was Congressman Leo Ryan. Several of the Temple's members came from Ryan's congressional district in south San Francisco. Houston persuaded Ryan to investigate the sect and find out what was going on in the Temple's South American settlement, Jonestown.

On 24 October 1978, Ryan received authorisation from the US House of Representatives' Foreign Affairs Committee to go to Guyana. With legal action pending which threatened to cut off the sect's American funds, Jones had no choice but to comply. However, Jones tried to lay down conditions. He would not allow Ryan into Jonestown if he brought any 'traitors' or the press with him. The feisty congressman would have none of this. He turned up in Guyana with four members of the Committee of Concerned Relatives, reporters and photographers from the San Francisco dailies and the *Washington Post*, and an NBC film crew. If he was not allowed into Jonestown, Ryan informed Jones, a film of him being turned away would be shown on NBC's network, coast to coast across America. A full-scale congressional investigation was sure to follow.

On the afternoon of 17 November, Ryan's party flew to the airstrip at Port Kaituma, a few miles from Jonestown. They were picked up by one of Jones's adopted sons, Johnny. Congressman Ryan, the relatives and the party of journalists entered Jonestown just before sunset on the back of the Jonestown dump truck. The reception was surprisingly friendly. Although Jones retired scowling to his hut, sect members had been instructed to smile. Dinner was served at eight and, afterwards, the Jonestown band began to play. Congressman Ryan made a speech. It was pure political genius. He told the Templars how much he enjoyed the band and that Jonestown looked like a pretty nice place to live.

'From what I have seen,' said Ryan, 'there are a lot of people who believe this is the best thing that ever happened to them.'

There was only one thing wrong with Jonestown, he said – it wasn't in his congressional district so its members couldn't vote for him.

The Templars who, despite their smiles and Sunday-meeting clothes were deeply resentful of outside interference, broke into spontaneous applause. The tension was broken. The band struck up again. The young people took to the dance floor. The older ones joined in clapping. Everyone seemed happy. But as the dance floor emptied that night a young black woman, Monica Bagby, passed a note to NBC journalist Don Harris. It asked him to arrange for her and her friend Vern Gosney to leave Jonestown with Congressman Ryan the next day.

The next morning things really started falling apart. At daybreak, nine sect members seized their chance to escape. They set off through the jungle towards the village of Matthew's Ridge, some twenty miles away. Dodging the official tour of Jonestown, some journalists began poking around on their own – almost provoking a riot. And Don Harris began interviewing Jones on camera. Jones talked openly about his mistresses and denied press reports that there was any ban on sexual intercourse among his followers. It was 'bullshit', he said. 'Thirty babies have been born since the summer of 1977.'

But this was not the smooth polyester-suited Jim Jones who had charmed politicians in California, dined with the President's wife Rosalynn Carter and flown in the private jet of Presidential hopeful Walter Mondale. He was fat, pale and sweaty. After only a few minutes of persistent questioning Jones began to crack.

'The only thing I regret is that somebody hasn't shot me,' he ranted. 'We're a small community, we're no threat to anyone, but they won't rest until they destroy us. I wish they would just shoot me and get it over with. But I guess the media smear is what they use now – in the long run it's as good as assassination.'

Other reporters began pressing Jones about John-John, who Jones still refused to return to his mother. By this time Tim Stoen had also defected from the People's Temple and was reconciled with his wife. Together they were trying to get John-John back. But as Stoen had so accurately predicted, the case was stalled in the Guyanese courts.

Reporters asked why the Jonestown security guards carried weapons and why threats were made to those who wanted to leave.

'It's all lies,' responded Jones wearily. But immediately he was caught in a lie. One of his henchmen brought news that Edith Parks, the grandmother of a family that had been planning to escape for some time, had asked Congressman Ryan to be taken out. Jones went to see them.

'I am betrayed,' he wailed. 'It never stops.'

Seizing their opportunity, another twenty people asked Ryan to take them with him. Jones, by this time, was hysterical: 'I've given my life for my people,' he cried.

Aides calmed him down and persuaded Jones to let them go. Such a small number of defections – thirty compared to the thousand who stayed – was not important. Even so, the atmosphere in Jonestown began to turn ugly. As the defectors left, a husky young man in his late twenties, Don Sly, pulled a knife from his pocket and grabbed Congressman Ryan. Two of Jones's aides, pulled Sly off, cutting his arm in the process. The blood spurted over Ryan.

At the last moment, another defector, Larry Layton, announced that he was 'pissed off with Jonestown' and joined the departing party. The early defectors were terrified. Layton was known as Jones's 'robot', the strictest of his security guards. Layton was searched before he boarded the plane at Port Kaituma. But somehow he had managed to smuggle a gun on board. Before the plane could take off, the Jonestown tractor turned up, blocking the runway. In its trailer there were twenty armed men. Inside the plane Layton started shooting, hitting Monica Bagby in the chest. The men from the trailer then opened up. Three of the defectors were hit. Out on the runway, Congressman Ryan and three of the NBC crew including Don Harris were caught in a hail of bullets. Once they were down, the Jonestown gunmen made sure they were dead with a shot in the head as they lay on the ground. Three other journalists were wounded. Then the tractor and trailer pulled away.

Meanwhile, back at Jonestown, Jim Jones called his followers together. He sat on his crude wooden throne, surrounded by nearly a thousand of his followers. He had bad news for them. They were about to die. He explained that one of their number, Larry Layton, had shot the pilot of Ryan's plane in the head and the plane had crashed in the jungle. That had been the original plan. The twenty men on the trailer were sent in case anything went wrong. Jones said that the CIA would force the left-wing government in Georgetown to send soldiers of the Guyanese Defence Force against them. These soldiers were their black socialist brothers. They could not fight back. The only answer was a solution they had long prepared – they should all kill themselves. One of the Templars asked whether it was not too late to escape to the Soviet Union. The Russians would not take them now, said Jones, though he had already despatched two of his henchmen to the Soviet Embassy in Georgetown with a suitcase containing half-a-million dollars in cash.

Jonestown medical staff prepared two fifty gallon drums of Kool-Aid, laced with Valium and cyanide. His followers were well prepared. Jones assured them that they would 'meet again in another place'. The Templars queued up in an orderly fashion. Mothers gave the cyanide to their children. Infants had it squirted in their mouths from a syringe. Even Jones's own children were happy to take the poison. The congregation had long been told that swallowing the poison would lead to a painless death. But when the children went into convulsions, panic broke out. Jones managed to calm the congregation.

'They are not crying out of pain,' he said, 'it's just a little bitter-tasting.' So the adults calmly took their poison from paper cups. They went out into the fields and lay down and died. Then came the turn of the armed guards. They too took their poison without resistance. When they were all dead, Jones took a pistol and blew his brains out. Annie Moore, one of Jonestown's nurses, shot herself in the head with the same gun moments later.

The only note that was found was a ghoulish tape-recording of that final meeting and the grisly mass suicide Jones himself had made. It did little to help explain to a shocked world how a charismatic leader had driven over 900 people to kill themselves. On the tape, Jones can be heard reassuring his followers: 'I don't care how many screams you hear ... how many anguished cries; death is a million times preferable ... Take the potion like they used to take it in ancient Greece. It is a revolutionary act.'

The children particularly were anxious.

'Can some people assure these children of the relaxation of stepping over into the next plane?' Jones says.

But despite the fact that he is committing mass murder, Jones is full of self-pity.

'The world was not ready for me,' he laments. 'The best testimony we can make is to leave the goddamn world.'

When the Guyanese army first arrived in Jonestown, they estimated that there were only about six hundred dead. It was hard to tell as bodies were piled on bodies.

And like most ordinary Guyanese they were not really interested in the new settlers and left them to their own devices. There had been two Guyanese soldiers at Port Kaituma when the shooting started. They did nothing to defend Congressman Ryan and his party. They later said that if two lots of crazy Americans wanted to shoot each other, what business was it of theirs? Ten days after the shooting, a US army mortuary team arrived at Jonestown. It was only then that the death toll was finally fixed at 914. Among the dead was Grace Stoen's son, John-John.

The mortuary team and the Guyanese coroner Dr Leslie Mootoo examined the bodies for blisters on their upper arms. They were looking for evidence that the cyanide had been administered forcibly to unwilling victims. But, with the exception of a few feeble old people, there were no signs of telltale blisters. Although the crowd of followers had been ringed by armed guards, they did not seem to need to coerce the Templars into killing themselves. In fact, the victims seemed not just willing but eager to drink the poison. According to one witness, the first victim, Ruletta Paul walked up to the dais with her child and took the cyanide without even being asked.

'She just poured it down the baby's throat. And then she took the rest herself,' said one witness. 'It didn't take them right away. She had time to walk outside . . . then the next woman, Michelle Wilson, she came up with her baby and did the same thing.'

And when Jones radioed to the office in Georgetown that liaised with the Guyanese government and instructed them to commit suicide too, the Temples's public relations officer took her three small children into the bathroom, killed them, then slit her own wrists. The other failed to follow suit.

But although the deaths seem to be voluntary, Jones had spent years cowing his followers into total submission. Not only would they do whatever he said, they would anticipate what he wanted and do it before he even asked. Had he lived, it would have been hard for Jim Jones to have denied responsibility for those who gulped down cyanide – and gave it to their children – at his behest.

But not everyone perished. The day after the massacre, Guyanese soldiers entering Jonestown found two survivors. Grover Davis was hard of hearing and missed the summons to the pavilion. When he finally went to see what was happening, he saw the first children in their death throes. He hid in a dry well. The next morning he climbed out and went back to his hut to sleep. He woke when the soldiers arrived and was nearly shot. They thought that he was a corpse coming back to life again. The other survivor, Hyacinth Thrush, slept through the whole thing. She was frail and bedridden and when her breakfast did not turn up the next morning she hobbled outside to find out what was happening. By the time she had reached the door, the terrible smell explained everything. Later she said that she was sorry to have missed the opportunity to die with her brothers and sisters.

Others escaped. One of them was Odell Rhodes who had been a heroin addict when he first encountered the People's Temple. They had turned his life around. They got him off drugs and put him in charge of the children. He became a teacher and for the first time had some status in life. He was happy to go to Guyana. When he heard that the CIA was going to attack he did not mind fighting and dying for the Temple. He was a Vietnam veteran. But he got fed up with the nightly meetings. After a long day in the fields he could not stand the hysteria, the sermonising, the sexual humiliation and the white nights. So he volunteered to work in the nursing cottage, which allowed him to skip the meetings. Not being as indoctrinated as the others, he was not prepared to take the poison.

At the final meeting, Rhodes found himself at the front – unable to move without drawing attention to himself. He was shocked how easily others took the poison. When the children started dying he volunteered to go to the hospital to get a stethoscope. He slipped out the back way and out into the jungle. When he reached Port Kaituma, he found it difficult to convince the police that everyone at Jonestown was dead. But eventually they put him on the phone to Georgetown, where a sceptical police inspector said he would be down the next morning with the army.

Another escapee was Stanley Clayton. He was working in the kitchen that evening, when he was told to forget about dinner. There had been white nights before, but no one had ever said forget about dinner before. When he reached the pavilion, he saw the children dying. But he was not prepared to take his own life because a few people had left the Temple. He would rather risk getting a bullet in the back. He pretended that he was looking for someone, slipped around the backs of the guards and made off into the jungle. He found a nearby house and told the occupants what had happened. They did not believe him. But when he said that they would be able to help themselves to the tools and supplies in Jonestown, they decided to check out what he was saying. They came back with arms full of stolen goods and a glazed look of horror in their eyes. When Clayton finally made it into town, he was arrested. News of the massacre had gone out and it was rumoured that one of Jones's last acts was to send out assassination squads. It was thought that Clayton was one of them.

Others survived because they were away from Jonestown at the time. One of them was Jones's nineteen-year-old son Stephan. He cannot forgive his father for what happened.

'I can almost say I hate the man. He has destroyed everything I have to live for,' he said.

There was a final, terrible irony in Jim Jones's death. Despite the fact that his father was a member of the Klu-Klux-Klan, Jim Jones had spent his whole life fighting against racial prejudice. He established his ministry in the ghettos and preached largely to black people. Until the People's Temple, it was rare to see black and white people worship together in America. In black ghettos, he got junkies off the street, helped unmarried black mothers, educated black children, helped house black people and provided day-care centres and food kitchens for black inner-city residents. He and his wife adopted eight Korean and black children. He saw himself as a great revolutionary leader in the mould of Martin Luther King and Malcolm X. To identify more closely with his black congregation, he claimed to have Cherokee Indian blood that gave him his swarthy complexion. But when the bodies were found, the cyanide had turned the skin of even his white followers black, while Jones, who had shot himself, had turned a deathly white.

Even with Jones dead, his followers were not safe. After the Jonestown Massacre, the Mertles and their teenage daughter were found murdered. No one has been caught and the police have no suspects and no active leads. Although the police say they have no reason to believe that their murders had anything to do with the People's Temple, other defectors do. Many have lived for many years in fear of the Temple's assassination squads.

Only one person went to trial for complicity in the Jonestown Massacre. It was thirty-five-year-old ex-Quaker Larry Layton. Extradited to the United States, he was charged with injuring US diplomat Richard Dwyer and conspiracy to kill Congressman Ryan. But the jury in San Francisco could not reach a verdict and the judge declared a mistrial.

Jim Jones's People's Temple was not the only weird and wonderful apocalyptic sect in America at the time – far from it. But others tend to be further to the right in the political spectrum. One of them was the Gospel Doctrine Church of Jesus Christ, the religious wing of a group called Posse Comitatus.

Posse Comitatus started in 1969 in Portland, Oregon. Its founder was retired dry-cleaning shop owner Henry L. Beach. During the 1930s, he was a member of the American Nazi group known as the silver shirts and believed that the Federal Government was part of an international Jewish conspiracy. Members of Posse Comitatus – which means 'power of the country' in Latin – took pride in opposing the government at every turn. They refused to carry drivers' licences or pay income tax. Throughout the Midwest in the late 1970s and early 1980s – when the collapse of farming was being laid at the door of the Federal Reserve Board – Posse Comitatus recruited followers throughout the farming states of the Midwest. And when the Japanese cars drove the US auto industry off the road, they turned their attention to Detroit where auto workers were being laid off in droves. With branches in twenty-three states, Posse Comitatus had an estimated following of over 20,000.

One member, a struggling farmer named George Kahl, came to Posse Comitatus by way of a religious group called Christian Identity. They believed that the Anglo-Saxon people were the lost tribe of Israel and they were involved in an apocalyptic struggle with the children of Satan – who just happened to turn out to be the Jews. Kahl believed that only white Christian males should have the vote and when he got married to a local farm girl, Joan Seil, he gave her as a wedding present a double-barrelled shotgun.

When he joined Posse Comitatus, he set up his own church, called the Gospel Doctrine Church of Jesus Christ. His eldest son, Yorie, was appointed its bishop and ran the church while his father was in jail for eight months for refusing to pay his income tax. He was paroled on the promise that he would pay up in future. This jail term made Kahl something of a hero and he went on a preaching tour of the Midwest. This did not amuse the authorities, especially as Kahl was still not paying up the taxes he owed. A warrant was issued for his arrest. Local police set up a road block to detain Kahl, but their efforts resulted in a shoot-out, during which Kahl's son Yorie was hit. Kahl injured two policemen and killed two more. One of them was shot twice in the head at point blank-range after already being injured and incapacitated during the exchange of gunfire. The survivors of the shoot-out were

243

taken to the medical centre in nearby Medina, North Dakota. After checking on the condition of his son, Kahl complained to the wounded policeman that they could have talked this matter over without a shoot-out. Then he stole a police car and disappeared.

While on the run, Kahl wrote to Posse members claiming that he had shot only in self-defence and was a victim of persecution by the 'Jewish-Masonic-Communist Synagogue of Satan'.

The struggle, Kahl wrote, was 'between the people of the Kingdom of God and the Kingdom of Satan'. The Jews, he said, were out to destroy Christianity and the white race. Across the Midwest he soon became a hero.

Eventually he was cornered in the Ozark mountains on the Missouri-Arkansas border, with a commune of survivalist families, numbering around a hundred, who believed the apocalypse was at hand. They called themselves the Covenant of the Sword and Arm of the Lord, which was the new paramilitary wing of Christian Identity. The FBI led the assault, but local sheriff Gene Matthews beat them into the small house where Kahl had taken refuge. In the resulting shoot-out, they were both killed. Then a tear-gas grenade hit the stove, which ignited some diesel fuel – the cabin went up in flames. Sheriff Matthews' body was rescued from the burning building, but Kahl's corpse had to be dug out of the ashes.

His family held a funeral service where Kahl was eulogised as a great American patriot along the lines of George Washington. Meanwhile, Posse members spread the rumours that Kahl was not dead. He had escaped the burning house and was now in hiding, they said.

The Covenant of the Sword and Arm of the Lord issued death threats to the judge who tried those who had harboured Kahl, though the hit squad despatched to finish him off was involved in a traffic accident on the way and the mission was cancelled. And Christian Identity spawned another armed offshoot called the Order – known to its members as *Bruder Schweigen* or the Silent Brotherhood.

Four members machine-gunned to death Denver talk-show host Alan Berg, a Jewish liberal, in June 1984.

The American Christian Movement for Life – more commonly known as Move – could not have been more different. It was a black group that equated satanic influence with 'the system'. It was headed by Vincent Leaphart, a middle-aged black man from West Philadelphia, who called himself John Africa. A high-school drop-out, Leaphart could barely read or write. But with white middle-class college lecturer Donald J. Glassey, he wrote a three-hundred-page diatribe called *The Teachings of John Africa*, known to followers simply as 'The Book'.

The two men met on a protest march in the early 1970s. In 1973, Leaphart established a commune in Glassey's house in the gentrified Powelton Village area of Philadelphia. By 1975, the commune had swelled to around thirty-five people – adults and children – and an unspecified number of cats and dogs. The group began protesting, but no one could tell what they were protesting about and the slogans they chanted were largely incoherent. Nevertheless, they managed to disrupt a bicentennial meeting of the governors of the thirteen original states of the Union. Donald Glassey quit the group, complaining of their growing talk of violence. He did not get his house back though.

Members of Move all adopted the surname 'Africa'. The men gave themselves ostentatious titles such as Minister for Information and Minister of Defence. Women on the other hand got no such exalted positions. They were there to propagate a new wave of Move supporters. According to Leaphart's back-to-nature manifesto, after giving birth, they were supposed to cut their umbilical cord with their own teeth and clean the baby with their tongue.

Leaphart and his bizarre philosophy controlled every element of his followers' lives and group solidarity was instilled at all-night meetings. The neighbours began to complain. The household was grossly overcrowded. It generated a huge amount of garbage that no one ever seemed to clear up. Huge herds of dogs and cats roamed around and naked toddlers wandered in and out seemingly at will. The place was becoming a public nuisance. The police were called, but there was little they could do.

The hostility of the neighbours increased the level of paranoia among the members of Move. They built a high security fence around the house and mounted loudspeakers outside so they could taunt the police. They even boasted that they were building an atomic bomb. This led to inevitable scuffles – followed by the charge issued over the booming PA system that the police had broken into the house and beaten a child to death. While the police vehemently denied the charge, Leaphart invited community leaders and the press to the house. They were shown the dead body of a child, decaying on a bed of garbage. The child had died earlier of natural causes, but at the time it was a propaganda coup.

Arrested for the possession of marijuana, Donald Glassey revealed that Move were in the business of making bombs and led the police to a number of stockpiles. Under hardline Mayor Frank Rizzo, former police chief and scourge of the Black Panthers, the police were forced to act. They surrounded the house, while Move members appeared in combat fatigues, brandishing rifles and shotguns. While Rizzo made plans to storm the house, Move used the PA system to taunt him. When the police did go in, they found Move members holding babies and children as shields. Meanwhile, one policeman was shot dead, while three other policemen and four firemen were wounded. Move members were arrested and, on Rizzo's orders, the house was bulldozed to the ground. Charges resulting from the shoot-out put nine Move members behind bars for life. But Leaphart was not one of them. He had slipped out of the house before the bullets had started flying.

The remaining Move members scattered and Leaphart took refuge with them. Three years later, in 1981, the police caught up with him in Richmond, Virginia. He stood trial for firearms charges that had been outstanding since the Philadelphia siege in 1978, but was acquitted. Leaphart moved into his sister's house in Philadelphia and began building up the commune again. Soon the situation was much like it had been before the shoot-out in 1978. But this time, the windows of the house had been boarded up and a pill box was being built on the roof. Neighbours again complained about the filth and the noise from the loudspeakers mounted on the outside of the house. And when a man armed with a shotgun appeared on the roof, the police decided it was time to act.

Undeterred by the fact that no one had actually broken any laws, the police surrounded the house in force. They were taunted day and night by the loudspeakers. On 8 August, the anniversary of the 1978 shoot-out, more than three hundred policemen and fire-fighters were camped out around Move's new headquarters. The police maintained a siege of the house for eight months. They watched as Move members brought out the spoil from the reinforced bunker they were now excavating in the cellar. But, doubting the legality of any direct assault on the house, the new mayor, Wilson Goode, an African-American, stayed the police's hand. Meanwhile the city's press demanded action. The political pressure became irresistible. The authorities tried negotiation. Move conceded they 'wanted out', but then demanded the release of all Move members sentenced after the 1978 siege. This was not possible. The police then had no choice. They had to storm the house. The only question was how.

One plan to blast the house with high-pressure hoses had already been rejected as there were children in the house. A tear-gas generator had been brought in. Plans were made to breach the walls to the adjoining houses, which had already been evacuated, and pump the tear-gas in. But the police did not know whether Move members had already broken through and were lying in wait for them. Even if they hadn't, the police did not consider that the internal walls offered sufficient protection against any high-powered weapons Move members may have. The roof seemed a better option. But with the pill box up there now complete, scaling it was out of the question.

Move then started issuing threats. If the police came in, they would set the house on fire. They would burn but the police would burn with them and a lot of the neighbours would 'get fucked up', they said. If Move went down, the whole block would go down. The rumour spread that Move had been laying bombs in the underground excavations they were making. Police negotiators begged the authorities for one more chance. After all, the people in the house had done nothing and simply killing them would be unlawful and wrong. There was another round of dialogue. But Move were immovable. They said: 'Come in and get us.'

As the Move loudspeakers continued to taunt the police and threaten death to anyone who approached the house, the authorities evacuated the surrounding houses. Police sharpshooters sheltered behind sandbags as fire-engines drove into position. Police Commissioner Gregory Sambor again gave Move one last chance to give themselves up. They had fifteen minutes to come out with their hands up. Move's response was the suggestion that the police personnel check their life assurance, reminding them that one policeman had lost his life in 1978.

At 6 a.m. on 13 May 1985, the battle began. High-pressure fire hoses were turned on the roof-top pill box. It withstood the blast. Tear-gas grenades lobbed into the compound drew automatic fire. In the house next door, the police started drilling in the wall. Move members fired through the wall and the police responded with machine guns. An explosive charge was laid, but it was not enough to breach the wall. A second explosion made a small hole, but the tear-gas generator broke down. The police broke through the adjoining wall at the other side of the house more easily. They threw in tear-gas grenades. But when they followed them through, one man was hit by gunfire. His flak-jacket saved his life, but when news filtered back up the chain of command the action was called off. The guns fell quiet at around 7.20 a.m. Already the police had loosed off over 10,000 rounds of ammunition and they were no further forward. Mayor Goode held his head in his hands. The battle for the Move headquarters was going out on live television.

The police were at a loss what to do. They called up a crane and wrecking ball to knock the house down. But the crane would not get down the narrow street and the Commissioner was not overwhelmed with volunteers who wanted to operate it. The stand-off continued for the rest of the day. Members of the families of Move members were put on the bull horn and begged their loved ones to come out. There was no response. Soon after 5 p.m., the fateful decision was made. They were going to bomb the building. This was unprecedented. Never before had the American civil authorities dropped a bomb on a city. The idea was to dislodge the roof-top pill box, blow a hole in the roof and pump in tear-gas. But the police sadly misjudged their mission. They packed a bag with a commercial explosive used in mining and, at around 5.30 p.m., they dropped it from a helicopter on to the roof of the house.

The explosion sent wreckage flying ten metres into the air. Some of the huge crowd that had gathered cheered. But the cheers were mixed with cries of horror. The authorities are bombing babies, people said. When the dust cleared, the pill box was still standing. The explosive had not been powerful enough. But worse, explosives used in mining created an enormous amount of heat – enough to melt rock and certainly enough to set a house on fire. Soon flames were leaping a hundred feet into the air. But the firefighters could not move in because the Move members kept up a withering barrage of fire. Police snipers tried to pick off the gunmen they saw silhouetted against the flames. At the back of the house, a thirty-year-old woman and a thirteen-year-old boy managed to escape. They were badly burned but the police could not move in to help them. Eventually, when the police had laid down intense covering fire, they were rescued and arrested. They were the only two that got out alive.

By the time the fire brigade got the fire under control at midnight, the entire block had burned down and the fire had spread to adjoining streets. In all, nearly sixty houses were gutted. In the cellar of the Move headquarters, among the charred remains of dogs and children, the police eventually found what they were looking for – the body of John Africa.

Another black radical named Hulon Mitchell Junior formed a murderous cult in 1981. Satan to Hulon Mitchell – who renamed himself Yahweh Ben Yahweh – was the white race. But the people he picked out for special venom, like right-wing racist Gordon Kahl, were the Jews and their 'synagogue of Satan'.

Mitchell was born in the segregated town of Kingfisher, Oklahoma in 1935. After leaving high school, he joined the Air Force, then used his service entitlements to take a BA in psychology. Like every young American heading for the top, Mitchell went on to law school, but he soon became involved in the racial politics of the time. He dropped out and moved to Chicago where he joined the Black Muslims. Like Malcolm X, he dropped his 'slave name' and became Hulon Shah. But his racial views were too violent even for the Black Muslims and he was expelled.

Mitchell moved slowly south under various religious guises – Father Michel, Brother Moses. Though his religious affiliations changed as often as he changed name and address, one thing remained the same – the white man was the Devil. When he reached Miami, Mitchell took, ironically, the Hebrew name Yahweh Ben Yahweh – God, Son of God – and founded the Temple of Love in a supermarket that had been burnt out in the 1980 race riots. His message was simple. Black people's nobility had been stolen by the satanic white race. This was expressed most clearly in the Temple's pamphlet 'You Are Not a Nigger – The World's Best Kept Secret'. The twin themes of Black pride and retribution hit a chord with both the dispirited and dispossessed in the ghetto and the nascent Black middle class.

Mitchell had already learned to dress up his simple message with theatrics. He surrounded himself with staff-wielding bodyguards who were swathed in white robes. Yahweh Ben Yahweh himself wore a turban and an outfit covered in jewels. And to increase the sense of paranoia, the supermarket temple was turned into a fortress. All went swimmingly at first. The sect used minority-enterprise loans and preferential government contracts to set up businesses. They opened shops and a school. Drug houses were taken over and turned into residences for the Temple of Love. However, there was a dark side to this very positive initiative. The Temple's elite, called the Circle of Ten, strictly enforced discipline. Members had to give up their individual surnames and take the name Israel instead. And Yahweh Ben Yahweh had the pick of the women, some as young as fourteen.

Dissent was forbidden and defectors hounded. As early as 1981, just two years after the Temple of Love was formed, the mutilated, headless corpse of former Temple of Love member Aston Green was found in a field. Apparently, when Green had told Yahweh Ben Yahweh that he wanted to leave, he was beaten. Then he was bound and gagged and taken to the field where he was beheaded with a machete. Green's two flatmates told the police that they suspected Green had been executed by Temple of Love members to prevent him leaving. When they returned home they were shot and slashed with swords by men wearing balaclavas. Only one of them survived. The police had other evidence that linked the killings to the Temple of Love, but no one at the Temple would talk. Besides, like Jim Jones before him, Yahweh Ben Yahweh was building up powerful political friends.

In 1983, twenty-two-year-old Leonard Dupree was beaten to death in the temple after a dispute with a woman member. Yahweh Ben Yahweh watched and ordered Dupree's body to be dumped in the Florida Everglades. Several witnesses had the courage to go to the police. But this time the police could do nothing. It is hard to bring a murder charge without a corpse.

In the mid-1980s, the Temple of Love were in all-out war with local drug dealers. The followers of Yahweh Ben Yahweh started petrol-bombing drug dealers' homes, while Yahweh Ben Yahweh himself calmly told the *New York Times*: 'I am the Messiah, I am the Word. I am incarnate.'

The Temple of Love then decided to increase its property empire. It took over a run-down apartment block and ordered the tenants – who were black – to leave. When some refused, Yahweh's praetorian guard turned up with clubs. Two men were beaten and decapitated. A Temple-member calling himself Neariah Israel was arrested and charged with the murders. He claimed to be over four hundred years old. In fact, he turned out to be thirty-three-year-old former professional American football player Robert Rozier.

While Rozier rotted in jail, Yahweh Ben Yahweh excommunicated him. This gave the District Attorney a chance to cut a deal with him. In exchange for his life, Rozier gave detailed information on how the sect was organised. He told the police how Yahweh Ben Yahweh had an inner circle of followers called the Brotherhood. The price of admission was the murder of a white person. The proof required was an ear and Yahweh would often carry the ears around with him to show people. The spate of dead vagrants found with their ears missing had been puzzling the police for some time. After pleading guilty to four murders, Rozier was sentenced to twenty-two years in jail – instead of going to the electric chair. But still the authorities did not feel they had enough evidence to proceed against the Temple of Love.

In fact, following renewed rioting in Miami in 1989, Yahweh Ben Yahweh was being courted by politicians even more assiduously. With an empire of shops, apartment blocks and businesses worth over $9 million, he was

252

being exalted as a symbol of Black enterprise and in 1990 Miami Mayor Xavier Suarez designated 7 October 'Yahweh Ben Yahweh Day'. The man himself modestly proclaimed that he was 'the world's greatest attraction'.

But exactly a month later, Federal prosecutors charged Yahweh and fifteen of his inner circle with racketeering and conspiracy. The indictment also mentioned murder, firebombing and the sexual exploitation of minors. Yahweh Ben Yahweh was arrested in New Orleans, the handcuffs making a curious contrast with his gaudy robes. At the police station, he identified himself solely as the 'first begotten son of God'.

A SWAT team broke down the door of the Temple of Love and other members, including the financial mastermind Judith Israel, were arrested as far afield as Atlanta, Georgia, North Carolina and Louisiana. The remaining members of the sect accused the authorities of religious persecution. And they told the press that a number of natural disasters – fires, earthquakes, hurricanes and plagues of locusts – had been caused by Yahweh Ben Yahweh's arrest.

At the trial, the defence painted Yahweh Ben Yahweh as Ghandi, performing good works among the poor. But Yahweh was anything but humble. He announced that he was 'Grand Master of the Celestial Lodge' and 'Architect of the Universe'. He said he had known about the murders. But his followers had told him about them only after they had occurred, in the way of a confession – and he claimed the sanctity of the confessional. But sixty-three witnesses, including his own sister, testified that he had ordered killings, including that of Leonard Dupree.

Yahweh Ben Yahweh and six of his followers were found guilty of conspiracy to murder. The judge sentenced him to eighteen years in prison. The maximum sentence he could have imposed was twenty years but, he explained, he gave Yahweh two years off for the good works he had done in the community.

* * *

Mormonism seems like a cosy middle-class religion when clean-cut young men in polyester suits knock on your door. In fact, it is another apocalyptic faith. It preaches that the end of the world is at hand and that Satan and the righteous will be joined in battle at Armageddon. And there are those among its followers who would kill to that end.

The Church of Jesus Christ of the Latter Day Saints, as the Mormon Church is more properly known, is a uniquely American institution. It began in 1838, when Joseph Smith Jr dictated his account of the discovery of the Book of Mormon.

Smith was the son of an impoverished New England farmer. The area of upstate New York where he was born was called the 'burned-over district' because of its frequent religious revivals. At the age of fourteen, Smith claims to have had a vision of Christ while praying in the woods. Several years later, in 1827, he said he was visited by an angel named Moroni who gave him a book engraved in ancient hieroglyphs on gold plates. Smith translated the book, using special stones. The angel told him that the book had been 'delivered by the Saviour'. It told of how the lost tribe of Israel had moved to the New World and colonised it.

Though many of Smith's early followers left him, Mormonism grew. They moved to Kirtland, Ohio, where Smith established their first temple. Then they moved on to Missouri and Illinois. There Smith built the city of Nauvoo and became mayor and lieutenant general of the militia.

The Mormon's self-assurance in business and their practice of polygamy provoked hostility among non-Mormons. And Smith was arrested and murdered by Illinois militiamen in 1844. The Mormons then split. The majority followed Brigham Young to Utah where they built a settlement at Salt Lake City. The minority, including Smith's wife Emma and his son Joseph Smith III, stayed in the Midwest where they founded the Reorganised Church of Jesus Christ of the Latter Day Saints. Other splinter groups set up churches, including one in Kirtland, Ohio, established by David Whitmer and Martin Harris, two other men who claimed to have been witnesses to the golden plates.

Jeff Lundgren was a member of the Reorganised Church. Born in Independence, Missouri, in 1950, he developed an enthusiasm for the scriptures as a youth. At the age of twenty, he married a local girl named Alice. Like him, she was a religious fanatic and claimed that Satan had come to her bed while she was at summer camp. After their first son was born, Lundgren joined the US Navy and was posted to San Diego. But the young couple did not enjoy the relaxed lifestyle of California and formed a prayer group which Lundgren led.

Lundgren's ship was sent to Vietnam. The US Navy formed a firing line in the Gulf of Tonkin, giving artillery support to their ground troops ashore. As the Vietnamese navy consisted of little more than a couple of gunboats which were blockaded in the harbour at Haiphong, US ships were never under any serious threat. However, in 1972, a few shells fell in the water near Lundgren's ship. He was convinced that they were the work of Satan, but that God had protected him, sparing his life for some higher purpose.

After his discharge, the Lundgrens returned to Independence. By then he had four children who he supported by doing odd jobs and bouncing cheques. He was beginning to sense that he was a failure at everything he turned his hand to. Around that time the Reorganised Church of the Latter Day Saints was going through something of a crisis. Its activities were being swamped by those of the Utah branch and, in an attempt to broaden its appeal, it was proposed that women be allowed to become priests. This, Lundgren knew, was the work of Satan. He gathered around him a number of like-minded Mormons and together they prepared for Armageddon.

Studying his Book of Mormon, Lundgren read that he should 'go to Ohio ... there you shall be endowed with

255

power from on high'. And that is what he did. He and his family drove to Kirtland, Ohio, where he and Alice took jobs as tour guides at the Mormon temple. They rented a large farmhouse. Some of their followers from Independence moved there with them, taking jobs around town to help with the household expenses. Lundgren and his wife recruited more followers from among the visitors to the temple. They were invited to join the prayer group that Lundgren ruled with a rod of iron and some joined the commune at Lundgren's farmhouse.

Lundgren and his wife supported themselves by embezzling from the visitors' centre at the temple and used the money to build up a formidable arsenal of guns at the farm. Meanwhile Lundgren slowly became convinced that he was the eighth and last of the prophets of God and the great battle with Satan was going to be there in Kirtland. He put his group into paramilitary training, ready to storm the temple to wrest it back from the clutches of Satan.

Eventually it was discovered that the Lundgrens had been stealing and they were sacked. The elders of the temple also became concerned about the heretical ideas Lundgren was teaching in his prayer group and he was excommunicated. Lundgren's response was threats of death against the leaders of the Reorganised Church. But the bloodshed would occur closer to home.

With the income from the temple shut off, the group began to turn in on itself. For no real reason, Lundgren took a special dislike to Dennis Avery. He, his wife Cheryl and their three daughters had sold up in Independence to join Lundgren's commune. Lundgren expected the money from the sale of their house to be donated to the group – in other words, given to him. But the Averys only handed over half of it. The rest had gone to settle bills. The preparations to storm the temple were now nearing completion. But Lundgren insisted that only those without sin could take part. The Averys, he said, were not without sin.

Dennis and Cheryl Avery were offended by this. They withdrew from the nightly meetings Lundgren held in the draughty barn. This was a mistake. In their absence, Lundgren suggested a way they could atone for their sins. They would become a blood sacrifice. The plan was simple. The Averys would be slaughtered, then the righteous ones would head off into the wilderness where they would await a sign from God that they should begin their assault of the temple. To this end, Lundgren acquired a credit card and began buying camping equipment. The men in the group began digging a pit in the barn, then Lundgren invited the Averys around for dinner. They were delighted, thinking that the animosity between the two families was now over.

The evening was pleasant enough with the two families sitting around the large table talking and eating. Dennis Avery was still eating a second helping when Lundgren went out to the barn with the other men. Then one of them was sent in to tell Avery he was wanted in the barn. When he came through the door, he was grabbed. He was stunned with an electric stun gun. His mouth, arms and legs were taped. He fell to his knees as Lundgren put the gun to his chest and pulled the trigger twice. Then Cheryl was called. Her husband wanted to see her in the barn, she was told. She too was bound and gagged. Thrown into the pit on top of her husband's body, she was shot three times. Fifteen-year-old Trina was next. She was told it was a game when she was bound and blindfolded. But even with a shot in her head, she would not lie down. She was trying to clamber out of the pit when Lundgren shot her two more times in the back. The two youngest children were told they could go and see the horses in the barn – one at a time. Thirteen-year-old Rebecca clung to her mother's body as Lundgren shot her. And six-year-old Karen was sat on the edge of the pit and used as target practice before she toppled in dead with the rest of her family.

While other men in the group shovelled lime over the corpses, Lundgren went outside to pray. God, he soon decided, had found his sacrifices acceptable. And now that they had been cleansed of sin they could begin their divine mission.

As the group wandered from camp-site to camp-site, Lundgren discovered that he was Moses. He began to make sexual demands on all the women in the group. This was a relief for his wife Alice who had long been appalled by his perverted behaviour in the bedroom. He claimed that she was frigid. But she said he liked to tie her up and defecate on her breasts. He would masturbate with his own faeces and would dress up in women's clothing and demand to be 'raped' with a dildo. Slowly, people began defecting.

The police had long taken an interest in the goings-on at Lundgren's farm. And when the group suddenly disappeared they decided to investigate. They found the communal grave in the barn. A bulletin was sent out and soon the Lundgrens and their followers were in custody.

Defence counsel tried to present Lundgren as the victim of an abused childhood, but Lundgren insisted on declaring himself the prophet of God and threatening the jury with divine retribution. He was sentenced to the electric chair and is now on death row. Other members of the cult, including Lundgren's eldest son, were given long prison sentences. Lundgren's wife Alice claimed that she knew nothing of what was going on. She was convicted of conspiracy and sentenced to 150 years in jail.

Seventh Day Adventism is another apocalyptic religion. It was founded in the nineteenth century by former US Army officer William Miller. From his studies of the book of Daniel and the Book of Revelations, he worked out that Christ would make his Second Coming between 21 March 1843 and 21 March 1844. When Christ did not turn up between the appointed dates, Miller came up with a second date of 22 October 1844. His 100,000 followers, many of whom had sold up all their wordly goods, waited all night but Christ and his fiery conflagration did not turn up then either. This is known among Adventists as the 'Great Disappointment'. Miller himself was so disappointed he died four years later.

In 1845, the Adventists got together to figure out what to do next. The Mutual Conference of Adventists decided that Miller had indeed got the date right, but that his interpretation was off. In fact, God started 'cleansing the heavenly sanctuary' on that date – in other words, he was spring-cleaning heaven ready for the righteous to turn up. After that he would have to go through all the names in the Book of Life and investigate all the sins listed. Only after that would he make his judgement and send Christ back to Earth to separate the righteous from the wicked. So he could be some time yet. Meanwhile those Adventists who had already died were in a state of 'conditional immorality' awaiting the judgement when they would either be extinguished with the wicked or live forever on Earth under Christ's millenial reign.

Seventh Day Adventists also believed that celebrating the Sabbath as God ordained on the seventh day – that is, Saturday – rather than the first day – Sunday – would help speed the Second Coming. Refusing to work on Saturdays means that Seventh Day Adventists suffer some job discrimination.

One of the original Adventists who had suffered the Great Disappointment, Ellen Hamond White, found she had been given the gift of prophecy and was told by God to take the church to Australia, which she did in 1894. She introduced dietary laws that discourage the eating of meat and the intake of intoxicants. This leaves Seventh Day Adventists somewhat marginalised in the land of steaks, barbies and Fosters and was, no doubt, a contributing factor in the famous 'Dingo Baby Case'.

In August 1980, thirty-two-year-old Lindy Chamberlain and her thirty-six-year-old husband Michael, a Seventh Day Adventist parson, were on a camping holiday near Ayers Rock in central Australia when a dingo entered their tents and dragged away their baby, nine-week-old Azaria. Despite an extensive search, no trace of the baby could be found. However, at an inquest, the coroner ruled that the Chamberlains were not to blame and took the unprecedented step of allowing the TV cameras into his court-room to broadcast their innocence.

However, Ayers Rock is sacred to the Aborigines. At the base of it is the Cave of Fertility, said to be the birth passage of the world. The Rock is also a place of death, a burial ground guarded by stone warriors as the ancient ancestors sleep. The Australian public were intrigued by the child's name Azaria. It had an Old Testament ring to it and rumours circulated that it meant 'blood sacrifice'. The talk of Australian dinner tables was that Azaria was the product of an adulterous affair and had been killed in some bizarre religious rites at Ayers Rock. But search as they may, the newspapers could not find a single shred of evidence to that effect. However, the police did not give up. They contacted a forensic scientist in England, who had never even seen a dingo. He claimed that a dingo could not possibly make off with a child – despite the fact that twenty-seven attacks had been reported in the area, several on the night that baby Azaria went missing.

The finding of the first inquest was quashed. A second inquest recommended that Lindy and Michael Chamberlain be sent for trial. The trial of the Chamberlains' case was unique in the annals of modern murder trials. Here was a prosecution case where there was no body, no murder weapon, no eyewitness and no motive. In their opening statement, the Crown admitted that it was not even going to suggest a motive. But what prosecuting counsel Ian Barker QC did say attacked the very core of the defence case.

'The dingo story was a fanciful lie, calculated to conceal the truth,' he said.

Outside the court building, pretty girls wore T-shirts emblazoned with the slogan: 'The dingo is innocent.'

The trial turned into a battle between forensic scientists. The defence effectively shredded the prosecution case. They demonstrated that the prosecution's witnesses were mistaken and incompetent. Even the judge in his summing up said that the jury must allow for the possibility that a dingo had indeed taken the baby. The jury were out for just three hours. When they filed back, they found Lindy Chamberlain guilty of murder and Michael Chamberlain of being an accessory after the fact.

The next morning, the judge sentenced Michael to eighteen months hard labour, but under his powers as a judge in the North Territory he was able to suspend this sentence and bound Michael over for three years on a bond of $500. With Lindy though, he had no choice. For murder the sentence of life at hard labour was mandatory.

How did the jury make such a heinous mistake? An anonymous juryman explained later why they had reached such an astounding decision.

'It really came down to whether you believed it was the dingo or not,' he said. Plainly, the jury did not.

Lindy, who was eight months pregnant during the trial, went straight to Berrimah jail in Darwin where, less than three weeks later, she gave birth to a second daughter, Kahlia. The baby was taken from her after four hours and given into the care of Michael.

The defence were so shocked by the unexpected guilty verdict, they were ill-prepared for an appeal. There was little new they could say when the Federal Appeal Court convened in Sydney in February 1973. After a month's hearing and two months' deliberation, the three appeal judges unanimously rejected the appeal. In a final appeal to the High Court of Australia, the judges let the judgement of the lower courts stand on a majority verdict of two to one. Lindy turned to her faith and resigned herself to spending the rest of her life in prison. But Michael resigned the priesthood. A crisis of faith was rumoured. Many felt that if they had been through what Michael had been through they would have been atheists by then.

But letters of support still poured in. Pleas for Lindy's release appeared in the press. A film was made showing two versions of the story – the prosecution's and the Chamberlains'. Somehow they could not get the Crown's case to hang together dramatically. A prison psychologist who examined Lindy publicly proclaimed that he found himself unable to account for any 'criminal behaviour on her part'. Newspapers employed their own analysts, handwriting experts and the like, who all proclaimed Lindy innocent. Prominent scientists protested at the interpretation of the forensic evidence. A petition was organised. The Plea of Justice Committee was formed and travelled the country, campaigning on Lindy's behalf.

Then, in February 1986, David Brett, a British tourist who was climbing on Ayers Rock, slipped and fell to his death. When it was found, his body had been partially eaten by dingos. Near his body a baby's jacket was found. It was identified as Azaria's. Organic material that could have been the remains of Azaria's body were also found. This was all consistent with a dingo taking the baby.

That should have been an end to it, but there were rumours that Brett had Azaria's name tattooed on his arm. His mother believes that both her son and baby Azaria were victims of black magic. His parting words when he left Britain, she said, were: 'If anything happens to me, I have been made a sacrifice.'

Nevertheless Lindy was released on licence and T-shirts began appearing in Australia bearing the slogan: 'Watch out, Kahlia – mummy's home.'

A judicial inquiry set up under Federal judge Mr Justice Trevor Morling exonerated the Chamberlains. His 380-page report blamed erroneous and unreliable forensic evidence.

However, the apocalyptic vision offered by the Seventh Day Adventists *has* played its part in murder. Lapsed Catholic Roch Theriault became a Seventh Day Adventist, before going on to establish his own murderous cult.

Theriault was born in 1947 in a remote part of Quebec province. The only business there was tourism and as a young boy Theriault learned to carve native ornaments with a knife. When he was about ten, his parents moved to the asbestos mining area north of Montreal. Life there was grim. Things at home were little better. His father was a strict Catholic and belonged to a secret organisation called the White Berets who opposed any reform in the church. At night, he and his three sons would play a game called Bone. The idea was to kick each other's shins until the loser called 'assez' – enough. To escape, the young Theriault would walk in the woods and fields, dreaming he was back out in the wilds of Quebec. He used his time to study plants and roots and became a self-taught homoeopath. Despite his love of solitude, he was a great talker. He had a large number of friends – especially girls – and treated them all for minor ailments.

At twenty, he married a local farmgirl and settled down in a wooden house down the road from his parents. Soon he was the father of two children and he supported his family selling carved wooden ornaments to tourists who stopped to see the asbestos mines. The marriage worked well for a time. But then, Theriault began insisting that his wife dress in the puritan style of the early pioneers. The next minute he would want her in the very latest microminiskirt. He asked her prudish parents whether he could hire one of their fields to build a nudist camp. Theriault, it seems, had become fascinated with the human body. His parents-in-law turned him down. Soon after, his wife took their two children and moved back in with her parents, leaving Theriault to study anatomy on his own.

To improve his social life, Theriault joined a Catholic youth group. He pushed to become its leader and suggested that members wear robes with supernatural emblems on them. The other members did not think this was entirely suitable. Theriault was upset by the snub and quit not only the group but the Catholic church.

Instead he joined the Seventh Day Adventists. He took their claim that the world was about to end very seriously and bought a special monk's habit, complete with cowl, for the event. He was soon announcing to the small, deeply conservative congregation of the local Seventh Day Adventist Church that he was a prophet and should be made their leader. But he had one great drawback as a Seventh Day Adventist pastor. He drank like a fish.

Theriault decided that a true prophet should spend his time in the wilderness. He headed back to northern Quebec where he set up as a healer. His shop, which specialised in natural foods and homoeopathic medicines, was a huge success. He started giving lectures on healing and became something of a guru, especially to the local women. He married one of them, twenty-six-year-old Giselle Lafrance in 1977. Another couple who fell for his natural approach to life were Jacques and Maryse Giguère. They gave up their jobs, sold their home and moved in with Theriault and his new wife.

The following year Theriault had what he called his 'Great Vision'. In it, God vouchsafed unto him that the world was about to end. Theriault was to collect around him a commune of 'the chosen' and flee into the wilderness. He did as he was told and moved to the north shore of the Gaspe Peninsula at the mouth of the Gulf of St Lawrence. He took with him there his little band of followers – four children, nine women and four men. When they got there, he revealed to the group his real name – Moses.

The conditions that far north are harsh. Members of the commune had to toil day and night during the summer to keep themselves through the long winters. Moses did none of the work though. He slept until mid-afternoon. When he awoke, he would start drinking. In his drunken rages, he would shout at the children and beat them. And he would intimidate the adults. Sometimes, when sober, he would sob with remorse and pray. It did not good. The rest of the time he ranted on about the second coming. Most of his apocalyptic philosophy came straight from Seventh Day Adventism. But he also began to get interested in the teachings of the Church of Jesus Christ and the Latter Day Saints. Or at least, one of their early teachings – polygamy.

Despite his constant drunkenness, Theriault demanded exclusive sexual rights to all the women in the commune. The other men, he explained, should remain celibate. After all, they were monks. To strengthen his theological claims, he visited Mormon polygamist Alex Joseph, who lived with his nine wives in Utah. The two got on well and Joseph crowned Theriault 'King of the Israelites'. Back in Canada, Theriault demanded that he not just bed all the women individually, but that he sleep with them two or three at a time. He would arrange competitions to see who had the most orgasms. The men and the women were forced to strip naked and fight for Theriault's amusement and they would have to suffer his harangues at the nightly prayer meetings.

But life was even harder for the children. One of them, the two-year-old son of Jacques and Maryse Giguère, was found badly beaten. Instead of blaming Theriault, they asked for his help as a healer. He examined the child and concluded that he was suffering 'pressure' in the testicles that needed to be relieved. He pulled out his hunting knife and cut into the two-year-old boy's scrotum. The child died in agony.

A new member, twenty-three-year-old Guy Veer, had joined the commune recently and was not fully under the thrall of Theriault yet. When the two-year-old died, Veer demanded that Theriault be reported for murder. Instead it was Veer who was tried in a hastily organised communal court. He was found not guilty, but insane. Theriault concluded that Veer must be prevented from having children himself. While commune members held him down, Theriault sliced off his testicles.

Veer managed to escape from the commune and get medical assistance in a nearby town. He reported the murder of the child and his own mutilation to the police. Theriault and six of his followers were found guilty, not of murder, but of criminal negligence in the case of the child. Theriault was also convicted of the malicious wounding of Veer. But he only served eighteen months on both counts.

In 1984, he was released. His parole conditions forbade him from associating with his followers. So he skipped the state and set up a new commune in the wilderness of Ontario. There, his old followers came back to him and attracted new wholefood freaks to his group. While they awaited Armageddon, they supported themselves selling wood carvings, hand-knitted woollens and organic food. Theriault spent much of his time drinking and satisfying his indefatigable libido with the eight 'wives' he had amassed. They, in turn, were involved full-time in giving birth and child rearing.

The social services started keeping an eye on the cult in 1985 after a child died of what a coroner decided were natural causes. By the end of the year, they had enough evidence of child abuse to raid the commune. Fourteen children, all fathered by Theriault, were taken into care. Girls as young as six told their foster parents that they had been forced to perform sexual acts with Theriault. The women were given a straight choice. They could leave Theriault and get their children back, or stay with him and lose them. They chose to stay with him. After all, they could always have more children. In the next two years, Theriault fathered another nine children, all of whom were taken into care.

Theriault maintained his interest in sexual mutilation and makeshift surgery. One man was punished for a minor offence by having a rubber band tightened around his testicles. When they swelled up, Theriault insisted that he operate. While members of the commune held the man down, Theriault slit open his scrotum and removed one swollen testicle. Then he cauterised the wound with a red-hot poker.

Theriault was drunk when one of his wives, thirty-two-year-old Solange Boillard, complained of a stomach ache. Instead of the usual preparation of herbs and roots he prescribed, Theriault had her strip naked and lie on a table in front of the assembled commune. Then he began a thorough examination. This consisted of violent prodding and a punch in the stomach. Then he turned her over. The treatment began with an enema of hot vegetable oil and molasses administered via a plastic tube rammed roughly up her anus. When Theriault arbitrarily decided that this had not worked, he tried a radical intervention. He turned her on her back again, grabbed his hunting knife and sliced

266

open her belly. Despite her screams, Theriault plunged his unwashed hands into the unfortunate woman's stomach. He pulled out a portion of her intestine, cut it off and threw it away. He left his other wives to sew up the huge wound. Solange Boillard lived for several hours, then died in agony. She was buried in the yard.

Theriault could not believe that his surgery had failed. What appeared to be death was, in fact, only a state of unconsciousness. A week later, he ordered his followers to dig her up so that he could bring her back to life. However, when they opened the grave, they found that the corpse was already in an advanced state of decay. Theriault operated again. This time he broke off a rib, which he wore in a bag around his neck. The body was reburied. His failure to revive Solange Boillard troubled Theriault. After a prolonged drinking session a couple of weeks later, her body was dug up again. This time Theriault tried chanting. When that failed, he tore off the head and cut the top of the skull off with a hack saw. Then he got one of the women to masturbate him into the festering brain. Even Theriault's life-giving seed did not revive Solange Boillard. So, in despair, her remains were cremated.

After that other commune members tried to keep quiet about their ailments. But Gabrielle Lavallée made the mistake of complaining about toothache. Theriault extracted eight of her teeth. Later she was having trouble doing her work in the field and it came to light that she had a slight stiffness in the joints of her fingers. Theriault pinned her hand to a table with his knife while he began to 'operate'. Gabrielle endured an hour of agony, terrified of losing consciousness. She knew if she blacked out he would kill her. Unfortunately, during the operation, her arm turned black and blue. Theriault had the cure for that too. He hacked the arm off with a blunt meat cleaver. Crude stitching did not close the wound properly and, when the stump continued bleeding for a couple of days, Theriault heated up an old drive shaft from a broken-down truck with a blowtorch and cauterised the wound.

267

After this, Gabrielle had had enough. She escaped. With her good arm, she hitched a ride to Toronto, where she checked into hospital. The medical staff reported her unusual injury to the police, who raided the commune. But Theriault and his followers had already fled. Using helicopters and tracker dogs, they caught Theriault camping out in the wilderness with two of his wives. He pleaded guilty to assault on Gabrielle Lavallée and was sentenced to twelve years. Eventually other members of the commune trickled into custody. One of them mentioned the operation on Solange Boillard.

Police found Boillard's burnt remains and Theriault was charged with murder. He pleaded guilty, but did not manage to sound contrite. He believed that his operations had been carried out with the best intentions. He got life. This did not discourage his wives. One of them, Francine Laflamme, enjoys conjugal visits with Theriault. She claims to be deeply in love with Theriault who, she claims, is a pleasant man when he is not drinking or performing operations. Two of his other 'wives' live with Laflamme and are waiting patiently for Theriault to be released. Roch Theriault is eligible for parole in the year 2000, when it is to be hoped that his wives are in good health.

Seventh Day Adventism spawned another murderous spin-off cult – the Davidians. It was founded in 1930 by a Bulgarian immigrant named Victor Houteff. He had been an Adventist preacher, but was defrocked for not adhering to the strict line laid down by the church. He believed that there was hidden meaning in the Bible that would be unlocked by breaking a series of scriptural codes. These naturally told him that the apocalypse was at hand and that he, Victor Houteff, had been chosen personally by God to lead a band of the Elect who would rule the Earth along with Jesus Christ in the thousand years that followed.

Earning his living as a part-time washing machine salesman in California, Houteff began to collect a band of followers around him. He bought two hundred acres of low-cost farmland in Texas, near a small town called Waco, where he established a Bible school teaching his own eccentric interpretation of the scriptures. Houteff's great task was to cleanse the world of wickedness prior to God's coming. But his forty devoted followers were not the slightest bit phased by the fact that their leader died before the last trumpet had sounded.

Instead, another prophet, Ben Roden, took over the sect. He wisely avoided making the mistake that other apocalyptic cult leaders had done. He did not set a date for the Second Coming – it so often leads to disappointment. Instead he enforced compulsory daily worship and began churning out religious pamphlets. One, bizarrely, claimed that the Pope had masterminded Watergate. When Roden died in 1978, his wife Lois Roden took over. Their son George Roden waited patiently in the wings for his mother to die. He was extremely fat and the Davidians wittily dubbed the heir apparent the Prince of Whales.

Three years later, twenty-three-year-old Vernon Howell joined the sect. He was the illegitimate son of a Dallas schoolgirl. His mother, Bonnie, was just fourteen when she had him, but she was allowed to keep him. He was a slow learner and dropped out of school in ninth grade. He also failed to develop as a bodybuilder and was an excruciating heavy metal guitar player. The only thing in the world that he was good at was memorising the Bible. He knew the whole of the New Testament by heart by the time he was thirteen. He joined the Seventh Day Adventists, but was expelled for ranting and raving in services. Then, after a series of menial jobs, fate led him to Waco.

Howell was already an accomplished con-man by the time he applied to join the Davidians. His comprehensive knowledge of the Bible now stood him in good stead, as did his knowledge of human nature. He told Lois Roden that he wanted to join the Davidians as part of a spiritual quest. Then he threw himself on her mercy. He was in the grip of a terrible vice, he confessed – excessive masturbation. She approved his application.

The conservative cult members were somewhat wary of Howell at first. They saw him as a hippie, a wastrel. But he soon won them round with a quick smile and a willingness to help. He worked hard fixing the ramshackle ranch buildings, repairing cult members' cars and running errands. And they could not fail to be impressed by his knowledge of the scriptures and his religious zeal.

After two years, Howell was ready to make his bid for power. Lois Roden was seventy years old and her grip was slipping. The twenty-five-year-old Howell went to her and told her that he had had a vision. God had told him that they must conceive a son together. He would be the last prophet. Even though her age precluded the possibility of conception, Lois Roden and Vernon Howell became lovers. When rumours of the relationship spread through the Davidians, there was disquiet. One cultist came up with a parody of the Lord's Prayer which began: 'Our Mother, which art in heaven.'

However, Howell used his new position to begin a religious revival. He was a natural showman. His hellfire-and-damnation sermons put new life into the sect. And he told them what they wanted to hear – that the apocalypse was at hand and they must cleave to a new prophet. Lois Roden was now marginalised. So Howell dumped her and took a fourteen-year-old bride. She bore him two children. He also had sex with other girls in the sect, some as young as ten. The reason for this was simple, he told his flock: he was the ultimate sex machine.

All this was too much for Lois Roden. At the age of seventy-one, she died. Her son George stepped into her shoes. He rounded on Howell, accusing him of being a worshipper of Satan. His passion for heavy metal music was proof of this. And Howell and his offspring were expelled from the sect 'unto the tenth generation'. To everyone's surprise, Howell accepted this. He left. But he took with him twenty-five sect members, including almost all of the young blood. As they had split from the Davidians, Howell and his followers called themselves Branch Davidians.

A period in the wilderness is *de rigueur* for a bona fide prophet. Howell and his followers wandered the Midwest in a couple of beaten-up trucks, supporting themselves with social security cheques and odd jobs. In fact, they did rather well. They soon had enough to send Howell to Israel, where his prophecy was confirmed. He came back saying he was indeed the chosen leader who would fight the world's last great battle against Satan. His next trip was to Australia where he recruited more followers. Back in the US, he gathered around him a core of mediocre rock musicians. Having moved on from the teachings of Houteff, Howell saw hidden messages from God encoded in rock songs, especially the blues classic 'The House of the Rising Sun'.

Howell had built his following up to over sixty when he moved back to Texas. His inner circle were a number of bodybuilders who called themselves the Mighty Men. They seized control of the ranch at Waco. In a last-ditch attempt to retain control, George Roden issued what can only be described as a satanic challenge. On Hallowe'en 1987, he had the body of an eighty-five-year-old Davidian disinterred. Howell could call himself the prophet, Roden said, only if he could raise the corpse from the dead. Instead, it was simple enough for Howell to proclaim that Roden was Satan. Digging up the dead was proof enough. So, doing God's will, Howell and his Mighty Men simply took over. There was a short altercation, during which Roden was shot. It was only a flesh wound, but it was enough for Roden. He ran for it. Howell and his men were charged with the shooting, but acquitted. They fortified the compound at the Waco ranch, so there was no chance of Roden staging a counter-coup. Howell's new Branch Davidians now numbered well over a hundred.

Vernon Howell changed his first name to David – after King David – and took the surname Koresh. That was the Hebrew name for the Babylonian King Cyrus who allowed the Jews to return to Palestine. The ranch at Waco was re-named Ranch Apocalypse. It would be the battlefield where Armageddon would begin. Satan, Koresh told his followers, would attack there, probably under the guise of the US Army.

His rule became absolute. The sense of paranoia was increased by the nightly harangues about what a hostile place the outside world was and a diet of war videos. Discipline was rigidly enforced. Everything, right down to the children's games, was regulated and any hint of dissent was snuffed out. The Branch Davidians were the Army of God. They lived under martial law.

Everything in the commune belonged to him, Koresh maintained, right down to his followers' underpants. If he came into their quarters and demanded their possessions in the name of God, they were to strip naked. Naturally all the women belonged to Koresh. The prophet had to multiply. His many wives – picked from among the wives and daughters of his followers – wore Star of David pendants. Many of them were under-age. The other men were denied sex altogether. They were housed in separate dormitories and to ease their sexual frustration they were encouraged to drink heavily. Somehow the men managed to rationalise this situation. Sexual intercourse was aggressive and incursive, they said, and they expressed gratitude to Koresh for taking that burden upon himself. But then, they believed it when Koresh said that God was going to come down in a spaceship and fly them to heaven in it.

While the bulk of his followers were kept corralled in Ranch Apocalypse, steeling themselves for the battle ahead, Koresh and his Mighty Men were out and about having a good time in local bars and restaurants. Meanwhile, they were amassing a huge arsenal of weapons at Ranch Apocalypse. They managed to amass over eleven tonnes of arms – firearms, grenades and tactical weapons such as anti-tank guns.

The US authorities were not unaware of what was going on at Waco. This was due to the courage of one man. Mark Breault was one of Koresh's original Mighty Men and he was not happy about the way things were going.

His wife had already quit the sect and had gone back to Australia. Now he was beginning to feel disquiet about the situation. Koresh had just taken up with a thirteen-year-old girl, who was lording it over the place. This was too much for Breault to handle. He managed to slip out and phone his wife. She promised to send him the airfare home. All that remained was for Breault to get to Los Angeles where he could catch a plane for Melbourne. Claiming that the mixer in the commune's recording studio needed replacing, he said he would have to drive to Los Angeles to buy a new one. Koresh said he would come along too. He brought with him his thirteen-year-old lover and a Kalashnikov assault rifle. The Branch Davidians had a house in California where the three of them stayed. Somehow the denizens got wind of Breault's plans and told Koresh. He ordered Breault to fly back to Waco where he would be punished. Instead, Breault seized his chance and flew to Australia.

Mark Breault had kept a detailed diary of his time at Waco. He and a group of other Australian defectors got together and warned the American authorities that Waco was another Jonestown in the making. Australian TV picked up on the story and devoted an edition of a current affairs programme to the goings-on at Ranch Apocalypse. But it still took the US authorities two years to get round to doing anything about David Koresh and his apocalyptic army.

The US Bureau of Alcohol, Tobacco and Firearms – the ATF – eventually responded to reports of the huge amount of arms that the Branch Davidians had accrued. They tried to infiltrate the group, but any ATF agent stood out like a sore thumb. The ATF's activity only increased the Branch Davidians' paranoia. Now they were ready to die – and kill – for Christ.

On 28 February 1993, the ATF moved in. In the utmost secrecy, agents moved into the area concealed in cattle trailers. The bureau's press office had already prepared a press release trumpeting the successful capture of David

Koresh. When they arrived at Ranch Apocalypse, the place was eerily quiet. It was a Sunday and the Davidians were at prayer. Seeing no guns in the windows, ATF officers were given the go-ahead. They streamed out of the cattle trucks. With ladders, they tried to scale the walls of the main building. Then suddenly, they came under withering gunfire from all around the compound. Some ATF agents fell. Plainly they had been expected.

In fact, everyone in the county knew that the raid was imminent. You cannot assemble hundreds of law enforcement officers in a sparsely populated area of Texas without someone noticing. The ATF had hired a van to supply coffee and doughnuts to their men. But other customers included Davidians and the women who ran it heard them discussing their defence plans. Even the local TV station had been given advance warning and were spotted setting up their cameras before the raid.

The first battle lasted nearly an hour. The ATF were hopelessly outgunned. Four ATF men were killed and twenty-four were wounded. The Davidians lost six, one wounded member shot by colleagues 'to put him out of his misery'. Koresh called police headquarters complaining that they had killed some of his children. Then he launched into a sermon. Later he called his mother, telling her that he was hit and would see her real soon 'in the skies'.

The ATF's publicity backfired on them. They were now seen on network TV to have bungled the operation. The FBI were put in charge instead. They knew that the Davidians had stockpiled food which would keep them going for a year and enough fire power to defend themselves. Worse. They were led by a madman. So they called in their hostage negotiators. This conciliatory approach showed some success at first. After a week, two older women and twenty-one children were allowed to leave the compound. But the authorities knew that there were still probably over a hundred people left inside, and at least seventeen of them were children.

The real problem was that FBI hostage negotiators had

274

been trained to deal with Muslim fanatics, criminal gangs and other politically motivated terrorists. They did not understand the jargon of apocalyptic Christians. When Koresh talked of the seven seals of the Book of Revelations, the FBI men thought he was a militant environmentalist concerned with the clubbing of baby seals. Mark Breault tried to put them right. In Koresh's theology, the fifth seal was mass suicide, he told the Bureau. But FBI psychological profilers did not consider this a possibility. Koresh, they concluded, was a physical coward and they did not believe that he inspired the same fanatical devotion as Jim Jones.

As the siege dragged on, psychological tactics were employed. Spotlights were played on the windows to try and disrupt the cult members' sleep. Loudspeakers blasted the compound with the chanting of Tibetan monks, the screams of dying rabbits and loud rock music. The Davidians simply countered this by blacking out the windows and deadening the sound by piling bales of hay against the walls. Months of these tactics brought no results and a more gung-ho faction in the FBI began to find favour. There was also new US Attorney General, Janet Reno. She was concerned about the welfare of the children. She knew they had been sexually abused and was now worried about the sanitary conditions they were suffering. She told President Clinton that she intended to authorise the FBI to use tear-gas to flush the Davidians out – despite the catastrophic failure of these same tactics with Move in Philadelphia.

At 4 a.m. on 19 April 1993, after fifty-one days of siege, two tanks fitted with battering rams rumbled into position. As they moved forward, the FBI called the compound and told them that this was not an assault. Holes were going to be knocked in the outer walls and tear-gas was going to be injected into the compound. But if they came out with their hands up they would not be harmed. Instead the Davidians put on their gas masks and prayed. Loudspeakers repeated the message, but the advance of the tanks was met with gunfire. The tanks reached the compound unscathed, knocked holes in the walls and began pumping in the tear-gas. After half-an-hour, Koresh refused to negotiate so more gas was pumped in. Three hours later, the process was repeated. Still Koresh did not want to make peace. Instead, he was glimpsed briefly inside fixing his followers' gas masks. The FBI had high-tech listening devices that picked up some of what was going on inside Ranch Apocalypse. Around midday, eavesdroppers heard instructions being given to set fires. Wisps of smoke were seen. Then suddenly the wind whipped across the prairie turning the Ranch into a conflagration. A few members managed to run clear as the burning watchtower collapsed. Then the ammunition dump went up in a huge series of explosions. FBI eavesdroppers then heard one member inside say in earnest: 'What is the plan?' Koresh replied with sardonic humour: 'Well, you always wanted to be a charcoal briquet.'

Eight members of the sect managed to escape the flames, some with their clothes on fire, and were arrested. Over a hundred people perished, not all of them voluntarily. Twenty-five of the charred bodies dug out of the ashes of Ranch Apocalypse belonged to children; twelve of them were Koresh's. A two-year-old boy had been stabbed to death and a woman had been shot in the back. Another seventeen members died of gunshot wounds. Five of them were children. Koresh shot himself through the forehead.

One survivor, Kathryn Schroeder, turned state's evidence and testified that the Davidians had long planned to kill anyone who tried to storm the compound. Murder and conspiracy charges were laid against eleven surviving members of the sect. However, the jury found that the ATF had so bungled the raid that they were largely responsible for the death of their own agents. Five Davidians were found guilty of involuntary manslaughter. Two more were convicted on firearms charges and four walked free.

The faith of the Branch Davidians did not die in the all-consuming flames of Ranch Apocalypse. One member who was away from the Ranch when the siege began sees Koresh's departure as a sign from God and is eagerly awaiting his resurrection. Another who lost a son, two daughters and four grandchildren in the conflagration, still believes in Koresh's prophesies of the Second Coming. Even more frightening, there are many who believe that the deaths of David Koresh and his followers were avenged in the Oklahoma bombing in 1995, which took place on the second anniversary of the end of the siege.

Luc Jouret's Solar Temple was not an off-shoot of a more conventional Christian sect. Its apocalyptic vision claimed roots in the Knights Templar, one of the roots of modern Satanism. But thirty of its members lost their lives in a mass murder-suicide in October 1994.

Jouret was born in what was then the Belgian Congo in 1947. After a stretch in the Belgian Army, he studied medicine at Brussels University. He had intended to specialise in obstetrics but, during his course, he became interested in New Age ideas, especially homoeopathy. Gradually his interest began to spread to mysticism and the occult. During the 1970s, he joined the Renewed Order of the Templars, which had neo-Nazi overtones and was led by an ex-Gestapo officer named Julien Origas. But when Origas died in the mid-1980s, the Renewed Order fell apart in a squabble over finances. Jouret left to form the International Chivalric Order Solar Tradition in Switzerland, which peddled a mixture of environmentalism, homoeopathy and mysticism. This group soon amalgamated with a sect called the Foundation Golden Way, led by Joseph DiMambro, who largely believed in a New Age approach to high finance. Together they led the Solar Temple, a cult that seemed to have the answer for everything in the 1980s.

Jouret was the high priest and he preached that the apocalypse was at hand. It would come in the form of a great ecological disaster. This being the age of the Yuppie, cult fees were high and members would be served champagne at cult meetings. The Solar Temple were not interested in recruiting the drop-outs and hippies that were lured into other sects. They wanted to attract people with money. Jouret found new members through his expensive homoeopathic clinic in Geneva. Jouret also toured the world lecturing on environmental politics. This gave him new openings to prominent people who, at the time, would swallow anything as long as it was wrapped up in the politically correct green packaging.

The Solar Temple were not interested in the heavy-handed discipline that other sects employed either. Their members were far too sophisticated for that. But Jouret had mugged up on all the latest management techniques. He freelanced as a corporate motivator and perfected elegant techniques of control and coercion.

In 1986, Jouret and DiMambro branched out and formed a Canada wing of the Solar Temple. They bought an old monastery north of Montreal and started an organic farm there. Meanwhile, Jouret continued his corporate career. He gave lectures and seminars on man-management, motivation and self-realisation to large Canadian corporations. This gave him a chance to recruit high-flyers. He picked up other recruits by travelling around small towns, giving lectures on homoeopathy and wholefood. And he sold inspirational tapes through New Age shops. Using these methods, Jouret managed to lure people such as Robert Ostiguy, the mayor of the town of Richelieu and Robert Falardeau, an official in the finance ministry of Quebec, into the Solar Temple.

Membership of the Solar Temple cost $50. That allowed a follower to attend lectures and seminars. For $150 a week, you got the club-class 'Club Arcadia' membership. This entitled – or, rather, obliged – you to work on the Temple's organic farm, recruit new members and join in the Temple's religious rites. And for $200 a week, you joined the inner 'Golden Circle'. Then you were allowed to join in the secret, occult rituals. Naturally, you would also be expected to donate all your savings and your property. Enlightenment does not come cheap.

While members of the Solar Temple toiled in the fields producing organic vegetables, Jouret and DiMambro maintained a playboy lifestyle, skiing and travelling the world. Jouret slowly tightened his grip on the group. He assumed the right to approve marriages and arbitrarily dissolved existing unions. And he kept discipline by maintaining that only a hundred cult members – the Elect – would survive the apocalypse.

Details of what was going on in the sect began to come out when a member left in disgust and went to the papers after handing over savings of $500,000 to the sect. Then in 1993, Jouret was fined $750 on weapons charges. By that time there was growing disquiet in the Canada branch of the Temple. During the 1980s, DiMambro had invested heavily in property, but the market was in decline. The Yuppie dream was over and so was its New Age religion. Soon Jouret began to talk of mass suicide.

In the hope of a spiritual revival, Jouret visited sympathetic groups in Australia with a view to holding religious rites at Ayers Rock. However, the Aborigines who now controlled the rock and the surrounding Uluru National Park refused them permission. There were also rumours of links with right-wing terrorist groups and that the Solar Temple were stockpiling weapons. Then suddenly it all came to an end.

On the night of 5 October 1994, a farmhouse in the farming village of Cheiry in Switzerland caught fire. A neighbour raced to the scene. He broke into the burning house and found the owner, retired businessman Albert Giacobino, dead in the bedroom. He had been shot. When firemen had quenched the flames, they searched the farm. They found that the spacious barn had been converted into a temple of sorts. A pentagram had been drawn on the floor. Over a triangular pulpit was a picture of Christ holding a chalice, but the face in the painting was that of Luc Jouret. Around the base, spread out in a sunburst were twenty-three dead bodies – ten men, twelve women and DiMambro's twelve-year-old daughter. The men were wearing robes in white, black and red; the women wore white and gold. The Templars seemed to have been well prepared for their send-off. Empty champagne bottles were strewn around. Around half of the bodies had plastic bags tied over their faces. Some also had their hands tied. Others had been shot up to eight times. Although three rifles were found in the barn, the Templars had been despatched with a pistol – a .22. Over fifty shell casings were found on the floor.

Four hours later, three chalets in Granges-sur-Salvan, fifty miles away, caught on fire. Inside, there were twenty-five bodies, five of them belonging to children. The bodies had been badly burned, but plastic residue indicated they had died with bags over their heads. None had been shot, though some had been badly beaten. The remains of drugs and syringes indicated that they had been heavily sedated before they were killed. The .22 hand-gun used in the Temple at Cheiry was also found in the ashes.

Later that day in Canada, an explosion went off in a house used by the Solar Temple. In the bedroom, the firemen found the bodies of a man and a woman. Around their necks were medallions with a double-headed eagle on it. They were members of the Solar Temple. In the basement, the bodies of Antonio Dutoit, DiMambro's Swiss chauffeur, and his British wife Nicki were found. They had been dead before the fire started. And wedged behind the immersion heater was their three-month-old son Christopher. The child had a plastic bag tied over his head and a stake through his heart.

Investigators soon discovered the cause of the fire – a crude timer had been set to ignite cans of petrol. Former sect members claimed that DiMambro had been annoyed that the Dutoits had given birth to a baby without permission. The child, DiMambro said, was the anti-Christ and cult members had been ordered to kill it in a ritual a few days earlier. Jouret and DiMambro were seen leaving the house early the day before the fire. They seem to have taken the 10 a.m. flight to Geneva, then gone about finishing off the rest of the cult in Switzerland.

At first it was thought that Jouret and DiMambro were involved in some murderous financial swindle and had escaped to live a life of luxury with the proceeds. Rumours circulated that they had more than £90 million salted away in a Swiss Bank. However, dental records demonstrated that Jouret and DiMambro were among the victims of the fire at the chalets in Granges-sur-Salvan.

They had been telling followers that the cataclysm was imminent for some time and, two days before the murders, DiMambro took twelve members of the Solar Temple out to an expensive restaurant for a last supper. Apparently, they believed that they would be reborn on a distant planet called Sirius if they underwent a fiery death on Earth. But a local priest in Cheiry put the proliferation of sects such as the Solar Temple down to 'demonic influence'. Satan, it seems, is abroad in the world.

15

Devil Worship Italian-style

In 2007, priests went to work alongside Italian police in an attempt to stem the rising tide of crimes linked to devil worship. The clerics were seconded to the *Squadra Anti Sette* (SAS) – Italy's crack anti-sect squad – by the Vatican after a number of churches were desecrated by Satanists. There have also been a string of murders that have been linked to devil worship. One of the Vatican's leading experts on Satanism and the occult, Don Oreste Benzi, was also brought in to liaise with police. Don Oreste said that the natural curiosity of young people often attracted them to the occult. Drugs were also used to give sects a psychological grip over the young and lure them away from traditional social values. Many of the new wave of Satanists in Italy indulge in a potentially lethal blend of black magic, hard drugs, sex, and heavy metal music. The nationwide operation is controlled from Rome by police chief Gianni de Gennaro and a special freephone hotline has been set up to report occult activities. The church estimates that there are more than 8,000 Satanic sects in Italy with over 600,000 members and there are fears that the numbers are growing.

One recent murder case that dominated the headlines was the so-called "Beasts of Satan" trial of a group of Satanists who murdered nineteen-year-old Chiara Marino and sixteen-year-old Fabio Tollis. The double homicide took place in in the woods near Somma Lombardo, north-west of Milan in January 1998. The couple had last been seen drinking in The Midnight, a Milan pub that is the centre of the city's heavy metal scene. They never returned home. After a cursory investigation, the authorities concluded that they had run away together. However, Fabio's father, Michele Tollis did not believe this and began his own investigation. He discovered that, through their interest in black metal and death metal music, they had become deeply involved in the occult and Satanism. Over six years he steadily built up a file on their activities and those of the bands they played in, and concluded that they were involved in the wider Satanic sect. But nothing came of it until a third murder was committed in January 2004. Twenty-seven-year-old Mariangela Pezzotta, the girlfriend of group member Andrea Volpe, was shot and buried alive in a forest. Volpe was arrested shortly afterwards, and confessed to that crime. Volpe's name had come up in Tollis's investigation and he took his file to the police. During the interrogation of Volpe, he admitted the existence of the sect and led the police to where the bodies of Chiara Marino and Fabio Tollis had been buried. The couple had been sacrificially stabbed and beaten in a drug-fuelled occult rite involving sex and heavy metal music. Authorities said there had been a previous attempt to kill the two by burning them alive in a car on New Year's Eve. As the investigation continued, Mario Maccione, a childhood friend of Fabio Tollis, admitted beating him to death with a hammer. Additionally sect members were accused of pushing their drummer, Andrea Bontade, to commit suicide. Police believe that there may be other victims of the sect buried in the woods, as several people are missing. They also think that the group is connected to a wider network of Satanists in Italy.

On 22 February 2005, Andrea Volpe and fellow sect member Pietro Guerrieri were sentenced in the northern city of Busto Arsizio to sixteen years in prison for the murders of Chiara Marino and Fabio Tollis. Volpe was given another fourteen years for the slaying of Mariangela Pezzotta. Although Mario Maccione had also confessed to the murders, he was cleared due to his secondary role in the crimes. Five more members of the group went to trial in June 2005. In early 2006 Nicola Sapone, leader of the group and the person suspected of being the mastermind behind the killings, received a life sentence. Paolo Leoni, Marco Zampollo, Eros Monterosso and Elisabetta Ballarin received sentences of between 24 and 26 years for their role in the murders.

Following the trial, a Roman Catholic university began offering a two-month course on diabolical possession and exorcism for priests and seminarians, and priest Don Aldo Buonaito called for death metal music to be banned. The police say that Satanists are particularly active in Piedmont, Veneto, and Emilia Romagna in the north, and Tuscany, Umbria, Calabria, and Puglia further south. A Satanic sect is thought to be behind one of Italy's most famous cases. Pietro Pacciani, the man convicted of being the "Monster of Florence" – a serial killer who murdered courting couples over three decades – had his conviction overturned on appeal and was himself murdered before he could face a second trial. The police now believe that Pacciani was the head of a gang of Satanic killers, some of whom are still at large.

The killings began one hot night in the summer of 1968. Thirty-two-year-old Barbara Locci, from the town of Lastra a Signa, just to the west of Florence, and her lover Antonio Lo Bianco were found shot dead in his Alfa Romeo. Barbara was married with a child, but she was a notoriously promiscuous housewife. She had taken several lovers and was known locally as "Queen Bee."

On the night of 21 August 1968 she had gone to the cinema with Lo Bianco and her young son Natalino. On the way home, the boy had fallen asleep in the back of the car so the couple seized the chance to stop at a secluded cemetery to make love. Antonio had just started removing Barbara's clothing when the killer crept up on them and fired eight shots, killing them both. He then grabbed the boy – who must have been woken by the gunfire – and carried him to a nearby farm before fleeing into the darkness. The farmer was awakened by knock on his front door. When he opened it, he found the young boy standing there with tears streaming down his face.

"My mother and my 'uncle' are dead," the boy said.

The farmer called the police.

At the crime scene, the Carabinieri found a white Alfa Romeo "Giulietta" with licence plates from the neighbouring province of Arezzo. The car was registered to Antonio Lo Bianco. They also found eight .22-calibre shell cases beside the car.

From the state of the bodies, it was clear what had been going on when the couple were shot. Detectives immediately suspected Barbara Locci's cuckolded husband, Stefano Mele. They sent a patrol car that arrived as Mele's front door between six and seven in the morning. At that moment, Mele came rushing out with a suitcase, as if making a quick getaway. When told of his wife's murder, he showed little reaction and was taken to police head-quarters.

At the police station, Mele told detectives that he had not felt well the previous day, and had stayed at home. Two people had visited, Antonio Lo Bianco and Carmelo Cutrona, another of his wife's lovers. Mele also mentioned a third lover of his wife, Francesco Vinci, who had been jailed briefly following an accusation of adultery by his own wife. Then it came out that Barbara had been the lover of Francesco Vinci's two brothers, Giovanni and Salvatore, as well. Mele said that his wife's killer could easily have been one of her numerous lovers. The police now had more suspects than they could easily handle.

But the following day, 23 August 1968, Mele confessed to the murder. He also incriminated Salvatore Vinci who, he said, had given him the gun. Mele said that when his wife and son had not returned home by 11.20 p.m., he went looking for them. When he reached the town square of Lastra a Signa, he met Salvatore Vinci who told him that Barbara had gone to the cinema with Lo Bianco and Natalino. Vinci chided Mele for allowing his wife to cuckold him so publicly. He told him that he had to put a stop to the situation. Vinci had a gun with him, Mele said, and the two of them drove to the Giardino Michelacci movie theatre in Signa on the other side of the Arno.

They found Lo Bianco's Alfa Romeo parked outside and waited for the couple to come out of the cinema. When Lo Bianco and Barbara, with Natalino in her arms, appeared and drove off in Antonio's car, Mele and Vinci followed. They stopped at the cemetery just outside Signa. When they started to make love, Vinci pulled out the gun and handed it to him, Mele said.

Mele then walked up to the car and started firing, continuing until the gun was empty. Afterwards they drove to the bridge in Signa and threw the gun in the Arno, then went home.

"I killed my wife and her lover because I was tired of continually being humiliated," Mele concluded. "My wife had been cheating on me for a number of years, but it was only a few months ago that I decided to do away with her."

There were great holes in this confession. The most glaring was that he had failed to mention how Natalino had turned up at the farmhouse. If the boy had been woken by the gunfire, surely he would have recognized his own father. Nevertheless Mele was formally arrested and held pending formal charges.

The police then tried to find the weapon, but when a prosecutor questioned Mele about the gun again, he changed his story. Instead of throwing it in the Arno, Mele said, he had given it back to Salvatore Vinci. Soon after Mele retracted his entire confession and began accusing Vinci's brother Francesco of the double murder. It was Francesco who had owned the weapon, Mele said, and Francesco who had killed Barbara and her lover.

This change of story did not help him in court and, in 1970, Mele was found guilty of the double murder and jailed for fourteen years – a lenient sentence was handed down on the grounds of partial insanity. And that was thought to be the end of it. Then there was another double murder.

On the moonless night of 14 September 1974, with Stefano Mele safely in jail, 19-year-old Pasquale Gentilcore and 18-year-old Stefania Pettini parked up in Pasquale's father's Fiat 127 overlooking the River Sieve in Borgo San Lorenzo, just north of Florence and eighteen miles from Signa. They were enjoying a romantic moment when someone began firing at them. The next day a passer-by found the car and called the police.

Detectives found the half-naked body of Pasquale Gentilcore in the driver's seat. He was peppered with gunshot wounds. Copper-jacket shell casings surrounded the scene and there was no evidence of a struggle.

Outside the car to the rear was the naked body of Stefania Pettini. She had been stabbed and mutilated. Her corpse was posed with her arms and legs spreadeagled, and with a branch protruding from her lacerated vagina. Her handbag was found in a nearby field, its contents scattered.

A post mortem showed that Pasquale had been shot five times, killing him. Stefania had been shot three times, but she had still been alive when the killer carried her from the car and began slashing her. She had died of one of 96 stab wounds inflicted on her naked body. The knife had a single-edged blade 1.5 cm wide and between 10 and 12 cm long. The gun was a model 73 or 74, .22 automatic Beretta, while the bullets were of a distinctive Winchester type made in Australia in the 1950s.

A mentally unstable man named Giuseppe Francini walked into the police station and confessed to the murders, but he was unable to describe in detail how the killings had been carried out. The police also suspected Guido Giovannini, a voyeur reported to have been spying on couples in the area, and a 53-year-old self-proclaimed healer, Bruno Mocali. But they could find no evidence linking either man to the crime, and both suspects were eventually ruled out. The perpetrator was clearly a sexually deviant maniac, but the police, who had not yet made the link to the 1968 murder and with no clues or leads to pursue, filed the case away as unsolved.

Seven years later, on another warm summer's night, yet another double murder took place. On 6 June 1981 an unknown gunman fired eight shots into a Fiat Ritmo. Inside were 30-year-old Giovanni Foggi and his lover, 21-year-old Carmela De Nuccio. The following morning, a police sergeant on a country walk with his young son spotted the copper-coloured Ritmo parked at the roadside. The sergeant then noticed a woman's handbag lying beside the driver's-side door with its contents scattered on the ground. Taking a closer look, he noticed that the driver's-side window had been smashed. At the wheel was a young man whose throat seemed to have been slashed.

When detectives arrived, they found the body of a female victim in a ditch some twenty yards away from the car. She had been stabbed in the abdomen and her T-shirt and jeans had been slashed. Her legs were spread and her genital region cut out and removed. It seems the perpetrator had had plenty of time to perform this crude surgery. There were no witnesses and no tracks.

The post mortem demonstrated that both had died of multiple gunshot wounds while in the car. The young man had then been stabbed once in the chest and twice in the neck. The woman's dead body had then been carried to the ditch. The medical examiner concluded that the girl's genitals had been excised with an extremely sharp instrument, which the killer had clearly wielded with some skill.

Ballistics tests revealed that the bullets had been fired by a .22-calibre automatic pistol. Again they were the same distinctive Winchester rounds that had been found previously. Veteran detectives quickly made the connection with the Gentilcore and Pettini case. The bullets from all four bodies matched. Florence, it seemed, had a serial killer on its hands – though even now no-one had yet made the connection with the 1968 crime.

The red Ford of known peeping Tom Enzo Spalletti had been seen parked near the scene of the most recent crime. When questioned Spalletti gave a confused alibi. Detectives' interest was further piqued by the fact that he mentioned a copper-coloured Ritmo and two dead bodies to his wife at 9.30 a.m. on the morning they had been discovered, telling her that he had read the story in the newspaper – though the papers had not reported the murders until the following day. Spalletti was arrested and jailed pending trial.

Four months later Spalletti had to be freed when another couple were murdered in exactly the same way; as he was behind bars, this was plainly a crime he could not have committed.

On 23 October 1981, 26-year-old Stefano Baldi and his 24-year-old girlfriend Susanna Cambi decided to spend the evening parked in their Volkswagen at a beauty spot near Calenzano, five miles north of Florence. Later that evening, another courting couple found their bodies.

Stefani Baldi was found next to the car. Half-naked, he appeared to have been shot and stabbed many times. Susanna Cambi was lying on the other side of the car. Her wounds were similar to Baldi's, but her genitals had also been excised like those of Carmela De Nuccio.

The medical examiner concluded that both victims had been shot through the front windscreen of the car, but that both had still been alive when they were stabbed. The same .22 Beretta as before had been used. The knife used to stab the victims had a single-edged blade, between 5 and 7 cm long and approximately 3 cm wide.

The instrument used to excise Susanna Cambi's genitals appeared to be the same as the one used on Carmela De Nuccio, but the murderer seemed to have been rushed. The killer had performed the operation with less precision and a larger area had been excised. He had cut through the abdominal wall and punctured the intestine.

The press now dubbed the killer the "Monster of Florence" and two separate couples came forward and reported that they had seen a lone male driver speeding from the crime scene in a red Alfa GT. However, despite the growing press coverage no further leads were forthcoming.

The following summer another couple were targeted. On

19 June 1982, 20-year-old Antonella Migliorini and her boyfriend, 22-year-old mechanic, Paolo Mainardi, were making love in a parking spot off the Via Nuova Virgilio, near Montespertoli, twelve miles south-west of Florence. They were just putting their clothes back on when the killer appeared out of the bushes and started shooting.

Antonella Migliorini died instantly but Paolo Mainardi survived the initial burst of gunfire. Although badly injured, he started the Seat, switched on the headlights and slammed the car into reverse. But he ended up in a ditch. The killer walked over, shot out the headlights and emptied the pistol into the wounded driver. Then he pulled out the ignition keys and threw them into the undergrowth.

When the killer left, Paolo Mainardi was still alive. Unfortunately he was not found until the next morning and he died a few hours later, without having regained consciousness and before he had been able to give the police any vital clues.

However, Silvia Della Monica, the prosecutor assigned to the case, persuaded the newspapers to report that Paolo Mainardi had been alive when he reached hospital and that he had given a description of the killer before he died. All of the reporters agreed, and the information appeared in the afternoon papers.

The idea was to rattle the killer. It worked. After the afternoon papers hit the streets, one of the paramedics who had accompanied Paolo Mainardi to the hospital received two telephone calls from a person who first claimed to be with the prosecutor's office. The second time he identified himself as the killer and he wanted to know what Mainardi had said before he died.

A few days later, police Sergeant Francesco Fiore made the connection with the 1968 murder of Barbara Locci and Antonio Lo Bianco, when he had been seconded to Montespertoli from Signa, ten miles away. Fiore began to wonder if there was a connection with the crimes of the Monster. At his insistence, the bullets were compared. They matched. Not only had all the bullets been fired by the same .22 Beretta, they were also from the same distinctive Australian batch and they all came from a single box of 50 shells. It was clear that the Monster of Florence had killed Barbara Locci and Antonio Lo Bianco in 1968 – or, at least, was using the same weapon and bullets.

Plainly Stefano Mele, Locci's jealous husband, could not be the

Monster since he had been in jail ever since. But he was not released. The Carabinieri simply assumed that he had an accomplice for the original crime who had continued killing after Mele was imprisoned. They interviewed Mele again, but he continued to claim his complete innocence and refused to co-operate with the investigators. Nevertheless, in August 1982 police arrested Francesco Vinci, who Mele had first accused 14 years before.

On 9 September 1983, Wilhelm Horst Meyer and his friend Uwe Rusch Sens, both 24, were asleep in a Volkswagen camper van some 19 miles south of Florence when the Monster paid them a visit. He fired through the window killing the German holiday-makers instantly. The bodies were not mutilated, so the police did not immediately associate the murders with the Monster. It was only when ballistics found that the bullets were from the same batch as those used in the other killings that the connection was made.

The police wondered whether the killer had changed his pattern. Or perhaps he had simply made a mistake. One of the victims had long blond hair and could have been mistaken for a girl, especially at night. There were reports that the two men were homosexual lovers, though there is no evidence of that. It may also have been that when the killer realized that he did not have a dead girl on his hands, he abandoned his plans to stab and mutilate the bodies.

However, the murder of Horst Meyer and Uwe Sens brought to light some other common features of the crimes. The killer usually struck on a Friday or Saturday night, and when the moon was hidden by clouds. The victims had all spent their last evenings at a discotheque – with the exception of Barbara Locci and Antonio Lo Bianco, who had been to the cinema. The killer had also rifled through each female victim's belongings. Was he looking for something that might connect him to the victim? Or was he hunting for some macabre souvenir?

Although Francesco Vinci had been in custody at the time of the murder of Horst Meyer and Uwe Sens, his lawyer failed to persuade the judges to release him, even though he clearly could not have committed the latest murders. State Prosecutor Mario Rotella now believed that the crimes were committed by a gang of Sardinian-born peasants, of which Mele and Vinci were members. They arrested Mele's brother Giovanni Mele and a friend Piero

Mucciarini. Both remained in custody until a few months after the next murders.

Other bizarre theories were doing the rounds. Religious historian Massimo Introvigne pointed out that Florence, home of Dante's "Inferno", had long been linked to sorcery. Occult sects, he said, were stalking lovers' lanes to commit ritual murders. Detectives had already toyed with the idea that the killer had taken the women's genitals to be used a trophy by some religious cult.

There was more unsettling news. Shortly after the murder of the two German campers, the paramedic who had accompanied Paolo Mainardi to the hospital in 1982 got another phone call from the killer, demanding to know that Mainardi had said before he died. Disturbingly, the paramedic was in Rimini at the time. How did the killer know that Mainardi was on holiday and how to contact him?

At 9.40 p.m. on 29 July 1984, 18-year-old sales girl Pia Rontini and 21-year-old university student Claudio Stefanacci were parked in a sky-blue Fiat Panda off a provincial road between Dicomano and Vicchio, just north of Florence. They were just about to make love when the killer began firing at them.

Claudio's body was found on the back seat of his car dressed in only underpants and a vest. He had been shot four times and stabbed ten times. Not far from the vehicle, behind some bushes, lay the naked body of Pia. She had been shot twice and stabbed twice in the head. The killer had then dragged her by the ankles some ten yards into the bushes. As before she had been left in a spreadeagled position and her genitals had been excised. This time the killer had also cut off her left breast and slashed her body more than a 100 times. The police then asked, did the removal of the left breast have any occult significance? Or was the killer becoming more sadistic?

Again the knife used was single-edged. Both victims had been shot through the car window. The weapon was the familiar .22 Beretta automatic and the bullets matched those used in the previous crimes. No fingerprints were recovered from the scene and detectives had come to believe that the killer wore surgical gloves during the murders. Sixteen years had passed since the first murder and, despite the arrest of four suspects, the police were no closer to stopping the "Monster of Florence."

The killer struck again over a year later. On 8 September 1985 he murdered a French couple as they camped in the San Casciano area just south of Florence. The murderer slashed open their tent and fired several shots into the bodies of 25-year-old Jean-Michel Kraveichvili and 36-year-old Nadine Mauriot. According to the medical examiner, they had been making love at the time with the man lying on his back and the woman on top of him.

Nadine Mauriot had been shot four times. Three bullets had penetrated her skull; a fourth had passed through her throat. Kraveichvili had also been hit four times – twice in the upper arm, once in the mouth and once in the right elbow. Even so, he managed to get to his feet and scrambled out of the tent, but, after about 30 yards, the killer had caught up with him and stabbed him to death. He then pushed him down a bank into some bushes. The killer then returned to the tent, dragged out Nadine Mauriot's body and began to mutilate it.

According to the medical examiner, the shots had been fired at close range – from no more than 20 inches away. Once again the woman's genitals and left breast had been removed. It was estimated that this would have taken around ten minutes. In that time, the killer was not disturbed.

Soon after detectives thought they had got lucky. A copper-jacketed Winchester bullet was found on the pavement in front of a hospital nearby. The idea that the killer used surgical gloves and his evident interest in dissection led the police to question the hospital staff. But no suspect emerged and the trail went cold again.

The following day an envelope arrived at the office of assistant public prosecutor Silvia Della Monica. The address was made up of letters cut from a newspaper or magazine in the style of a ransom note. It contained a single spelling mistake. Inside the envelope was a folded sheet of paper that had been glued along its edges. Inside the paper was a small plastic bag. Inside the plastic bag was a cube of flesh cut from from Nadine Mauriot's missing breast. The killer was now taunting the authorities.

In 1986 the police admitted that their strategy of focusing on the idea of a Sardinian peasant gang was wrong. They began again from scratch and, over the next eight years, questioned over 100,000 people.

By 1991 several leads seemed to point in the direction of Pietro

Pacciani, a 68-year-old semi-literate farm labourer in San Casciano whose hobbies included hunting and taxidemy. In 1951, Pacciani had killed a travelling salesman he had caught sleeping with his fiancée. He had stabbed the man 19 times. He had then trampled the man to death and sodomized his corpse. Released from prison after 13 years, he married, but was jailed again from 1987 to 1991 for wife-beating and the sexual molestation of his two young daughters.

Anecdotal evidence suggested that Pacciani was involved in the Satanic group with Giancarlo Lotti, Giovanni Faggi, and Mario Vanni – all well-known voyeurs who haunted local lovers' lanes. Pacciani and Vanni were also said to have participated in black masses, using female body parts, at the house in San Casciano. Nurses at a clinic where Pacciani had worked as a gardener claimed he had told them that a mysterious doctor presided over these occult ceremonies.

Florence's head of detectives, Michele Giuttari, had his doubts. He believed that the semi-literate Pacciani was not sufficiently organized to have planned the crimes and was too slipshod to have got away with them. Nevertheless, on 17 January 1993, Pacciani was arrested.

Pietro Pacciani finally went on trial on 1 November 1994 charged with 14 counts of murder – the 1968 murder of Barbara Locci and Antonio Lo Bianco were left off the indictment. Determined to vindicate themselves the prosecutors demanded that the trial be televised. It became compulsive viewing. Although the evidence was grisly – one police guard collapsed during a particularly gory session – the case against Pacciani was largely circumstantial. He protested his innocence throughout. Nevertheless, he was convicted of 14 murders and sentenced to life imprisonment. As he was dragged from court, he screamed: "I am as innocent as Christ on the cross."

In February 1996 the court of appeal overturned Pacciani's conviction after the public prosecutor admitted that the evidence against him was unsound. But just hours before Pacciani was released, his friends, 70-year-old Mario Vanni, 54-year-old Giancarlo Lotti, and 77-year-old Giovanni Faggi, were arrested for their involvement in five of the double murders.

Detectives had returned to the theory that the Monster of

Florence was not a lone killer, but a gang. According to the police, Lotti had confessed that he and Pacciani were responsible for the killings. On 12 December 1996, the Court of Cassation cancelled Pacciani's acquittal and ordered a new trial.

Pacciani never made it to his retrial for the Monster of Florence murders. On 23 February 1998 he was found dead, face down on the floor of his home, with his shirt up around his neck and his trousers down around his ankles. His face was blue and disfigured, and the police thought that the 71-year-old Pacciani had died of a heart attack. But the post mortem revealed that a combination of drugs had caused his death. The investigating magistrate, Paolo Canessa, believed that Pacciani had been silenced in case he revealed more details about the murderous cult at his retrial.

On 24 March 1998, Mario Vanni and Giancarlo Lotti were sentenced for their involvement in five of the double murders. Vanni got life; Lotti 26 years. Giovanni Faggi was acquitted.

That should have been the end of it. But in 1994 Thomas Harris, author of *The Silence of the Lambs*, had attended Pacciani's trial and he set his third Hannibal Lecter book, *Hannibal*, in Florence. While this was being filmed in the city, it stirred memories of the Monster of Florence and people began to ask, if Pacciani had been murdered, surely the Monster of Florence himself, if he was an individual, or another member of the Satanic sect, if he was not, was still at large. As it is, the case remains officially unsolved.

16

The Juarez Ripper

In Ciudad Juarez, Mexico, directly across the border from El Paso, Texas, there is a killing spree that has lasted for more than a decade and which shows no signs of abating. In February 2005 Amnesty International put the body count at over 370, with more than 400 potential victims listed as missing. In that year alone the death toll topped 28, according to the BBC. Even so, in August 2006, Mexico's Federal Government dropped its investigation in *El Depredador Psicópata* – "the Juarez Ripper." It has long been thought that the murders committed in London by Jack the Ripper had some occult overtones. But, despite the best efforts of Patricia Cornwell, the truth about Jack the Ripper has been lost in the mists of time. However, the killings in Juarez are now thought to be the work of members of the Satanic cult of Adolfo de Jesus Constanzo that operated in another border town, Matamoros, seven hundred miles to the east of Ciudad Juarez.

The first official victim of the Juarez Ripper was Alma Chavira Farel, whose body was found on 23 January 1993 in an empty lot in a middle-class neighbourhood of Campestre Virreyes. She had been raped both vaginally and anally, beaten and strangled. There was a bruise on her chin and she had a black eye. She was wearing a white sweater with a design on it and short blue pants. No mutilations were reported at the time, but later victims were said to have suffered slashing wounds to their breasts similar to those of Chavira. In all likelihood she was not the killer's first victim at all. Juarez is a city of transients where disappearances exceed recorded homicides each year and a Satanic cult could operate without any interference from the authorities.

No one is even sure how many people live in Ciudad Juarez. Official estimates hover around one million, while there are probably more like two million people there at any one time. Many are street people who don't show up in the official statistics. For many people, it is a stopping off place on their way to the United States which lies just across the Rio Grande. It is also home to numerous drug traffickers and other criminals who use it as a temporary base for cross-border operations.

Under the North American Free Trade Agreement, Mexico has set up over 330 *maquilladoras* in Juarez. These are factories that use cheap labour to produce goods to sell over the border. The wages range between US$3 and US$5 a day. Nevertheless thousands of young uneducated female workers from southern Mexico, known collectively as *maquilladoras,* flock to work in these factories. The owners prefer hiring women because they are less trouble. They also put up with the squalid work conditions, sexual harassment, and violent shanty towns where they are forced to live. Some 70 per cent of the labour force is female.

This piques Mexican men's traditional Latin *machismo*. It also drives men into crime or finding work in that the other traditional male preserve – the police force. However, the police earn so little that bribery is an accepted practice and there is enough drug money flowing through the city to ensure that the legal system is thoroughly corrupt. Any offence can be overlooked for the right price. Individual murders are largely overlooked, but it was hard to hide the fact that overall murder rate for women in Juarez were twice that of Mexico as a whole. The rate for woman aged between 15 and 24 in Juarez is five times the rate of Tijuana, another border town, and more than ten times that of El Paso on the US side.

In May 1993 a second victim was added to the Juarez Ripper's list when a body was found on the slopes of Cerro Bola, a hill where a sign reads: "Read the Bible." The victim had been raped and strangled. A third corpse appeared in June; the female victim had been stabbed and her body set on fire. On 11 May another anonymous victim was found partially naked in the playground of Alta Vista High School on the way to a dirt road at the edge of the Rio Grande. She had been tied to a stake, raped, stabbed and had her head beaten in.

By the end of the year, 16 more murders had been added to the list. The last, on 15 December, was "solved," along with three others – though the Juarez police had an unfortunate reputation for torturing confessions out of innocent suspects. In the dozen cases that remain unsolved, five of the victims remain unidentified. At least four had been raped. Four had been stabbed to death and four strangled. One had been shot and one beaten to death. In two cases, the body was so badly decomposed that a cause of death could not be established.

The following year the Juarez police had eight unsolved murder cases involving women. In three other cases they named "probable suspects," but none of these men were arrested. Three of the victims remain unidentified today. The ages of those identified ranged from 11 to 35. In the cases where the cause of death could be determined, one was beaten to death, one burned alive, two were stabbed and six strangled. At least four of the victims were also raped. State criminologist Oscar Maynez Grijalva was already warning that, in at least some of the cases, a serial killer was at work.

His words would be remembered the following year when a killer began to reveal a signature. Three of the four bodies found in September 1995 had had their left nipples bitten off and their right breasts severed. By then, at least 19 women had been slain – making 1995 the worst year yet. Eight of the victims are still unidentified. At least four had been raped. Where it was possible to establish the cause of death, one had been shot, one stabbed, and six strangled. Again in two cases, "possible suspects" were named and the police claimed to have "solved" one of the murders. In October, they arrested Abdul Latif Sharif, an Egyptian chemist living in one of Juarez's wealthier neighbourhoods.

Sharif was arrested in 1995 after a prostitute accused him of raping her at his home. She claimed that Sharif had also threatened to kill her and dump her corpse in Lote Bravo, a desert region south of town where the bodies of other victims had been found. But these charges were dropped after the police discovered that Sharif had dated 18-year-old Elizabeth Castro Garcia, who had been found raped and murdered in August.

In custody Sharif allegedly confessed to five *El Depredador Psicópata* murders. But publicly he has always maintained that he was innocent.

"They are pinning this all on me because I am a foreigner," he claimed. "I'm just a drunk, I'm not a murderer."

Sharif was born in Egypt in 1947. Later, he claimed to have been sexually abused as a child, sodomized by his father and other male relatives. In 1970, he emigrated to America and settled in New York City. He was known for drunken womanizing. Lovers thought him charming and funny. Years after the event, it was said he had an obsessive interest in young girls.

Sacked for suspected embezzlement in 1978, he moved to New Hope, Pennsylvania. A former friend there named John Pascoe claimed that on a deer-hunting expedition Sharif had tortured a wounded buck. Pascoe also claimed that girls seen in Sharif's company often disappeared later, though no missing person reports tied to Sharif ever surfaced. The friendship ended in 1980, Pascoe said, after he found possessions of a "missing" girl in Sharif's home and a spade caked in mud on the porch.

By 1981, Sharif had moved to Palm Beach, Florida. A talented chemist and engineer, Sharif was hired by the oil company Cercoa Inc., who gave him his own department. But then on 2 May 1981 he beat and raped a 23-year-old woman neighbour, later claiming that it was consensual sex that got a little rough. Afterwards, he showed remorse, saying: "Oh, I've hurt you. Do you think you need to go to a hospital?"

Cercoa hired a top lawyer for Sharif's defence who plea bargained the rape charge down to sexual battery and five years' probation, though the law called for the deportation of aliens convicted of crimes involving "moral turpitude." On 13 August, the night before he was to plead guilty, he attacked a second woman in her home in West Palm Beach. This time he kicked and threatened to kill her, before asking her to fix him a drink and for another date the following night.

The prosecutor of the first case was not informed of the second and, as soon as Sharif was paroled, he was re-arrested, then bailed again. On 11 January 1982, Sharif was sentenced to 45 days in jail for the second attack and Cercoa finally sacked him.

Sharif moved to Gainesville, Florida, where he set up a company and was married briefly. The short-lived marriage ended in divorce when he beat his bride unconscious. On 17 March 1983, he beat and repeatedly raped a 23-year-old college student who answered his ad for a live-in housekeeper, telling her: "I will bury you out back in the woods. I've done it before, and I'll do it again." He was arrested and held without bail pending trial. Sharif escaped from the Alachua County jail, but was soon recaptured. However, other women who had told the police that he had terrorized them now refused to co-operate further in case he escaped again. On 31 January 1984 Sharif was sentenced to 12 years imprisonment for rape. The prosecutor told local reporters that Sharif would be deported when he was released, though the authorities were seeking to tie him to unsolved murders in Florida and New Jersey. In January 1977, the body of pretty 30-year-old brunette called Sandra Miller had been found at the side of the road. She had been killed by a single stab wound. Sharif worked at a chemical plant just two miles from the remote farmhouse where Miller lived with her five-year-old daughter and Sharif and Miller frequented the same bar. He was a prime suspect in the case.

However, when Sharif was paroled in October 1989, he was not deported. Instead, he moved to Midland, Texas, when he got a job with Benchmark Research and Technology. His work there was so exceptional that the US Department of Energy singled him out for praise, and he was photographed shaking hands with US Senator Phil Gramm.

Sharif was arrested again in 1991, this time for drink driving. It then came to the attention of the authorities that Sharif was liable for deportation. Hearings dragged on for two years. Then Sharif was arrested for holding a woman captive in his home and repeatedly raping her. His lawyers cut a deal. Sharif would leave the country voluntarily if the charges were dropped and, in May 1994, Sharif moved across the border to the exclusive Rincones de San Marcos district of Ciudad Juarez and worked at one of Benchmark's *maquilladora* factories.

On 3 March 1999 Sharif was convicted of the 1994 rape and murder of Elizabeth Castro Garcia, though six other murder charges were dropped. He was sentenced to 30 years in prison. The police named Sharif as the Ciudad Juarez serial killer, but the murders continued – even escalated – after his arrest. Between Sharif's arrest in October 1995 and the first week of April 1996 at least 14 more female victims were slain in Ciudad Juarez. Their ages ranged from ten to 30. In cases where the cause of death was established, one had been shot, one strangled, and ten stabbed. At least four had been mutilated after death. Significantly, one victim – 15-year-old Adrianna Torres – had had her left nipple bitten off and her right breast severed. The scale of the slaughter was staggering. The police admitted that of the 520 people who had disappeared over the past 11 months, most were adolescent females. The populace was terrified.

The police then came up with a bizarre theory to explain why the killing had continued while Sharif was in jail. After the raped and mutilated body of 18-year-old Rosario Garcia Leal was found on 8 April 1996, they picked up members of a street gang called *Los Rebeldes* – "The Rebels." One of them, Hector Olivares Villalba, said that the gang's leader Sergio Armendariz Diaz – aka *El Diablo*, "The Devil"– and half a dozen Rebels had raped and murdered Rosairio Garcia Leal on 7 December 1995. Although Olivares' confession was made under torture and he later recanted, the police used it to move against *Los Rebeldes*, raiding their club and arresting 200 of the Rebels.

Armendariz, Juan "*El Grande*" Contreras Jurado, Fernando Guermes Aguirre, Carlos Barrientos Vidales, Romel Cerniceros Garcia, Erika Fierro, Luis Adrade, José Juarez Rosales, Carlos Hernandez Molina, and Olivares were all accused of being in the pay of Sharif. The police said that he had hired them to rape and murder at least 17 women in copycat killings to make it look as if the original "Ripper" was still at large. Juan Contreras told police Armendariz had sent him to collect "a package" from Sharif in prison. It contained $4,000 in cash. Then, Contreras said, he had joined Armendariz and other Rebels in the rape and murder of a young woman known only as Lucy. Contreras also later recanted, and the charges were dropped against suspects Ceniceros, Fierro, Guermes, Hernandez, and Olivares. However *El Diablo* remained in jail serving a six-year sentence for leading the gang-rape of a 19-year-old fellow inmate in February 1998.

The Rebels themselves had Satanic overtones. They liked to torture their victims on a sacrificial slab before stoving their heads in. Several victims had bite marks on their bodies. Chihuahua's medical examiner claimed that dental casts from Armendariz matched bite marks found on the breasts of at least three of the victims. However, the Rebels claimed they were tortured by police and displayed burn marks on their bodies caused by cigarettes and cigars. And in 1999 a Mexican court ruled that there was insufficient evidence to charge Sharif with conspiracy in any of the murders attributed to *Los Rebeldes*.

By then the police theory was already looking distinctly threadbare as the murders continued despite the round-up of the Rebels. Between April and November 1996, at least 16 women were killed. Three were shot, five stabbed, and one was found in a drum of acid. In some cases advanced decomposition made it impossible to determine the cause of death or whether the victim had been sexually assaulted. Eight could not be identified.

The following year there were another 17 unsolved murders involving females aged from ten to 30 years. Sexual assault was confirmed in only four cases, but other corpses were found nude and in positions that suggested that there had been a sexual motivation for their killing. Where the cause of death could be established, three were shot, three strangled, five were stabbed, and two beaten to death. Seven of the dead were never identified.

The murder rate continued to climb. In 1998 there were 23 unsolved murders following the same general pattern. There was the usual mix of shootings, stranglings, stabbings, beatings, and burnings. Six remained unidentified. Not only were the police helpless, but they were also complicit. On 21 September 1998 Rocio Barrazza Gallegos was killed in a patrol car in the parking lot of the city's police academy by Pedro Valles, a cop assigned to the Ripper case.

The spate of murders in Ciudad Juarez was now attracting international media attention. In May 1998 the Associated Press reported that more than 100 women had been raped and killed in Ciudad Juarez. In June they put the figure at 117, while the women's advocacy group Women for Juarez said it was somewhere between 130 and 150.

On 10 June 1998 Mexico's Attorney General Arturo Chavez told the Reuters newsagency that, with Sharif still safely behind bars, "police think another serial killer may be at work due to similarities in three crimes this year." The story was taken up again by AP who reported on 9 December 1998: "At least 17 bodies show enough in common – the way shoelaces were tied together, where they were buried, how they were mutilated – that investigators say at least one serial killer is at work. And 76 other cases bear enough similarities that investigators say one or more copycats may be at work."

However a team of three profilers from the FBI's National Center for the Analysis of Violent Crime in Quantico, Virginia, spent a week reviewing the cases and concluded that "the majority of the cases were single homicides . . . It is premature and irresponsible to state that a serial killer is loose in Juarez."

The first quarter of 1999 began with eight more victims. Then, while Sharif went on trial for the rape and murder of Elizabeth Castro Garcia in March 1999, another suspect emerged. Before dawn on 18 March a 14-year-old girl named Nancy arrived at a ranch on the outskirts of Ciudad Juarez. Sobbing and covered with blood, she said she had been raped, strangled, and left for dead. Miraculously she had survived. The attacker, she said, was the bus driver who had picked her up when she left work at the *maquilladora* at 1 a.m. When he had dropped off all the other passengers, he drove out into the desert and stopped, claiming the bus had mechanical problems. Then he grabbed her by the neck and asked her if she had ever had sex. The last thing she remembered before she lost consciousness was him telling her that he was going to kill her.

The bus driver's name was Jesus Guardado Marquez, aka *El Dracula*. A check of the records revealed that the 26-year-old Guardado had a previous conviction for sexual assault. But by the time police went to arrest him, he had fled with his wife. Guardado was arrested a few days later in Durango, some 550 miles to the south. He claimed that he was beaten by the police when he was returned to Ciudad Juarez. However, the police said that Guardado had confessed to a number of the murders and named four accomplices who were also *maquilladora* bus drivers – Victor Moreno Rivera (*El Narco*), Bernardo Hernando Fernandez (*El Samber*), Augustin Toribio Castillo (*El Kiani*) and José Gaspar Cerballos Chavez (*El Gaspy*). Together they were called *Los Choferes* – "The Chauffeurs." More sinisterly, they are also known as *Los Toltecas* – "The Toltecs," the blood-thirsty forerunners of the murderous Aztecs. Moreno was the leader of the gang, the police said, and he too was in the pay of Sharif.

They were charged with 20 murders, but protested their innocence. The only evidence against them was their own confessions which had been extracted under torture. Sharif denied having had any contact with the Chauffeurs and maintained he knew nothing of any conspiracy.

Again, the arrest of *Los Choferes* did nothing to stem the murders. By May 1999 it was reported that "nearly 200 women" had been murdered since 1993 – a substantial leap from October 1998's figure of 117.

Celebrated profiler Robert Ressler, who heads the Virginia-based corporation Forensic Behavioral Sciences, visited Juarez at the invitation of the authorities and concluded that his former employer, the FBI, were wrong. He found that 76 of the murders fitted a pattern. The victims were all women aged between 17 and 24. Most of them had been raped and strangled, and more that a dozen had been killed on their way to, or on the way home from, work at a *maquilladora*. But he concluded that the killings were not the work of a lone serial killer.

"I think it's probably two or three," he said. One of them, he thought, was an American coming across the border to take advantage of the situation in Juarez. The police had already demonstrated their inability to catch one killer. There were plenty of dark streets and abandoned buildings, and with a transient population of young women there were plenty of victims to choose from.

"It's an ideal situation for an American with money," said Ressler.

The founder of the Citizens' Committee against Violence Astrid Gonzales Davila said: "The failure to solve these killings is turning the city into a Mecca for homicidal maniacs."

Candice Skrapec, the Canadian-born professor of criminology at California State University in Fresno, also identified 67 cases where she thought serial killers were involved. She told the *Toronto Star* she believed that three or four killers were at large in the 182 post-1993 cases she had studied and "there may be even more murders that could be tied to the three suspected serial killers, and that they were operating in 1992".

Skrapec believed that "Railway Killer" Angel Maturino Resendez, was one of the perpetrators as he had lived in the barrios there and much of his family – including his uncle, Rafael Resendez-Ramirez, whose name he had used as one of many aliases – still live in Juarez. On 13 July 1999, at the urging of his brother and sister, Resendez crossed the Ysleta Bridge over the

Rio Grande into the United States and surrendered to the Texas Rangers after a six-week televised manhunt that made him the most wanted man in America. The US authorities had held back on charging Resendez, fearing the Mexican government would prevent the suspect's extradition if he was liable to face the death penalty – in Texas he would receive death by lethal injection. But a $125,000-reward had been offered for his capture and his family feared that he might by shot by a bounty hunter. Instead, they brokered his surrender and claimed the reward themselves.

Resendez was charged with nine counts of murder. The first was the murder of a 21-year-old college student who was bludgeoned to death while walking with his girlfiend along a railway line in Kentucky on 29 August 1997. After that eight more bodies were found in victims' homes along the railroad track from Texas to Illinois as he travelled from state to state. His last two victims were a 51-year-old woman and her 79-year-old father who were found dead in their home near the line in Gorham, Illinois, on 15 June 1999. Although Resendez could be a suspect in a least some of the Juarez killings it is unlikely that he was responsible for the majority of the unsolved cases. Indeed, they continued after his arrest.

In December 1999, a mass grave was found outside Ciudad Juarez. It contained nine corpses – three belonging to US citizens. This invited renewed attention across the border with some, again, suspecting the involvement of the Mexican police. The *Dallas Morning News* wrote: "Still a mystery is what happened to nearly 200 people, including 22 US citizens who, in many cases, vanished after being detained by men with Mexican police uniforms or credentials."

These missing persons became known as *Los Desaparecidos* – "The Disappeared." Some were thought to be victims of Juarez's drug wars. But the Association of Relatives and Friends of Disappeared Persons in El Paso believe they may have been kidnapped by the police.

Maquilladoras still went missing and on 6 November 2001 a mass grave containing the skeletal remains of eight women were found in an empty plot just three hundred yards from the headquarters of the Association of Maquilladoras, the organization that represents most of Juarez's US-owned export assembly plants. Police then announced creation of a new task force to investigate the murders and a $21,500 reward for the capture of those responsible.

Three days after the grave had been opened bus drivers Gustavo Gonzalez Meza, *La Foca*, and Javier Garcia Uribe, *El Cerillo*, both 28, were charged with killing the eight women. The prosecutor claimed they "belonged to a gang whose members are serving time for at least 20 of the rape-murders." The victims were identified as 15-year-old Esmerelda Herrera, 17-year-old Laura Ramos, 17-year-old Mayra Reyes, 19-year-old Maria Acosta, 19-year-old Veronica Martinez, 20-year-old Barbara Martinez (no relation to Veronica), 20-year-old Claudia Gonzales and 20-year-old Guadalupe Luna.

The suspects claimed that their statements had been extracted under torture. Their lawyers received death threats. On 5 February 2002, one of them was killed by police after a high-speed chase. The police claimed they "mistook him for a fugitive" and a judge ruled that the shooting was in "self-defence." Meanwhile it was revealed that DNA tests had failed to confirm the police's early identifications of the victims. New DNA tests apparently confirmed the identification of Veronica Martinez, though it threw no light on the other seven cases. Then Gonzalez died in jail, ostensibly from complications arising after surgery.

By now 51 suspects were in jail, but still the killing did not stop. Ten days after Garcia and Gonzalez and Garcia were arrested, the body another young woman, who had been stripped and beaten to death, was found in Ciudad Juarez.

Maquilladora protesters were reportedly harassed by police and the Inter-American Commission for Human Rights moved in to investigate. The new Mexican President Vicente Fox sent in "federal crime specialists." Resentful local prosecutors told the *Dallas Morning News* that "27 of the 76 cases" were resolved, while "the other killings involving women have been isolated incidents."

On 9 March 2002 members of the Texas state legislature joined a protest march through El Paso. Then a federal deputy attorney general in Mexico City claimed that the killings were committed by "juniors" – the sons of prosperous Mexican families whose wealth and influence had protected them from arrest. He was quickly found another job. Later that year the FBI returned to lend a hand but have so far failed to further the investigation.

Juarez's leaders are particularly conscious of the effect the killings are having on the image of the city. When a large wooden cross was erected as a memorial to the murdered women, the mayor received a letter from the chamber of commerce, complaining that this would damage tourism.

The day that letter was received – 23 September 2002 – the bodies of two more women were found in Ciudad Juarez. One victim had been strangled and partially undressed; the other, the police said, had died of a drug overdose. Special investigator David Rodriguez was "sceptical" of that claim. Another young woman was found beaten to death two weeks later. Then Martha Sahagun de Fox, Mexico's new first lady addressed more than a thousand women dressed in black who marched through Mexico City in protest at the deaths.

In January 2003 residents of Lomas de Poleo reported finding three corpses, but the Attorney General Jesus Solis and the police refused to confirm or deny whether they were connected to *maquilladoras* murders. These were not the first corpses found in this desert area near a rundown suburb. Two others had been found nearby in October 2002. One of them was identified as 16-year-old Gloria Rivas.

On V-Day, 14 February 2004, in Ciudad Juarez, busloads of female students from around the world calling themselves "vagina warriors" marched into town for special performances of *The Vagina Monologues*, performed by such film stars as Jane Fonda and Sally Field, to highlight and denounce what was now being dubbed "femicide." It did no good.

On 17 February 2003 two teenagers searching the wasteland for cans and bottles found three more bodies. When the police turned in to Mimbre Street at 2 p.m., they found the remains of three women dumped there. While the bodies were being removed, an onlooker found a fourth.

At a press conference two days later the police said that they had identified three of the victims – 16-year-old Esmeralda Juarez Alarcon who had vanished on 8 January 2003, 17-year-old Juana Sandoval Reyna, who had been missing since 23 September 2002, and 18-year-old Violeta Alvídrez Barrios who had disappeared on 4 February 2003. All three had last been seen alive in downtown Juarez. When asked about the fourth victim, the police refused to acknowledge that there was another body and called a halt to the press conference. With no end to the killings in sight, the authorities are in a state of denial.

There is no shortage of suspects. Along with those already in jail, a number are still at large. There is Armando Martinez, alias Alejandro Maynez, who was arrested in 1992 for the murder of a woman in Chihuahua City, some 220 miles to the south of Juarez. He was released "by mistake" and then conveniently vanished along with his police file. Ana Benavides, who was accused of killing and dismembering a couple and their child in Juarez in 1998, claimed that Martinez committed the triple-murder and framed her.

Then there is Pedro Padilla Flores. Convicted in 1986 for the rape and murder of two women and a 13-year-old girl, he confessed to other killings but was not charged. Padilla escaped in 1991 and is still at large.

The police themselves remain under suspicion. At least ten women have accused Juarez police officers of sexual assault and kidnapping over the past five years. No charges have been brought, but an unnamed policeman is being sought in connection with the murder of 27-year-old Laura Inere and 29-year-old Elizabeth Gomez in 1995.

In April 1999 Julio Rodriquez Valenzuela, the former police chief of El Sauzal, Chihuahua, was accused of attempting to rape a 16-year-old girl near where two previous murders had been committed. Chihuahua authorities report that he fled "to El Paso or New Mexico." He remains a fugitive. Also on the run are ex-Mexican federal agents Jorge Garcia Paz and Carlos Cardenas Cruz. They are sought for questioning in the disappearance of 29-year-old Silvia Arce in 1998 and the death of 24-year-old Griselda Mares, who was allegedly killed in error by police in a dispute over stolen guns. Former Chihuahua state policeman Sergio Hernandez Pereda fled in 1998 shortly after the murder of his wife. He is still at large. Former Ciudad Juarez policeman Dagoberto Ramirez was fired in 1999 after he was accused of murdering his lover. He claimed that she had committed suicide and was released, but police officials did not reinstate him. Melchor Baca, a former federal policeman, has been on the run for eight years. He disappeared after killing a male friend of his wife at the courthouse where they both worked. And then there is Pedro Valles, the cop who was assigned to investigate the Ciudad Juarez murders and killed his girlfriend at the state police academy in 1998. He is still at large.

As drug gangs are at work in the area, it had been mooted that the missing women were addicts or small-time mules, who were executed because they knew too much. In November 2004 the FBI report accused unnamed narcotics traffickers of the torture and death of 17-year-old Lilia Garcia in February 2001. Her body was found 100 yards from the spot where eight other victims had been discovered. Then there are the juniors, or perhaps a cabal of rich and powerful sadists whose wealth puts them above the law.

Others maintain that the murders are the work of organ harvesters who are collecting spare parts for transplants. But the theory that is gaining the most ground is that they are the work of a Satanic cult like the one run at Matamoros by Adolfo de Jesus Constanzo who died in a shoot-out in 1989. Some of his cannibalistic followers are still thought to be at large and could easily have moved to Juarez to continue their murderous ways.

Meanwhile Abdul Sharif won a judicial review in the Elizabeth Garcia case. The murder conviction was upheld, but his 36-year sentence was reduced to 20 years. However, the prosecutors say that Sharif may be charged with other murders. But as he is already been in jail for over 11 years, fresh charges are hardly likely to stop the killings.

In 2004, a federal special prosecutor was appointed. Her remit extends to investigating the incompetence of the local police. But so far she has drawn a blank. However, a $2.7-million fund to aid the families of the victims has been established. Amnesty International has criticized the Mexican Government's efforts to investigate these crimes and the United Nations has condemned Mexico's record on violence against women. But nothing has helped. There were more than 28 related murders in 2005.

On 15 August 2006 Edgar Alvarez Cruz was arrested by US Marshals in Denver, Colorado, and charged with 14 of the murders. José Francisco Granados and Alejandro Delgado Valles, aka *El Calá*, have also been arrested in connection with these 14 murders. Two of the men are said to be drug addicts and the third a psychopath. Even if these men are found guilty as charged, it seems that there are plenty more killers at large in and around Ciudad Juarez.

Even if they are caught, many will escape justice as much crucial evidence has been lost, incinerated, or even intentionally destroyed, some in exchange for money for suspects seeking to clear their names, according to a recent report from Mexico's National Human Rights Commission. In the winter of 2003, homeless men took refuge from the harsh cold inside the warehouse housing many of the case files. To keep warm, the men used the files as fuel, or so the story goes.

The following year, an official was appalled by the smell that permeated the warehouse. He discovered the source of the stench was clothing, caked with blood, worn by one of the victims, a ten-year-old girl whose corpse had been dumped in the desert. Nauseated by the odour, the official, a crime scene investigator, ordered the clothes washed and deodorized with fabric softener.

"I was aghast," said an investigator for the Human Rights Commission. "We lost crucial hair, fibre, prints, semen, and God knows what other vital potential evidence."

Far from being an isolated incident, this is part of a pattern of mishandling evidence that will make solving the killings even more daunting for a fresh crop of investigators and will probably ensure that the perpetrators remain at large. In a review of the investigation by the special prosecutor's office, some 177 state officials were found to have been responsible for negligence or omission in the original investigations. However, none of these officials has been brought to justice by the state authorities as the statute of limitations has been applied in their favour. Others have been forced to resign after refusing to fabricate evidence or documenting the use of torture in the investigation.

17

The Butcher of Mons

On 20 May 1998 Belgian police in the city of Ranst, outside Antwerp, found the skeletal remains of what were thought to be seven bodies in a container, along with five human heads. They feared that this might be the reappearance of the "Butcher of Mons," a unidentified killer who had dumped 30 bags containing body parts of at least three women, possibly six, in places around the city of Mons, sixty miles away, in 1997.

The killer left police scientists a gruesome anatomical jigsaw puzzle. Some of the remains were so badly decomposed that it was an almost impossible task to discover how many victims there had been. The authorities were under intense pressure to solve the murders from Belgian Justice Minister Stephane de Clerck after the outcry that had followed the discovery of the bodies of four young girls 20 miles away, victims of paedophile killer Marc Dutroux.

The killer, who plainly savoured the police officers' discomfort, played a grisly game with his pursuers, dumping the bags filled with body parts in places with chillingly evocative names. The first bags, containing 12 neatly-severed parts of an indeterminate number of arms and legs, were found on 22 March 1997 on the banks of the Fleuve Trouille – the Jitters River – a canal bordering Mons and neighbouring Cuesmes.

Two days later, a limbless upper torso was found on the banks of a tributary of the Fleuve Haine – the River Hate – next to a road called Chemin de l'Inquietude – the Path of Worry. The limbs had been severed in the same way as those of another torso found floating in the Haine the previous July. The police established that it was the work of the same killer.

The gendarmerie began an intensive search of Mons, using

helicopters, sniffer dogs, and infrared equipment. Then on 12 April another two bags were found in a lay-by on the Rue du Depot – Deposit Road. A week later another was found on the Rue St Symphorien – Symphorien was a Christian martyr who was beheaded in AD 200 – at a place called La Poudrière – The Powderkeg – near Havré.

The killer left numerous clues which allowed team of specialist psychiatrists to compile a profile. He is thought to be an intelligent, methodical, calculating and obsessive man, who takes pleasure in the ritualistic dismemberment of his victims and the careful distribution of their remains. Detectives believe that there might be a perverse religious motive for the killings. Mons is an ancient religious town with connections to a number of saints associated with decapitation.

A stone head of St John the Baptist can be found over the door of the oldest inn in Mons, which dates back to 1776. The inn was built by a monk, a member of the Catholic brotherhood of St John the Beheaded. The order was established in the Middle Ages to escort condemned men to the scaffold and still exists today. The head looks out over the Rue de la Clef – Road of the Key – a fact that investigators feel could be significant, given the clues the killer is volunteering. It may also be significant that relics of the decapitated St Symphorien are kept in a nearby church.

Two of the three victims whose names are known, disappeared on a Sunday, and the third may also have done so, though no one seems to have noticed that she was missing.

"We have not ruled out that he is a member of a Satanic sect," said Didier van Reusel of the public prosecutor's department. "The treatment of the bodies is very methodical, which is often the case with Satanists involved in ritualistic killings."

A song about the Butcher of Mons called "Bowels of Murder" appears on *Lovecraftian Dark*, the second album of the heavy-metal band Dawn of Relic.

It was initially thought that the killer was a surgeon or a butcher due to the precision of the dissection of his victims. But further investigation revealed that the killer had not dismembered the bodies by hand. He had run his victims through an automatic sawing machine with several circular blades at twelve-inch intervals – the kind of machine normally used for slicing chopping

311

logs into planks. The severed limbs were cut into sections exactly one foot long.

"There are not that many places you can carry out that operation, with the blood and the smell," said van Reusel. "And there are not that many people who own a machine like that."

The killer appears to have chosen his victims from a group of transients who congregate around Mons station and the string of cheap bars opposite. One of the victims was 43-year-old transexual Martine Bohn, a retired prostitute who had worked out of the bars. Having lost contact with her family years before, she disappeared on Sunday 21 July 1996 and it was her torso which was found floating in the Haine. Her breasts had been sliced off. It is thought that the killer may have been angry at discovering that his victim was not a real woman.

A second victim was 33-year-old Jacqueline Leclercq, a mother of four who had separated from her husband. After losing custody of her children, she had drifted into the station scene. She had disappeared on Sunday 23 January 1997.

A third victim was 21-year-old Nathalie Godart, who lived in a bedsit in Mons. Her young son had been taken into care, but no one had reported her missing. The staff at the Intercity, the Metropole, and the Café de la Gare, the bars opposite the station, knew her well.

"She was promiscuous, but not a prostitute," said one bar owner.

The police are aware that the killer is playing a complex game with them. Tests indicate that some of the first bags found on the bank of the Trouille had lain there undiscovered for months. They were only discovered when the last bag dumped there was hung conspicuously from a tree, drawing attention to it. The remains they contained were between one week and two years old which indicated that the killer had access to an industrial refrigeration unit.

The killer plainly enjoyed the publicity the discovery of his victims' remains brought and he became more audacious. Succeeding bags were placed in highly visible places, with evocative names, at a time when the police search was already fully under way.

Psychiatrists believe that the perpetrator relishes not just the killing but also handling the corpses. Each of the body parts found had been individually wrapped in its own white plastic bag which was then knotted tightly at the top. These white bags were then placed in larger, grey bags. Each grey bin-liner has been tied tightly in the same fashion, and the top of the knot had then been snipped off with scissors – "very neatly, very precisely, the work of an obsessive," said van Reusel.

One man was questioned, but then released. He has since left Mons, and is no longer a suspect. All the authorities could do was await the next piece of the puzzle and keep Rue des Sinistres, or Sentier des Morts under surveillance.